THE PERFECT TORAH

THE BRILL REFERENCE LIBRARY OF JUDAISM

VOLUME 13

THE PERFECT TORAH

BY

JACOB NEUSNER

BRILL
LEIDEN · BOSTON
2003

This book is printed on acid-free paper.

Library of Congress Cataloging-in-Publication Data

Neusner, Jacob
    The perfect Torah / by Jacob Neusner.
        p. cm.—(Brill reference library of Judaism ; ISSN 1566-1237 ; v. 13)
    Includes bibliographical references and index.
    ISBN 9004130330 (alk. paper)
    1. Bible. O.T.-Criticism, interpretation, etc., Jewish. 2. Judaism—Sacred books. 3.
Jewish law—Philosophy. 4. Aggada—Philosophy. 5. Narration in rabbinical literature. 6.
Rabbinical literature—History and criticism. 7. Judaism—Essence, genius, nature.
I. Title II. Series.

BM496.5 .N48155 2003   2003050221
296.1-dc21   CIP

CONTENTS

PREFACE

["Then I was beside him like a little child, and I was daily his delight [rejoicing before him always, rejoicing in his inhabited world, and delighting in the sons of men"] (Prov. 8:30-31). In the cited verse] the Torah speaks, "I was the work-plan of the Holy One, blessed be he."

In the accepted practice of the world, when a mortal king builds a palace, he does not build it out of his own head, but he follows a work-plan.

And [the one who supplies] the work-plan does not build out of his own head, but he has designs and diagrams, so as to know how to situate the rooms and the doorways.

Thus the Holy One, blessed be he, consulted the Torah when he created the world.

So the Torah stated, "By means of 'the beginning' [that is to say, the Torah] did God create..." (Gen. 1:1).

And the word for "beginning" refers only to the Torah, as Scripture says, "The Lord made me as the beginning of his way" (Prov. 8:22).

Genesis Rabbah I:I.2

The perfect Torah, written completed by oral, is the medium through which the one, unique God makes himself known. The statement of monotheism comes to expression in Scripture as perfected by the Oral Torah in two native category-formations, Halakhah, norms of behavior, and Aggadah, norms of belief. The Halakhah of the oral Torah conveys monotheism in a philosophical mode, and the Aggadah, monotheism in a mythic mode—a claim to be spelled out with some care in these pages. What is perfect about the dual Torah, written and oral, is the perfect match between the message and the medium, Halakhah for the philosophical monotheism, Aggadah for the mythic statement of the same proposition. chapters one and two explain the former, chapters three and four, the latter.

My proposition in this book is that for philosophical monotheism (defined in chapter two), Halakhah is the ideal medium sustained by the data of the written Torah (set forth in a large example in chapter one). For mythic monotheism (defined in chapter four), Aggadah is the ideal medium sustained by the data of the written Torah (identified in chapter three).

The question I raise, accordingly, concerns how one canonical corpus perfects its companion and produces in consequence perfection: the realization of the initial intent and program of the Written by the Oral Torah. That is a question not answered by a mass of details, however carefully crafted. It is addressed, rather, by the construction of large exemplary structures of comparison and contrast, as I do in the shank of the book. There I establish three principles. These are

(1) the perfection through the systematization of the law of the Written Torah by the Oral Torah, in chapter one;

(2) the perfection of the medium of the Halakhah for the message of philosophical monotheism, in chapter two;

(3) the perfection of Scripture's anomalous writings through the dismantling of one document and the systematic recasting of another, in chapter three;

(4) the perfection of the medium of Aggadah in its form of narrative for the message of theology concerning God's personality and activity, in chapter four.

Thus, in the probative, not merely illustrative, cases spelled out in the shank of the book I answer the question raised at the outset.

II

Let me unpack this proposition, starting with the definition of fundamental matters.

The Rabbinic sages received the Torah as a complete statement: the work-plan of creation in the language of Genesis Rabbah. That meant they viewed in retrospect, as a whole, not only as a collection of bits and pieces, the Written part of the Torah. In this work of theological apologetics[1] I show that, by criteria to be specified, from the sages' perspective, Scripture, the written component of the one whole Torah of Moses our Rabbi, required perfecting, and in

---

[1] The argument that the very beauty of a revealed writing argues for its perfection and consequently for the authenticity of its claim to originate with God is not unique to Judaism as I portray its canonical components. I got the idea for the exercise from Islam's argument for the perfection of the Quran, on which see most recently Navid Kermani, *Gott ist schön. Das ästhetische Erleben des Koran* (Munich, 1999: C. H. Beck), called to my attention by Professor William Graham, Harvard University. He further recommends Andrew Rippin and Jan Knappert, *Textual Sources for the Study of Islam* (Chicago, 1986: University of Chicago Press), pp. 49-59, for a full overview of the arguments. None so far as I grasp matters forms a counterpart to the claims set forth here as to the match of medium and message of the components of the Torah, which are particular to Rabbinic Judaism.

fundamental aspects—system (Halakhah, chapter one), structure (Aggadah, chapter three), and match of the message and the medium (the Halakhah in chapter two, the Aggadah in chapter four)—was perfected, by the oral component of that same one whole Torah.

By "the oral components of the Torah," I therefore refer to the oral tradition of indeterminate age and venue that was finally written down by the Rabbinic sages of the first six centuries of the Common Era, the canon comprised by the Mishnah, Talmuds, and Midrash-compilations of Judaism's formative age. Given the tasks contemplated for Israel by the Written part of the Torah, the oral part completed the prescription begun in writing. The originally-oral documents, viewed all together and all at once, completed the Torah, hence, together with Scripture yielded "the perfect Torah" in the precise sense defined at the outset.

III

The Rabbinic sages in the chain of tradition from Sinai received a complex corpus of writing that in the end they contemplated whole and complete. Their task, then, was to articulate the lines of structure and order that made of the Pentateuch, the Prophets, and the Writings a single cogent statement: a system and a structure that cohered in detail and as a whole. How do we know that that is so? From what those Rabbinic sages did, I reconstruct their view of what they thought they had to do. It was to complete the Written Torah and bring about the realization of God's full intentionality in revealing the one whole Torah to Moses our rabbi. Completing the work meant to regularize, systematize the whole and to complement the parts. Since the parts often enough came into conflict and appeared in disorder, they had also to be harmonized.

I cannot overstress: *they worked forward from the whole to the parts.* Everything they did, the purpose of all of their documents, was to respond to Scripture not only or mainly in bits and pieces, through ad hoc harmonization of details, but rather as a perfect and logical statement, unflawed by contradiction and confusion. To them that meant, to work their way from the grand design to the bits and pieces, each in detail always by implication adumbrating that grand design. To form their part of—to use their language "the one whole Torah of Moses our rabbi" that emerged at the end of the formative age, they did two things. First, they systematized the law in such a way as to expose its inner ontology. Second, developing Scripture's own media and matching the character and requirements of its data, they through narrative ordered and highlighted exemplary points of the theology they deemed to animate the entire structure.[2]

What the Written Torah began, the Oral Torah completed. Together, the written and oral components form the most perfect of all possible Torahs in its legal system (chapter one), in its theological structure (chapter three), and in its media of expression and of analysis, perfectly matched to the particular task, whether Halakhic, whether Aggadic, above all, whether analytical (chapter two and four, respectively). Thus the thesis: the Oral Torah completed the written to form the perfect Torah to say what God at Sinai wanted said, to do what God wanted done, in the manner best suited to the purpose.

IV

The meaning and criteria of perfection forthwith demand definition. Depending on the accent, "perfect" in American English serves as a transitive verb, "to perfect," meaning, "to *make* something perfect," without flaw; and as an adjective, "to *be* perfect," means the condition of lacking any flaw. The distinction between transitive verb and adjective makes a difference. The former entails active engagement, participation in the process of creation. The latter involves the outcome of activity, the result, the perfect realization of an intended

---

[2] In dialectics they also devised a medium of analysis for the law and the theology that would reveal the logical consistency of the whole, but dialectical analysis and argument come late in the process of perfecting the Torah and hardly characterize all documentary components thereof. I spell out the role of dialectics in the canon of the Oral Torah in *Jerusalem and Athens: The Congruity of Talmudic and Classical Philosophy*. Leiden, 1997: E. J. Brill. *Supplements to the Journal for the Study of Judaism*, which is based on *Talmudic Dialectics: Types and Forms*. Atlanta, 1995: Scholars Press for South Florida Studies in the History of Judaism. I. *Introduction. Tractate Berakhot and the Divisions of Appointed Times and Women; Talmudic Dialectics: Types and Forms*. Atlanta, 1995: Scholars Press for South Florida Studies in the History of Judaism. II. *The Divisions of Damages and Holy Things and Tractate Niddah; The Modes of Thought of Rabbinic Judaism*. I. *Types of Analysis*. Binghamton 2000: Global Publications. ACADEMIC STUDIES IN THE HISTORY OF JUDAISM SERIES; *The Modes of Thought of Rabbinic Judaism*. II. *Types of Argumentation*. Binghamton 2000: Global Publications. ACADEMIC STUDIES IN THE HISTORY OF JUDAISM SERIES. Second printing, condensed and revised; under the title, *Analysis and Argumentation in Rabbinic Judaism*. Lanham, 2003: University Press of America.

consequence. As is clear, I use perfect in its transitive sense. I propose that the framers of the Oral part of the Torah actively perfected the written part so that the two together yielded that condition of perfection that the one whole Torah of Sinai attained: divine instruction that realized its intentionality.

Second, as to criteria, how do we recognize perfection when we see it? The language of purpose and plan just now introduced, "realizing intentionality," answers the question in a concrete way. That object is perfect that accomplishes the declared and manifest purpose of its maker, who is judge of the condition of perfection. That action that is perfect fully executes the intentionality of the one who initiates and takes the action. Perfection then is defined by purpose, representing a judgment as to teleology. Statements of the end and goal of the Written Torah—statements concerning Israel's sanctification through God's imperatives, for example—both abound and cohere. And so too does evidence of their imperfect realization within the limits of the Written Torah. But the principal task of perfecting the Written Torah proves blatant: to read Scripture whole and complete, not (only) in bits and pieces. The Rabbinic sages possessed the whole and determined to reveal its perfection: coherence, cogency, consistency in all the parts. The shank of this book instantiates that claim.

True, in the teleological context perfection, defined in relationship to intentionality, is a relative, not an absolute, condition. Clearly, by some effort at an objective criterion, one may speak of "the perfect storm," or "the perfect wife,"—with perfection defined by a theoretical ideal and not by a determinate context and purpose. But in the realm of culture, writing for example, such ideal types are difficult to come by, and defining them yields banality and vacuity and in the end proves arbitrary. By contrast, once we know the requirements imposed by context and the intention of the maker signaled by the actual character of a thing he has made or an activity he has carried out, however imperfect, we may infer that to which the maker aspired. Then we judge whether the thing or activity realizes the purpose for which it is made or done. If it does, we call it perfect.

That represents an objective judgment about a matter relative to manifest intentionality. It is based on the actuality of the thing or activity and its potentiality or promise. Description of the norms of a writing and its goals then shades over into definition of the outer

limit of aspiration in that same writing. In this exercise by that teleological criterion we may discern the attainment of perfection—a
secular, this-worldly judgment of literary culture.

And what was that goal? Here, as I said earlier, the situation of
those who recorded the Oral Torah of Sinai comes into play: they
stand at the end and inherit the whole of the Written Torah. Confronted by so complex and diverse a corpus of writing as the Written part of the Torah, the Rabbinic sages took as a given that that
Torah formed a whole and uniform statement—and set out to make
it so.

Is the Written Torah on its own then flawed? We need not address that question. For within the normative theology that assigns
to the Oral part of the Torah an essential role in revealing the one
whole Torah of Moses, our rabbi, the argument of this book fits quite
well. The Rabbinic sages articulately validate the dual medium
meaning, oral as well as written, for revelation. In that context they
even accord greater authenticity to the Oral part of the Torah.
Accordingly, relying on their result to deal with the question of constructive theology, I propose to spell out what that role was and how
it was realized: the match of message and medium, why this, not
that?

V

So much for perfection in theory, now to the specific claim that the
Oral Torah perfects the written. The question that requires attention is, what unrealized intentionality left flaws in the Written Torah viewed wholly on its own? And what made necessary the initiative toward perfection accomplished by the Oral Torah? The
question is to be answered in this-worldly terms.

Working back from what they did in recording the oral tradition
of Sinai to what they thought they had to do, we may judge that in
the view of the Rabbinic sages, the Written Torah (Scripture) on its
own was incomplete. Its imperfection—as a matter of hypothesis in
these pages—consisted in lacking precisely those traits that the Oral
part of the Torah evinced. We may then reconstruct from the program of the Oral Torah an account of those flaws that the Rabbinic sages identified and corrected in perfecting the Written Torah.
I am guided by the native category-formations of the Rabbinic canon,
the division between the Halakhah, law, and the Aggadah, lore (nar-

rative, theology, exhortation). Each chapter—(1-2) the Halakhah, the Aggadah, (3-4) the match of the medium and the message for the Halakhah and the Aggadah, respectively—begins with the alleged incompleteness, the flawed character of the Written Torah, setting the problem solved by the oral one.

VI

Theological apologetics that defines the program of the present project requires attention to context and circumstance as much as to its contents. By context I mean, historical setting, and by circumstance, the cultural tasks of the social order that the Rabbinic sages in that context undertook to design. This brief account then appeals to established, familiar facts of history and culture and not to mooted matters that require extensive amplification.

VII

CONTEXT: By this I mean, the political setting in which the Israel contemplated by the Torah was imagined. It is a matter of conventional history. The documents that give form and permanence to the originally Oral Torah, deriving from inchoate traditions of indeterminate antiquity, took shape in the first six centuries of the Common Era. That marked the axial period in which ancient Israel in the Land of Israel witnessed the destruction of the old order and the definition of the new. The initial context (70-312) found definition in the ruin of the Temple of Jerusalem, the loss of political autonomy (independence was rarely an issue, the Land being incorporated into a succession of empires). The task concerned exteriorities of institutional restoration. It was one of reconstruction, reordering the social order in the aftermath of the loss of its center and focus and source of stability.

That context, defined by autonomy and stability and the absence of interior challenge to Israel's unique possession of Scripture, shifted with the advent of Christianity to dominance in the Land of Israel, from the legalization by Constantine to the Islamic conquest (312-640). The task then shifted to one of inner recapitulation, the definition and validation of the community within. What endured the destruction of 70 and calamity of the Bar Kokhba fiasco of 132-135—

the integrity of the Jews' claim to constitute the Israel formed by
the Torah—came under challenge. That is because catholic, ortho-
dox Christianity claimed to possess the very same Scriptures that
the Rabbinic sages designed "the Written Torah" but read them with
very different results. The permanent sanctification of Israel, never
doubted from 70 for some centuries, now required reaffirmation, new
media of expression.

The successive historical settings, then, required the Rabbinic sages
in recording and expounding the Torah to address the condition of
a defeated people, weak, subordinated, but now contending for the
possession of its very birthright in both Land and Scripture. And
here we identify a principal flaw in the Written Torah. Contempo-
rary Israel then found itself in the thrall of a Scripture that did not
contemplate, and could not have imagined, the political context in
which it found itself. So politics defines the exterior context. And
the solution to the problem of politics lay in law, thus chapter one
of this book, which explains the way in which the Rabbinic sages
reconstructed the civil law of Scripture. What of the interior circumstance?

VIII

CIRCUMSTANCE: by this I refer to the cultural tasks of the Israelite
social order that the Rabbinic sages envisaged: the givens of Israel's interior condition transcending politics and power. In the loss
of ancient institutions of culture—rites to which they imputed great
antiquity, hierarchies of ancient and enduring worth, which had
lasted for nearly a millennium,—they discerned also the disarray of
ancient patterns of culture, represented by the cessation of the sacrificial offerings of a cult then centuries old. Here the Rabbinic sages intuited the imperatives of regeneration and renewal. That was
to be in response to Scripture's own admonitions. A single story
captures the theological and cultural crisis:

THE FATHERS ACCORDING TO RABBI NATHAN IV:V.2
    A.   One time [after the destruction of the Temple] Rabban
Yohanan ben Zakkai was going forth from Jerusalem, with R. Joshua
following after him. He saw the house of the sanctuary lying in ruins.
    B.   R. Joshua said, "Woe is us for this place which lies in ruins,
the place in which the sins of Israel used to come to atonement."
    C.   He said to him, "My son, do not be distressed. We have

another mode of atonement, which is like [atonement through sacri-
fice], and what is that? It is deeds of loving kindness.

     D.   "For so it is said, 'For I desire mercy and not sacrifice,
[and the knowledge of God rather than burnt offerings]' (Hos. 6:6)."

Here, in a document possibly co-terminus with the Bavli, hence of
ca. 600 C.E., the perspective on the interior circumstance of Israel
comes to explicit expression, together with the Oral Torah's recapitulation of the pertinent passage of the Written Torah.

The urgency of the task defined by circumstance matched the
insistence of Scripture. For consider the task and program that Scripture had set. Specifically, Scripture's demands upon Israel in the
Pentateuch defined the circumstance in which the sages would work:
the requirement that they construct a kingdom of priests and a holy
people, an abode where God might dwell as he had dwelt in the
Temple, a life of holiness for the people defined by the Torah of
Sinai and addressed by God through that Torah.

The Written Torah, read whole, encompassing the narrative from
Genesis through Kings and the companion-guidance of the literary
prophets, Isaiah, Jeremiah, Ezekiel, and the Twelve, corresponded
to exactly the situation that the Rabbinic sages constructed, in their
imagination. Their broken-hearted Israel now recapitulated the initial
narrative and could then hope for a counterpart denouement: exile
and return. Scripture as they read it told the story of exile and return
through the narrative of the loss of paradise, the Land, by reason
of the sin of arrogance, but then the restoration to paradise, the Land,
by reason of repentance and atonement. Defeat and loss of the
embodiments of the divine favor had happened once, and now once
more.

And therein they found grounds for hope. That fact made all the
more urgent the message of Scripture—repent, atone, rebuild, re-
new. And by placing the media of atonement into the hands of every Israelite, all of them capable, after all, of acts of loving kindness
and of attaining knowledge of God in the Torah, as Hosea is understood to require, the Rabbinic sages empowered Israel to restore
its condition. The way forward as before once more led to restoration. But now—once more reading Scripture whole and its details
in a single pattern—it would be for the last time, within the pattern
already established in Scripture itself. The circumstance defined by
Scripture then establishes the criterion of perfection: effectively to
recapitulate Scripture's account of Israel's history and destiny—in
an effective, orderly way.

That is how the cultural task defined itself: turn to Scripture, particularly the parts set forth by Moses for guidance on how to regenerate Israel's social order. If culture defined the matter of circumstance, then the solution to the problem lay in the Aggadic theology, the construction of a structure of ideas to explain and accommodate the circumstance of the hour and the long future beyond, thus chapter two of this book, which spells out the theological solution to Scripture's flaws: its contradictions and conflicts.

IX

CONTENTS: So much for context and circumstance: a defeated people, undertaking reconstruction in accord with an established model. What of the challenge contained within the very contents—the intellectual workings of the Written Torah? The contents of the Written Torah—Scripture itself—presented traits that in context and circumstance presented blatant flaws. These fall into two classifications: contradiction and insufficiency. Only the briefest of amplifications is required, since everyone recognizes Scripture's contradictions and failures, however diverse the conclusions drawn from them.

As to the contradictions what needs to be said? None denies that, on the surface, the several codes of law in the Pentateuch require a process of harmonization of conflicting details. Deuteronomy 25:5-10 has a man marry his deceased childless brother's widow, which Leviticus 18:16 does not provide for. Deuteronomy wants all sacrifices to God to take place in Jerusalem, and so permits secular slaughter of beasts as well, while Leviticus wants all acts of slaughter to be sanctified, but allows sacrifice to take place anywhere. These Halakhic points of conflict have been recognized from antiquity, and the Oral Torah addresses them forthrightly.

And when we turn to the Halakhic insufficiency of the Written Torah's laws, we need only set the Mishnah's category-formations up side by side with Scripture and note the numerous tractates of the Mishnah, hence of the normative law, that rest on no solid foundations in Scripture at all—just as the Rabbinic sages did at Mishnah-tractate Hagigah 1:9 as amplified at Tosefta Hagigah 1:9—to recognize the formidable failures of the Written Torah in setting forth the Halakhic system fully exposed by the Oral Torah in the Mishnah.[3] Here is the amplification of the Mishnaic statement, given in italics, by the Tosefta's authorities:

TOSEFTA HAGIGAH 1:9

A. *The absolution of vows hovers in the air, for it has nothing upon which to depend in the Torah* [M. Hag. 1:8A].

B. But a sage loosens a vow in accord with his wisdom.

C. *The laws of the Sabbath, festal-offerings, and sacrilege are like mountains hanging by a string, for they have little Scripture for many laws* [M. Hag. I :8B].

D. They have nothing upon which to depend.

F. *Laws concerning civil litigations, the sacrificial cult, things to be kept cultically clean, sources of cultic uncleanness, and prohibited consanguineous marriages* [M. Hag. 1:8D],

G. and added to them are laws concerning valuations, things declared *herem*, and things declared sacred—

H. for them there is abundant Scripture, exegesis, and many laws.

I. *They have much on which to depend* [M. Hag. 1:8D].

J. Abba Yosé b. Hanan says, "These eight topics of the Torah constitute *the essentials of the laws* [thereof] [T. Er. 8:24]" [M. Hag. 1:8D-E].

This formulation leaves no doubt that the Rabbinic sages recognized the phenomena that have won our attention and addressed these matters of the (superficial) imperfection of the Written Torah.

But, what is more, take the blatant contradiction in Scripture's Aggadah, in its exercises in theology, in the representation of God and man. God both shows mercy to sinners who repent and commands the extermination of the Canaanites. Consider that man in the Torah is called to great accomplishment, "You shall be holy, for I the Lord your God am holy" (Lev. 19:2). But man in Qohelet/Ecclesiastes perishes from memory, whatever memorials he constructs in life, and nothing really matters. Note that God is subject to the law of justice, as Abraham shows at the gates of Sodom, but God in Job is capricious and arbitrary, not to be argued with. Recall the secular love poetry included in Scripture in the Song of Songs, the hopeless spirit of Qohelet. The Rabbinic sages considered and took note of them all, not only in exegesis of specific verses that presented a challenge to their system, but especially in the interpretation of entire Scriptural books that contradicted that system.

---

[3] I have done the systematic work on this problem in *Scripture and the Generative Premises of the Halakhah. A Systematic Inquiry.* Binghamton, 2000: Global Publications. ACADEMIC STUDIES IN ANCIENT JUDAISM series. I. *Halakhah Based Principally on Scripture and Halakhic Categories Autonomous of Scripture.* II. *Scripture's Topics Derivatively Amplified in the Halakhah.* III. *Scripture's Topics Independently Developed in the Halakhah. From the Babas through Miqvaot.* IV. *Scripture's Topics Independently Developed in the Halakhah. From Moed Qatan through Zebahim.* Second printing, revised and condensed: under the title, *The Torah and the Halakhah: The Four Relationships.* Lanham, 2003: University Press of America.

But what of the matter of analytical method? Now, as a matter of fact, Scripture lacked an analytical model that would permit sages to sort out confusion and remove contradiction. It presented its information in the form of declared law, encased in narrative, admonition, and prophecy. These supplied facts, but little guidance on how to transform the facts into rules exhibiting regularity, order, coherence, and cogency. Disorganization prevailed. Above all, the Written Torah contains laws but exhibits no cogent theory of category-formation for its laws, hence, laws but not principles instantiated therein and available to adduce more laws. The Torah's rules for the Israelite social order prove not only unsystematic but in topic are set forth in highly fragmentary condition. The laws of Deuteronomy 12-26, for example, cover topics in a seemingly random fashion, yielding no possibility of extrapolation and extension. But even the so-called Holiness Code of Leviticus 19 is topically miscellaneous, as are the Ten Commandments, with their egregious mixture of public and personal, civil and family law.

More to the point, the disorganization of the Written Torah's laws, their occasional and random character—these did not suffice for the task at hand. For what Israel most needed now was more than an editorial ordering of episodic laws and theological facts. In the work of reconstruction and restoration, Israel required a grand design, a coherent pattern, a cogent construction of the social order fully articulated in the middle range of detailed rules. These were matters that Scripture scarcely supplied. Scripture articulates episodic cases but proves remarkably poor in supplying the governing rules to be extrapolated for the everyday and the here and now. And that is why the cases emerge as haphazard and unsystematic. What does the Written Torah offer, then, to fill the gap between global generalization and acute particularization ("you shall be holy, for I the Lord your God am holy" and "when two men quarrel and the wife of one....")? Perfecting the Torah requires filling that gap. Scripture in both aspects—its design for the Israelite society, its account of the organization and governance of that society—proves episodic, not systematic.

What was required, then, was system, order, amplification, attention to coherence and cogency. And that is precisely where the Rabbinic sages made their contribution and how they perfected the Torah and produced the perfect Torah. They took as their task the regularization and the ordering of the Written Torah's imperatives and the correction of its narratives to conform to reasoned truth, thus chapter three of this book, which matches the message to the media—narrative to the Aggadah, on the one side, dialectical to the Halakhah, on the other—that truly perfect Scripture.

X

The perspective of this book is new. As is often the case, I found nothing to help me in designing the work, and little enough, beyond episodic details, in carrying it out. But the theological problem is familiar: precisely how is God's Torah perfect as alleged at Psalm 19:8? And in what does its perfection consist? There have been prior efforts at undertaking the same demonstration, for the issue raised here inheres in the Torah-narrative of the Judaism of the dual Torah, oral and written.

The work has been done in detail, and has found wide acceptance among those that concern themselves with Halakhic, theological Judaism. A century ago, in 1902, Baruch Halevi Epstein (1860-1942)[4] published a work under the same title, *Torah Temimah*, the perfect Torah. In the language of Moses Hacohen, he "correlated passages of the Rabbinic literature with verses of Scripture, showing how the Rabbinic interpretations were deduced." That aspect of the issue— the interplay of the two Torahs, verse by verse—clearly does not arise here. I have in mind viewing whole through exemplary cases and problems the two components of the Torah, on their own in relationship, through three probative cases.

XI

What are the imperfections in this study? To explain why I ask: I have worked in an absolutely straight line from my first scholarly project, my doctoral dissertation,[5] completed in 1960, to the present. Each project left me dissatisfied, not so much in result as in scope

---

[4] Moses Hacohen, "Epstein, Baruch Halevi," Encyclopaedia Judaica 6:825; M. G., "Rabbi Baruch HaLevi Epstein," *Great Leaders of Our People* (N.Y.).

[5] *A Life of Yohanan ben Zakkai*. Leiden, 1962: Brill. Awarded the Abraham Berliner Prize in Jewish History, Jewish Theological Seminary of America, 1962. Second edition, completely revised, 1970. French: *Vie de Yohanan ben Zakkai*. Paris, 2000: Clio. Italian: Ferrara, 2003: Gallio Editori.

and method. I concluded with a keen awareness of the problems that
by my own criteria of rigor I had not yet addressed, let alone solved.
As is my way, in this cumulative intellectual enterprise of mine, let
me then specify a problem that is not solved in these pages, the principal one that logically awaits attention. It is this: since I treat the
Halakhic message and medium as comparative with the Aggadic
ones, I have to ask whether and how the category-formations of the
Halakhah compare with those of the Aggadah.

Specifically, identifying the systemic message of the Aggadah presents problems that defining that of the Halakhah does not. For the
Halakhah, the topical category-formations of the Mishnah define the
topics that impose coherence on free-floating facts and so organize
facts into knowledge and give knowledge a focus, shape, and message. Scripture's other-than-topical-propositional organization of the
Halakhah thus is set aside by the topical-analytical program set forth
in the Mishnah and paramount from the Mishnah through the Tosefta, Yerushalmi, and Bavli.[6] And a fundamental act of perfecting the
Torah imposed the topical-analytical structure of the Oral Torah
upon the whole of the Halakhic corpus of both Torahs, written and
oral.

But how are we to identify the categorical media of the theological message of the Aggadah? Unlike the Halakhic counterpart, the

---

[6] I spell out the foundations of the Halakhic category-formations in the sys-
tematic study as follows: *The Hermeneutics of the Rabbinic Category-Formations: An In-
troduction.* Lanham, 2000: University Press of America. Studies in Judaism SERIES.
The Comparative Hermeneutics of Rabbinic Judaism. Volume One. *Introduction. Berakhot
and Seder Mo'ed.* Binghamton, 2000: Global Publications. ACADEMIC STUDIES IN
ANCIENT JUDAISM series. *The Comparative Hermeneutics of Rabbinic Judaism.* Volume
Two. *Seder Nashim.* Binghamton, 2000: Global Publications. ACADEMIC STUDIES IN
ANCIENT JUDAISM series. *The Comparative Hermeneutics of Rabbinic Judaism.* Volume
Three. *Seder Neziqin.* Binghamton, 2000: Global Publications. ACADEMIC STUDIES
IN ANCIENT JUDAISM series. *The Comparative Hermeneutics of Rabbinic Judaism.* Volume
Four. *Seder Qodoshim.* Binghamton, 2000: Global Publications. ACADEMIC STUDIES
IN ANCIENT JUDAISM series. *The Comparative Hermeneutics of Rabbinic Judaism.* Volume
Five. *Seder Tohorot.* Part *Kelim through Parah.* Binghamton, 2000: Global Publications.
ACADEMIC STUDIES IN ANCIENT JUDAISM series. *The Comparative Hermeneutics of Rab-
binic Judaism.* Volume Six. *Seder Tohorot. Tohorot through Uqsin.* Binghamton, 2000:
Global Publications. ACADEMIC STUDIES IN ANCIENT JUDAISM series. *The Comparative
Hermeneutics of Rabbinic Judaism.* Volume Seven *The Generic Hermeneutics of the Halakhah.
A Handbook.* Binghamton, 2000: Global Publications. ACADEMIC STUDIES IN ANCIENT
JUDAISM series. *The Comparative Hermeneutics of Rabbinic Judaism.* Volume Eight. *Why
This, Not That? Ways Not Taken in the Halakhic Category-Formations of the Mishnah-Tosefta-
Yerushalmi-Bavli.* Binghamton, 2000: Global Publications. ACADEMIC STUDIES IN
ANCIENT JUDAISM series.

Aggadah by its nature as a composite of free-standing narratives is inchoate, not neatly presented in explicit category-formations as the components of the Halakhic system are. What then will permit us to define the theological medium in the way in which the Halakhic compositions allowed us to identify the philosophical medium that sustained them? Nothing so clear and cogent as the exercise of hierarchical classification in the service of philosophical monotheism emerges in chapter four as a counterpart to the results of chapter two. The upshot is, chapter three shows markers of an implicit theological structure. But in chapter four I define components of that structure narratively, therefore episodically (e.g., elaborate accounts of God's justice, God's empathy for Israel) *but not systematically.* That is, I present the theological structure not as a complete, coherent construction with its own native category-formations but only partially and then, alas, intuitively. So the comparison and the integration of the two components of the perfection of the Torah effected by the Rabbinic sages in recording the Oral part of the Torah await realization.[7]

XII

In the present context and for the purpose indicated, I recapitulate prior findings, as follows:

Chapter one, "The Legal System," goes over findings first set forth in

> *The Halakhah: An Encyclopaedia of the Law of Judaism.* Volume III. *Within Israel's Social Order.* Leiden, 1999: E. J. Brill, chapters one through three;
>
> *Scripture and the Generative Premises of the Halakhah. A Systematic Inquiry.* III. *Scripture's Topics Independently Developed in the Halakhah. From the Babas through Miqvaot.* Binghamton, 2000: Global Publications. Academic Studies in Ancient Judaism series; and
>
> *The Comparative Hermeneutics of Rabbinic Judaism.* Volume Three. *Seder Neziqin.* Binghamton, 2000: Global Publications. Academic Studies in Ancient Judaism series.

---

[7] In the concluding chapter of *The Theology of the Halakhah* (Leiden, 2001: E. J. Brill), "The Halakhic Theology Seen Whole: Actualizing the Torah's Story," I outline the way in which the two sets of category-formations cohere, but that is only an elementary exercise.

Chapter two, "The Match of Message and Medium (1) Halakhic," refocuses and states afresh the findings of

> *Judaism as Philosophy. The Method and Message of the Mishnah.* Columbia, 1991: University of South Carolina Press, chapters ten through twelve.

Chapter three, "The Theological Structure," on Leviticus Rabbah's naturalization of Qohelet into the Rabbinic system is new. It goes without saying that a counterpart repertoire for Job and Proverbs would well have served, but Qohelet is singled out as anomalous, along with Song of Songs, by the Rabbinic sages themselves and hence their systematic attention to it seemed acutely relevant. The articulation of a theological structure in Song of Songs by Song of Songs Rabbah draws upon my

> *Judaism and the Interpretation of Scripture: Introduction to the Rabbinic Midrash.* Peabody, 2003: Hendrickson.
> *Introduction to Rabbinic Literature.* N.Y., 1994: Doubleday.

Chapter four, "The Match of Message and Medium (2) Aggadic," on Aggadic narrative recapitulates some of the findings of

> *Rabbinic Narrative: A Documentary Perspective.* Volume Three. *Forms, Types, and Distribution of Narratives in Song of Songs Rabbah and Lamentations Rabbah. And a Reprise of Fathers According to Rabbi Nathan Text A.* Leiden, 2003: E. J. Brill. THE BRILL REFERENCE LIBRARY OF JUDAISM.

The idea of a correlation between message and medium is fully exposed for the Halakhah—why this particular topic to make this determinate statement, whether philosophical or theological?—in a systematic exposition in my

> *The Halakhah: An Encyclopaedia of the Law of Judaism.*
> Volume I. *Between Israel and God.* Part A. *Faith, Thanksgiving, Enlandisement: Possession and Partnership.*
> Volume II. *Between Israel and God.* Part B. *Transcendent Transactions: Where Heaven and Earth Intersect.*
> Volume III. *Within Israel's Social Order.*
> Volume IV. *Inside the Walls of the Israelite Household.* Part A. *At the Meeting of Time and Space. Sanctification in the Here and Now: The Table and the Bed. Sanctification and the Marital Bond. The Desacralization of the Household: The Bed.*
> Volume V. *Inside the Walls of the Israelite Household.* Part B. *The Desacralization of the Household: The Table. Foci, Sources, and Dissemination of Uncleanness. Purification from the Pollution of Death.*

All: Leiden, 1999: E. J. Brill. THE BRILL REFERENCE LIBRARY OF JU-
DAISM.

It is further expounded in

The Theology of the Halakhah. Leiden, 2001: E. J. Brill. BRILL REFER-
ENCE LIBRARY OF ANCIENT JUDAISM.

XIII

Let me acknowledge the help of colleagues whom I consulted in
thinking through this project:

on literary theory, Professor Ben LaFarge, Bard College, and
Professor David Gunby, Canterbury University (Christchurch, New
Zealand);

on matters of philosophy, Professor Robert Berchman, Dowling
College;

on matters of the perfection of Scripture, Professor Mayer Gruber,
Ben-Gurion University of the Negev; Professor Ithamar Gruenwald,
Tel Aviv University, and Professor Galit Hasan-Rokem, Hebrew
University of Jerusalem.

On the perfection of the Quran as a theological exercise in Islam
I consulted Professor William Graham, Harvard University.

On the project as it unfolded, I talked from day to day with Professor William S. Green, University of Rochester, and Professor Bruce
D. Chilton, Bard College.

JACOB NEUSNER
BARD COLLEGE

CHAPTER ONE

THE LEGAL SYSTEM

i. *The Problem Scripture Presents*

Viewed as a single, harmonious document, Scripture's presentation of normative laws is episodic, haphazard, and topically disorganized. Its law codes are fragmentary and hardly lay out in a cogent manner the rules for the governance of a well-constructed social order. A random sample suffices. An example of an episodic representation of a law out of all context is at Gen. 32:33, which deals with the prohibition of eating the thigh muscle that is on the socket of the hip, "since Jacob's hip socket was wrenched at the thigh muscle." An instance of the haphazard character of the presentation of rules covers, in sequence, slavery (Ex. 21:2-6, 7-11), manslaughter and murder (Ex. 21:12-14), hitting parents (Ex. 21:15), kidnapping (Ex. 21:16), insulting parents (Ex. 21:17), and the like. An instance of the disorganization of the Scriptural presentation is at Lev. 19:3-37, which defines holiness in terms of respect for parents and the Sabbath, not worshipping idols, conduct of sacrifices, leaving gleanings for the poor, not stealing, not dealing deceitfully with others, not swearing falsely by God's name, not defrauding someone, not robbing; not withholding the wages of a laborer overnight; not insulting the deaf, and on and on, in no apparent order. An example of topical disorganization, were Leviticus 19 not to suffice, makes a massive appearance at Deuteronomy 12-26.

That is not to suggest there are in Scripture no well-construed compositions on coherent topics. Numbers 5 on the wife accused of adultery, Numbers 6 on the Nazirite, Numbers 19 on corpse-uncleanness, not to mention Leviticus 1-15 on types of offerings and sources of cultic uncleanness suffice to show what can have been accomplished. But apart from Leviticus 1-15, there is no clear program of systematic topical exposition, where one subject is unpacked and then logically leads to the next and forms a cogent composite therewith. So even when topics come under systematic exposition, the outcome is nothing approaching a code of law capable of extension and amplification for the governance of a community. With Scripture's laws and even whole codes in hand, one can hardly construct a coherent legal system for Israelite society. That is the judgment, we shall now see, of the framers of the Mishnah's code of civil law, which vastly transcends the Written Torah's provision in recording the Oral Torah.

ii. *The Oral Torah's Program: The Case of a Code of Civil Law*

If we take up Scripture's contribution to the civil law set forth in Mishnah-tractates Baba Qamma, Baba Mesia, and Baba Batra, we find that important topics covered by the Mishnah's Halakhah for civil rule rest on no scriptural foundations whatsoever. To perfect the Torah, the Oral tradition had to provide for a variety of transactions left without any law at all in Scripture. But that is only the superficial aspect of how the Oral Torah perfected the Written one in this context. The Rabbinic sages in fact constructed a system of civil law that embodied a cogent viewpoint, not just collected topical data, and the organization of the data itself formed a medium for the message of the civil law-code.

To demonstrate that fact, we first review the composition of the Halakhah set forth by the Mishnah (then amplified by the Tosefta, Yerushalmi, and Bavli, but these rest on and amplify the Mishnah and so need not detain us). Then we identify precisely the points at which the Written Torah contributes to the Halakhic structure. What we shall see is how the civil laws of Scripture omitted a broad range of topics deemed by the Mishnah to be essential to the exposition of a complete code of civil law. Here I show, for the case at hand, the perfection of the Written Torah by the Oral Torah through provision of new rules, not only through the systematization of the law. The important side is, to perfect the Torah, the Oral component had a task of not only exegesis of the received Scripture but augmentation thereof.

Now to the task: the three tractates of the Civil Law, Baba Qamma, the first gate, Baba Mesia, the middle gate, and Baba Batra, the last gate, form a single, continuous statement. The Babas aim at the preservation of the just social order, the preservation of the established wholeness, balance, proportion, and stability of the social economy realized at the moment of perfection This idea is pow-

erfully expressed in the organization of the three tractates that com-
prise the civil law, which treat first abnormal and then normal transactions. The layout is as follows:

> I. Illicit Transactions; Restoring Order
>   Baba Qamma
>   i.   Damage by Chattels 1:1-6:6
>   ii. Damages Done by Persons 7:1-10:10
>   Baba Mesia
>   iii. The Disposition of Other Peoples' Possessions;
>   Bailments 1:1-3:12
>   iv. Illicit Commercial Transactions. Overcharge, misrep-
>   resentation, usury 4:1-5:11
>
> II. Licit Transactions; Preserving Order
>   v.   Hiring Workers. Rentals and Bailments 6:1-8:3
>   Baba Mesia, Baba Batra
>   vi. Real Estate B.M. 8:4-10:6, B.B. 1:1-5:5
>   Baba Batra
>   vii. Licit Commercial Transactions 5:6-7:4
>   viii. Inheritances and Wills. Other Commercial and Legal
>   Documents 8:1-10-8

The framers deal with damages done by chattels and by human
beings, thefts and other sorts of malfeasance against the persons and
the property of others. The civil law in both aspects pays closest
attention to how the property and person of the injured party so
far as possible are restored to their prior condition, that is, the state
of normality disrupted by the damage done to property or injury
done to a person. So attention to torts focuses upon penalties paid
by the malefactor to the victim, rather than upon penalties inflicted
by the court on the malefactor for what he has done. For each of
the components of the continuous statement of Halakhah set forth
by the Babas, we shall consider the main points of the law and their
relationship with Scripture.

We shall consider the pertinent verses of Scripture only within
the framework of the exposition of the law as set forth in the Oral
Torah embodied in the Mishnah. That is because while the triple-
tractate draws heavily upon Scripture where Scripture pertains to
its program, the tractate sets forth its own topical agenda, following
the problematic defined in terms of the triple-tractate's own goals.
Here Scripture contributes some topics, not others. But the generative premises of the entire statement vastly overspread the limits of

Scripture's presentation of those topics that to begin with originate there. The Halakhic category-formation intersects with Scripture's discrete categories, but it is asymmetrical and only partly concentric.

iii. *Baba Qamma and Scripture*

When speaking of damages, the Halakhah, initially stated by the Mishnah in the terms of injury and misappropriation, takes as its principal concern the restoration of the fortune of victims of assault or robbery. In its account of damages inflicted by chattel and persons, the native category defined by tractate Baba Qamma incorporates facts supplied by Scripture and frames the topic in its own way but in response to Scripture. What is original to the Halakhah makes itself manifest only when we consider the three Babas together as a single coherent statement. To state the character of the Halakhah of the Oral Torah in the present category, it does not suffice simply to note that what Scripture presents episodically, the Halakhah portrays systematically, because a fair portion of the Halakhah works out topics not treated by Scripture at all. That accounts for classifying the triple-tractate as I do. The following outlines the category as set forth in the Halakhah:

  i.   Damage by Chattels
       A. The Fundamental Rules of assessing damages when the cause is one's property, animate or inanimate
       B. Damages done by chattels in the public domain
       C. Damages done by the Ox
       D. Damages done by the pit
       E. Damages done by the Crop-destroying Beast
       F. Damages done by fire
  ii. Damages Done by Persons
       A. Penalties for the theft of an ox or a sheep
       B. Penalties for Abuse of the Land
       C. Penalties for assault
       D. Penalties for damages done by persons to property; restoring what is stolen

We now turn to the principal concerns of the Halakhah, then reverting to the Scriptural foundations of those that rest on Scripture.

Baba Qamma takes as its task the exposition of how the victim of assault or robbery is to be returned to his prior condition, the thug or thief not gaining from his action. What question common to a range of sub-topics precipitates inquiry of a uniform character among those diverse sub-topics? By way of experiment, let us simply review a sequence of topical sentences of the several sub-divisions of the Halakhah and see whether we can identify a type of question that recurs, now dividing the sub-divisions between injury and misappropriation. This we do so as to ask whether a uniform program of analysis or exegesis governs:

INJURY

1.   There are four generative causes of damages.

2.   A beast is an attested danger to go along in the normal way and to break something. But if it was kicking, or if pebbles were scattered from under its feet and it thereby broke utensils—the owner pays half of the value of the damages caused by his ox.

3.   He who leaves a jug in the public domain, and someone else came along and stumbled on it and broke it—the one who broke it is exempt. He who pours water out into the public domain, and someone else was injured on it, is liable to pay compensation for his injury.

4.   Two oxen generally deemed harmless which injured one another—the owner pays half-damages for the excess of the value of the injury done by the less injured to the more injured ox.

5.   He who digs a pit in private domain and opens it into public domain, or in public domain and opens it into private domain, or in private domain and opens it into private domain belonging to someone else, is liable for damage done by the pit.

6.   He who brings a flock into a fold and shut the gate before it as required, but the flock got out and did damage, is exempt. If he did not shut the gate before it as required, and the flock got out and did damage, he is liable.

7.   He who causes a fire to break out through the action of a deaf-mute, idiot, or minor, is exempt from punishment under the laws of man, but liable to punishment under the laws of heaven. If he did so through the action of a person of sound senses, the person of sound senses is liable.

MISAPPROPRIATION

8.   More encompassing is the rule covering payment of twofold restitution than the rule covering payment of fourfold or fivefold restitution. For the rule covering twofold restitution applies to something whether animate or inanimate. But the rule covering fourfold or fivefold restitution applies only to an ox or a sheep alone

9.   He who injures his fellow is liable to compensate him on five counts: (1) injury, (2) pain, (3) medical costs, (4) loss of income [lit.: loss of time], and (5) indignity

> 10. He who steals wood and made it into utensils, wool and
> made it into clothing, pays compensation in accord with the value
> of the wood or wool at the time of the theft.

Nos. 1-7 in treating injury all work on assessing culpability and assigning responsibility. If a question recurs, it concerns how we sort out that mishap against which we can take precautions from what cannot ordinarily be foreseen and prevented. But a variety of givens predominate, and those givens involve facts, not principles of general intelligibility such as might pertain in other Halakhic categories altogether; the givens seem remarkably particular to their context. And the facts on the face of matters scarcely can be said to inhere in the topic at hand. Nos. 8-10 in addressing misappropriation want to know how we assess damages and pay for them. Here too, responsibility to restore the status quo defines the recurrent question.

The Halakhah categorized as Baba Qamma—the Halakhah of injury and misappropriation—in fact systematizes facts supplied by Scripture, identifying the general principles and utilizing those general principles as the basis for the orderly recapitulation of the established facts, now in an improved formulation. Not only so, but that work of secondary amplification of facts of Scripture encompasses nearly the entire tractate; I see little in the Halakhah that aims at more than to articulate what is implicit in facts set forth by the Written Torah. No Halakhic problematic deriving from the Oral Torah dictates the course of the presentation of the topic. To show that that is the case, let me return to the repertoire of topics given just now ask these specific questions and answer them. I ask the question required by the rough reprise given above, and I answer by a systematic demonstration that the Halakhah finds in the Written Torah not only its facts but also such a generative problematics as pertains. When we come to the other Babas, we shall see a very different picture.

1. How do sages know that there are four generative causes of damages (covering Nos. 1, 3, 5, 6, 7)?

> Ox (No. 1): "When one man's ox hurts another's, so that i t dies, then they shall sell the live ox and divide the price of it; and the dead beast also they shall divide. Or if it is known that the ox has been accustomed to gore in the past, and its owner has not kept it in, he shall pay ox for ox, and the dead beast shall be his" (Ex. 21:35-6)
> PIT (No. 5): "When a man leaves a pit open or when a man digs

up a pit and does not cover it, and an ox or an ass falls into it, the owner of the pit shall make it good; he shall give money to its owner and the dead beast shall be his" (Ex. 21:33)

CROP-DESTROYING BEAST (No. 6): "When a man causes a field or vineyard to be grazed over or lets his beast loose and it feeds in another man's field, he shall make restitution from the beast in his own field and in his own vineyard" (Ex. 22:5)

FIRE (No. 7): "When fire breaks out and catches in thorns so that the stacked grain or the standing grain or the field is consumed, he that kindled the fire shall make full restitution" (Ex. 22:6)

The secondary amplification of these generative causes, elegantly carried forward by the Tosefta's and Bavli's exegesis of the Mishnah's statement, leaves no doubt that, within the prevailing hermeneutics of the native category at hand, the sole task is to articulate the givens of Scripture. That fact becomes more blatant at the next stage.

2. Where do sages learn the distinction between a beast that is deemed harmless and one that is an attested danger (covering Nos. 2, 4, inclusive of (1) half-damages paid in the case of the goring of the former, full damages of the latter; and (2) of selling an ox and dividing the proceeds)?

"When one man's ox hurts another's, so that it dies, then they shall sell the live ox and divide the price of it; and the dead beast also they shall divide. Or if it is known that the ox has been accustomed to gore in the past, and its owner has not kept it in, he shall pay ox for ox, and the dead beast shall be his" (Ex. 21:35-6)

"When an ox gores a man or woman to death, the ox shall be stoned and its flesh shall not be eaten; but the owner of the ox shall be clear. But if the ox has been accustomed to grow in the past, and its owner has been warned but has not kept it in, and it kills a man or a woman, the ox shall be stoned, and the owner also shall be put to death. If a ransom is laid on him, then he shall give for the redemption of his life whatever is laid upon him. If it gores a man's son or daughter, he shall be dealt with according to this same rule. If the ox gores a slave, male or female, the owner shall give to their master thirty shekels of silver, and the ox shall be stoned" (Ex. 21:28-32)

The entire program of the specified chapters of the Mishnah's presentation of the Halakhah derives from Scripture; the exegesis of the implications of the facts, the invention of illustrative problems for solution, and the specification of theorems for demonstration—all depend upon the factual postulates supplied by Scripture.

3.   Whence the distinction between the rule covering payment of twofold restitution than the rule covering payment of fourfold or fivefold restitution (No. 7)?

> "If a man steals an ox or a sheep and kills it or sells it, he shall pay five oxen for an ox and four sheep for a sheep. He shall make restitution; if he has nothing, then he shall be sold for his theft. If the stolen beast is found alive in his possession, whether it is an ox or an ass or a sheep, he shall pay double" (Ex. 22:1-3).
>
> "If a man delivers to his neighbor money or goods to keep and it is stolen out of the man's house, then if the thief is found, he shall pay double" (Ex. 22:7).

The specified chapter does nothing more than take up Scripture's distinctions and explore their implications.

4.   How do we know that one compensates a person whom he has injured (No. 9)?

> "When men quarrel and one strikes the other with a stone or with his fist and the man does not die but keeps his bed, then if the man rises again and walks abroad with his staff, he that struck him shall be clear; only he shall pay for the loss of his time and shall have him thoroughly healed" (Ex. 21:18-19).
>
> "When men strive together and hurt a woman with child so that there is a miscarriage and yet no harm follows, the one who hurt her shall be fined, according as the woman's husband shall lay upon him; and he shall pay as the judges determine. If any harm follows, then you shall give life for life, eye for eye, tooth for tooth, hand for hand, foot for foot, burn for burn, wound for wound, stripe for stripe" (Ex. 21:22-25).

Sages derive the laws of misappropriation and torts from Scripture, the categories being defined out of the passage at hand.

5.   What is the basis for requiring compensation for what one has stolen (No. 10)?

> "If any one sins and commits a breach of faith against the Lord by deceiving his neighbor in a matter of deposit or security or through robbery, or if he has oppressed his neighbor or has found what was lost and lied about it, swearing falsely, in any of all the things that men do and sin therein, when one has sinned and become guilty, he shall restore what he took by robbery or what he got by oppression or the deposit that was committed to him or the lost thing that he found or anything about which he has sworn falsely; he shall restore it in full" (Lev. 5:20-24).

Here again, it is not the topic and its inherent logic but Scripture that has dictated the character of the Halakhah, within the obvious proviso that, both Scripture's and the Oral Torah's Halakhah concur on the justice of restoring stolen property as a principle of the ordering of society. The upshot is that we may account by reference to the Written Torah's laws for nearly the entire exegetical program brought by sages to the Halakhic topic of Baba Qamma. Sages chose as their question—the problematic they discerned in the topic at hand—how to organize and systematize Scripture's facts.

Given these facts, what shall we assess that the sages of the Oral Torah have contributed to their elucidation of the Written Torah? They clarified details and worked out the secondary and tertiary implications thereof. They spelled out the full range of responsibility ("In the case of anything of which I am liable to take care, I am deemed to render possible whatever damage it may do. If l am deemed to have rendered possible part of the damage it may do, I am liable for compensation as if I have made possible all of the damage it may do"). They defined the specifics required for applying Scripture's general rules ("a tooth is deemed an attested danger in regard to eating what is suitable for eating"). In the manner of geometry, they showed how, within a given set of postulates, a range of problems was to be solved to yield a proof of a set of theorems. But that is hardly the whole story of the code of civil law perfected by the Oral Torah in the Mishnah.

iv. *Baba Mesia and Scripture*

Continuing the topical program of Baba Qamma, Baba Mesia takes up where the former left off. Baba Qamma concludes with analysis of the Halakhah of restoring what has been stolen; Baba Mesia starts with restoring what has been lost. Then it shifts to a new topic, the Halakhah governing transactions of an equitable character between buyer and seller, then, employer and employee. In the former case the Halakhah focuses on the counterpart to theft, which is overcharging and usury. In the latter, we proceed to an account of what each party owes the other. We conclude with attention to real estate, specifically, relationships of partners in a given house (a condominium, in our terms), relationships between tenant and landlord or tenant-farmer and householder. Here is an outline of the category:

We begin with the paired questions, first, has Scripture defined what sages wish to know about the topics at hand? And second, if not, then how do the Rabbinic sages in recording the traditions of the Oral Torah know what they want to know about said topics? To answer these questions, we rapidly review the main points of an outline of the tractate. I indicate Scripture's contribution at each pertinent point. The exposition of the topic commences *in medias res*, being continuous with the foregoing. It furthermore is carried forward without interruption into the following tractate. But each of the sub-topics—the divisions of the law—covered in Baba Mesia possesses its own point of interest. Reviewing the topics and the questions sages raise in expounding them reveals the character of the problematics that governs sages' account of what, about the subject at hand, sages find urgent.

A.   Disposition of Property Not Held by the Rightful Owner But Lost, Subject to Conflicting Claims, or Deposited with a Bailee

1.   CONFLICT OVER PROPERTY: the character of the oath that resolves the matter, which responds to the nature of the claim of the competing parties. That depends, further, on what portion of the property a claimant alleges is his. The will of each party enters into the transac-

tion, therefore, embodied as it is in the extent of each party's claim.
2. RESTORING AN OBJECT TO THE ORIGINAL OWNER: several issues are pursued. The first is, the right of the householder over what his dependents acquire; the second, the likely disposition of diverse documents; the third, the attitude of the original owner toward the objects that have been found, specifically, has he given up hope of recovering the object, in which case, through despair, he has relinquished ownership of the object? Or can he reasonably hope to regain the object, in which case he retains ownership? The condition of the objects that are found testifies to the imputed attitude of the original owner. The subsidiary problems do not change the picture. The main point is that persons capable of exercising independent will acquire in their own, not in the householder's behalf, whatever they find. The further point is that the right of ownership depends upon an act of will. Stated negatively through the principle that despair marks relinquishing ownership, the principle of the primacy of intentionality governs.

Scripture is explicit that one must restore property owned by another person, when it states the following:

> "You shall not see your brother's ox or his sheep go astray and withhold your help from them; you shall take them back to your brother. And if he is not near you, or if you do not know him, you shall bring it home to your house and it shall be with you until your brother seeks it; then you shall restore it to him. And so you shall do with his ass, so you shall do with his garment, so you shall do with any lost thing of your brother's, which he loses and you find; you may not withhold your help. You shall not see your brother's ass or his ox fallen down by the way and withhold your help from them; you shall help him to lift them up again" (Dt. 22:1-4).

The requirement of Scripture does not account for the governing consideration, relinquishing ownership through imputed despair of recovering the object.

3. THE RESPONSIBILITIES OF A BAILEE: if the bailee accepted full responsibility for the object, he also receives restitution from a thief; a bailee should not lay hands on the bailment, but does not have to make up losses due to natural causes in the bailment; if the bailee disposes of the bailment for his own convenience, he is liable for damages, but if it is for the convenience of the bailment, he is not; if he takes proper precautions, he is not liable, but if not, he is. Here again, the outcome of the transaction is mediated by the extent to which a bailee is willing to assume responsibility, encompassing compensation, for the bailment. And, again, the attitude of the bailee in disposing of the bailment—for his own convenience, for the service of the bailment—affects the judgment of the case. In all three areas of law, therefore, intentionality enters in and assessing the effects of an act of will forms

the main criterion for deciding the types of cases dealt with here.

That the bailee is responsible to take an oath and not required to make restitution if he has not committed negligence is indicated in the following:

> "For every breach of trust, whether it is for an ox, for ass, for sheep, for clothing, or for any kind of lost thing, of which one says, "This is it," the case of both parties shall come before the God; he who God shall condemn shall pay double to his neighbor. If a man delivers to his neighbor an ass of an ox or a sheep or any beast to keep, and it dies or is hurt or is driven away, without anyone seeing it, an oath by the Lord shall be between them both to see whether he has not put his hand to his neighbor's property; and the owner shall accept the oath and he shall not make restitution. But if it is stolen from him, he shall make restitution to its owner. If it is torn by beasts, let him bring it as evidence; he shall not make restitution for what has been torn. If a man borrows anything of his neighbor and it is hurt or dies, the owner not being with it, he shall make full restitution. If the owner was with it, he shall not make restitution; if it was hired, it came for its hire" (Ex. 7:15ff.).

The distinctions among types of bailee and the rules set forth in the Halakhah systematize the laws of Scripture.

B.   Corollaries of distributive economics: commoditization of specie; true value and price-fixing; prohibition of usury

1.   THE BASIS OF A COMMERCIAL TRANSACTION: it is not the transfer of coins, deemed a mere commodity, that effects a commercial transaction between an informed seller and a willing buyer, but the transfer of goods. The act of acquisition is effected through a symbolic exchange of things of value, not of specie. Even though the buyer willingly parts with the money, and the seller with the goods, the transaction is null until the one effects physical possession with the consent of the other. So an agreed-upon exchange by itself plays no role in determining the ownership of the goods.

2.   TRUE VALUE: Objects (but not slaves, commercial paper, or real estate) have a true, or intrinsic, value, as distinct from a market value. What an informed seller and a willing buyer agree as the price of an object is measured against the true value of the object, and if too great a divergence—more than a sixth—from that true value marks an exchange, fraud results; it may be fraud committed by buyer, if too little is paid, or by seller, if too much. Adulterating commodities involves fraud—giving the impression of value that does not, in fact, inhere. Here intentionality in the form of agreement is null; an objective, autonomous true value intervenes. The market-transaction, based upon

the will of an informed seller and a willing buyer, gives way to the consideration of intrinsic value.

3.   USURY: Concomitantly, taking interest is forbidden in transactions among Israelites; it involves payment for waiting for the return of funds that have been borrowed, or paying a higher price for the volume of a commodity that has been borrowed at a lower price, or trading in naked futures. One may lend wheat to be repaid in wheat only if it is for seed, not if it is for food. Variation in price based on supply cannot enter into transactions of lending commodities. Exchanges of labor must be exact, e.g., weeding for weeding, hoeing for hoeing, not weeding for hoeing. Usury in kind, e.g., advantages accorded to the lender of an other than monetary character, is also forbidden. Speculation in commodities or trading in futures is forbidden. Factoring, by contrast, is permitted, if both parties—the capitalist and the proprietor—share in the risk and profit. Israelites may not enter into a factoring arrangement by which the proprietor takes all the risk, the capitalist being guaranteed return of his capital no matter what happens. As above, even though the borrower is willing to pay interest and the lender to accept it, or arrangements of factoring on other than equal terms are freely entered into, the transaction is null. Will alone does not suffice; the intrinsic character of the transaction, violating as it does the law of the Torah by arranging for "payment for waiting" for the return of funds, overrides the attitude of the parties to the transaction.

Scripture explicitly prohibits usury:

> "And if your brother becomes poor and cannot maintain himself with you, you shall maintain him as a stranger and a sojourner he shall live with you. Take no interest from him or increase, but fear your God; that your brother may live beside you. You shall not lend him your money at interest, nor give him your food for profit" (Lev. 25:35-27).

> "You shall not lend upon interest to your brother, interest on money, interest on food, interest on anything that is lent for interest. To a foreigner you may lend upon interest, but to your brother you shall not lend upon interest, that the Lord your God may bless you in all that you undertake in the land that you are entering to take possession of it" (Dt. 23:20-21).

But I do not see here the consideration that is important for sages, that is, the intrusion upon private agreements of an implacable prohibition against all sorts of "payment for waiting."

4.   PRICE-FIXING: The market price is set, then bargains can be made. The price is set by current, not past, production. Price-fixing based on speculation, not on market supply in hand, is forbidden. Exactly what has been said pertains here as well. Even though the willing buyer

and informed seller have come to an agreement, their act of will is null; the objective market-price, agreed upon when the crops are in hand and not before, overrides their act of will.

C.   Mutual obligations in labor, rental, bailment

1.   EMPLOYER-EMPLOYEE: Each party is responsible to the other to make up loss caused by failure to carry out an agreement. Whoever changes the original terms of an agreement is liable to make up the loss. The prevailing rules of the labor market govern and may not be changed by private agreement. Workers are permitted by right to eat produce on which they are working. The act of will on the part of one party cannot set aside the agreement entered into by freely-undertaken acts of will of the two parties. But, self-evidently, if both parties concur, the original terms of the agreement are set aside.

One detail of the foregoing derives from Scripture:

"When you go into your neighbor's vineyard, you may eat your fill of grapes, as many as you wish, but you shall not put any in your vessel. When you go into your neighbor's standing grain, you may pluck the ears with your hand, but you shall not put a sickle to your neighbor's standing grain" (Dt. 23:25-26).

This is taken to pertain to workers, as indicated.

2.   RENTALS: One who changes the original terms of a rental agreement is liable to make up the loss or pay damages consequent upon the change. But if there is an unavoidable obstacle, the lessor is not obligated to the lessee. Here, *force majeure* overrides the original agreement, since the unavoidable obstacle does not come about through an act of poor faith on the part of one or the other party.

3.   BAILMENTS: In transactions with craftsmen, craftsmen who receive materials from householders are in the status of paid bailees, responsible for negligence and theft. Once the job is done and the craftsman informs the householder, the craftsman is in the status of an unpaid bailee. We differentiate among four classes of bailees, by the criterion of compensation. One who is not paid bears only limited liability. One who is paid, who borrows, or who leases, bears greater liability to compensate the bailer for damages. Differentiation between damage done through negligence and damage that cannot have been prevented accommodates a range of cases. What has already been said pertains here.

D.   Real Estate

1.   CONFLICTING CLAIMS OF LANDLORD AND TENANT: If one sells trees but not ground, then unanticipated fruit in modest volume belongs to the

purchaser of the trees. Where the volume is substantial, the produce is divided. The landlord may not evict the tenant without notice. The landlord makes an implicit contract to provide those components of a building that a craftsman makes, but the rentee provides what is not ordinarily made by a craftsman. The lessor must provide a replacement for a house that collapses, and it must be equivalent to the one originally leased. We impute to the act of agreement of both parties the prevailing customs of the area, e.g., if a building ordinary includes certain appurtenances, then the agreement between landlord and tenant is assumed to encompass those appurtenances. An act of will on the part of the one or the other is null in the face of the legitimate expectations that both parties bring to the transaction.

2.   CONFLICTING CLAIMS OF LANDLORD AND TENANT-FARMER: The lessee must follow prevailing practice, farming the leased land as is customary, and returning the land in suitable condition. The lessee may not change the conditions of the lease in any way. The lessor must supply what is ordinarily included in the lease. The lessor is liable for damages that affect everyone. What has just been said applies here too.

3.   PAYING DAY-LABORERS PROMPTLY: Wages and fees must be paid at the end of the work-period, e.g., at the end of the day for a day-laborer, at the end of the night for a night-worker. The scriptural rules on not holding on to a pledge are recapitulated. But if the worker agrees to some other arrangement, the scriptural requirement may be set aside. His act of will, involving relinquishing established rights, is valid. Here the act of will on the part of the worker overrides the protections that the Torah has provided for all workers.

Promptly paying workers is explicit in Scripture:

> "You shall not oppress your neighbor or rob him. The wages of a hired servant shall not remain with you all night until the morning" (Lev. 9:13).
>
> "You shall not oppress a hired servant who is poor and needy, whether he is one of your brethren or one of the sojourners who are in your land, within your towns; you shall give him his hire on the day he earns it; before the sun goes down, for he is poor and sets his heart upon it; lest he cry against you to the Lord and it be sin in you" (Dt. 24:14-15).
>
> "If you lend money to any of my people with you who is poor, you shall not be to him as a creditor, and you shall not exact interest from him. If you take your neighbor's garment in pledge, you shall restore it to him before the sun goes down, for that is his only covering; it is his mantle for his body; in what else shall he sleep? And if he cries to me, I will hear, for I am compassionate" (Ex. 22:25-27).
>
> "When you make your neighbor a loan of any sort, you shall not go into his house to fetch his pledge. You shall stand outside, and the man to whom you make the loan shall bring the pledge out to you.

> And if he is a poor man, you shall not sleep in his pledge; when the
> sun goes down, you shall restore to him the pledge that he may sleep
> in his cloak and bless you, and it shall be righteousness to you before
> the Lord your God" (Dt. 24:10-13)
> "You shall not take a widow's garment in pledge" (Dt. 24:17-18).
> "No man shall take a mill or an upper millstone in pledge, for he would
> be taking a life in pledge" (Dt. 24:6).

Scripture has supplied the facts but not adumbrated the governing
problematics, so far as I can discern. The same is so in connection
with restoring the pledge.

> 4.   JOINT-HOLDERS OF A COMMON PROPERTY: Both parties are equally
> liable to repair damages suffered in common. If one property-holder
> depends upon the other, the latter must carry out his obligation, even
> in the property the latter himself holds.

Our reprise completed, we may now answer the questions raised at
the outset.

First, Scripture has supplied important facts, but on the strength
of Scripture we could never have predicted the entire topical program of the Halakhah's presentation of Baba Mesia. In some aspects the Halakhah simply clarifies and refines the Written Torah's
laws. But in most, even where Scripture defines the topic and dictates the substance of the law, the Halakhah concerns itself with issues that Scripture does not introduce, and that do not inhere in
Scripture's own Halakhah. So Scripture has not defined either the
topical program nor framed what sages wish to know about the topics
that they do treat. The Oral Torah here emerges as autonomous of
Scripture and self-evidently perfects the Written Torah by filling fundamental gaps in its program. But there is more to the matter than
that.

What is in play is that the Rabbinic sages work with their own
set of questions, and, in the present case, those questions derive from
a set of considerations in no way inherent in the Halakhic topic but
beautifully exposed by that topic. Sages found in the topic at hand
a remarkably appropriate arena for the exposition of a problem of
fundamental concern to them. Specifically, the entire exposition turns
out to form an exercise on the interplay between intentionality and
value, with specific attention to (1) where the attitude of participants
to a transaction governs, (2) where it is dismissed as null, and (3)
where it takes a subordinate position in an exchange. These three
readings of the role of the will of the parties to a transaction—(1)

paramount, (2) excluded, and (3) subordinated but effective—form the expository program that animates the presentation of the topic of Baba Mesia. And, we notice, the layout of the topics permits the law to organize itself around the three possible outcomes for an act of will or intentionality: decisive, null, and mixed, that is, +, −, +/− —a strikingly logical sequence, entirely characteristic of the Mishnah's exposition of variables where topics yield an equivalent range of possibilities, positive, negative, mixed. (Baba Batra will show us yet another approach to the same matter: when one's *idiosyncratic* intentionality is null.)

When it comes to resolving conflicting claims, we focus upon the attitudes of the participants to the conflict. First, we want conflicting parties to resolve conflict in a manner that is not only equitable but also that is *deemed* by all parties to be equitable. Second, in assessing rights of ownership, we take account of the attitude of the original owner, who gives up his title when he despairs of regaining his property. Third, in assessing liability of a bailee, we assign restitution in proportion to the responsibility that the bailee has accepted. In all three instances, therefore, the variables of the law respond to the attitudes of the participants in a transaction, to acts of will that determine the outcome of untoward consequences.

When we deal with market-transactions, we treat as subordinate or dismiss outright as irrelevant the attitude of the players—willing seller, informed buyer. Rather, we impose the criterion of a fixed or true value. Worth deemed intrinsic, not market-determined, overrides the agreement of the parties to the market-transaction. And the law goes out of its way to underscore that in the face of the fixed and true value that inheres in a transaction, the willingness of the parties to ignore true value is simply nullified. A borrower may willingly pay usury—in the innocent form of a warm greeting for instance or a gesture of friendship—but the transaction is illegal. Even though a purchaser is willing to pay a premium for an object, his attitude does not affect the value of the object. One may be willing to pay a premium for the use of capital, but such a premium is deemed not a return on capital but usury and is illegal. All transactions must conform to a measure of exact exchange of true value, and that extends to exchanges of labor. Indeed, unearned value may take the form of not only special concessions but even a polite or obsequious greeting and so is outlawed. It follows that prices will be fixed—in terms of market-conditions affecting what is immediately available—and private agreements cannot upset the public arrangements.

But private agreements can be taken into account in other exchanges. In transactions involving labor, rentals, and bailment, the attitude of the participants to an agreement fixes the terms of the agreement, which then cannot be unilaterally revised. Labor—like slaves, bonds, and other documents—has no true value in the way in which grain does; each party bargains in good faith without the constraints governing usury. But then the transaction involving such and such a wage for so and so a span of labor, once agreed upon by both parties, is binding. Here the initial agreement governs, each party having acceded willingly, and the attitude or intention of one party cannot then dictate changes not accepted by the other. In the matter of bailments, liability responds to the level of responsibility imposed by variable compensation of the bailee; he is assumed to be willing to take greater precautions and accept more substantial liability in response to greater compensation.

What about what is not articulated but only assumed? Here too, we impose upon the parties an imputed attitude, that is, we assume that all parties accept the prevailing norms and make those norms their own. In resolving conflicts in real estate, certain implicit agreements are assumed. Prevailing attitudes or expectations are imputed to the parties, custom then defining what we assume the players to have accepted.

It follows that the Halakhah of Baba Mesia both sets forth information about the topics at hand and also works out a theoretical concern through the presentation of those topics. That concern focuses upon the attitude of parties to a conflict or transaction. To what extent does the intentionality of attitude of a participant in an exchange govern, and to what extent do immutable rules override the will of the individual?

(1) In certain situations of conflict, we take full account of the attitude of all parties. When two persons claim ownership of the same object, either because both have grabbed it at the same moment or because one has lost what the other has found, or because one has accepted responsibility in proportion to the other's inveiglement (good will, a fee, and so on), then intentionality reigns supreme. That is to say, we settle the conflict by a weighing or a matching of wills.

The Torah requires fairness, and, no other considerations' intervening, all parties have a say on what is equitable.

(2) But the willingness of two persons, e.g., a buyer and seller, to come to an agreement is set aside by other considerations. The will cannot overcome the law of the Torah. The Torah prohibits usury, which involves the concept of distributive economics that inherent in an exchange is a set valuation, which the participants may not set aside. A theory of static wealth comes into play when we maintain that true value inheres in things. God's will overrides man's, and what God does not want, man cannot legitimate merely by an act of will, even in an exchange involving mutual consent. Intentionality or attitude—willingness to evaluate at a higher or lower value than the intrinsic one—no longer enter into the disposition of a transaction. God's will outweighs man's will, hence intentionality plays no part in settling these transactions.

(3) Established custom modifies intentionality, in that people are assumed to conform to a common norm. In exchanges not of conflict nor of fixed value but of service, attitude or intentionality is subordinated to expectations that are broadly accepted. Intentionality plays its part, but idiosyncrasy does not, and we do not impute to an individual an intention or expectation that diverges from the norm. The parties may willingly enter a valid agreement to exchange service—work, rental of property, and the like—but their agreement cannot violate fixed procedures, any more than a buyer and seller may ignore true value. Custom in intangible relationships matches inherent worth in tangible ones.

What emerges from the presentation of Baba Mesia, therefore, is a coherent exercise on the three dimensions of will or intentionality: where man's will defines the norm, where God's will overrides man's will, and where custom and the social norm enter into the assessment of man's will and turn out to exclude unarticulated idiosyncrasy. We shall now see that Baba Batra works on yet another aspect of intentionality, cases in which intentionality is simply irrelevant to transactions of a certain order. Then we eliminate all consideration of individual preference or will. That completes the picture.

v. *Baba Batra and Scripture*

Baba Batra begins in the middle of Baba Mesia's concluding topical unit, the rules governing joint holders of a property. It proceeds to further licit real estate transactions: not infringing the property rights of others, establishing title through usucaption, transferring real estate and movables through sale. The next major section turns to licit commercial transactions and unstated stipulations in commercial transactions. The final unit turns to inheritances and wills and other commercial documents. Here is an outline of the category:

I. REAL ESTATE (CONTINUED)
    A. Joint Holders of a Common Property [continuing Baba Mesia VI.E]
    B. Not Infringing upon the Property Rights of Others
    C. Establishing Title to a Field through Usucaption
    D. Transferring Real Estate and Movables through Sale
II. LICIT COMMERCIAL TRANSACTIONS
    A. Conditions of Irrevocable Transfer of Goods
    B. Unstated Stipulations in Commercial Transactions 6:1-7:4
III. INHERITANCES AND WILLS. OTHER COMMERCIAL AND LEGAL DOCUMENTS
    A. Inheritance
    B. The Preparation and Confirmation of Commercial Documents, e.g., Writs of Debt 10:1-6
    C. Concluding Miscellany

Once more we want to know both the topical program and how Scripture has shaped that program.

A. RIGHTS OF JOINT HOLDERS OF A COMMON PROPERTY
    1. PARTITIONING PROPERTY: Apart from the equal contribution of each party to the property that the law requires, the main concern is to affirm the prevailing custom of the region. A secondary concern is that if a person benefits from a project, he must pay his share of the project. A tertiary concern of the law is, what is done for the community must be generally available (as with the produce of the seventh year) and not used in a selfish manner.
    2. NOT INFRINGING ON THE PROPERTY RIGHTS OF OTHERS: One may not utilize his own property in such a way as to damage the rights of the other. One has a right to expect others to respect his property rights and to enforce those rights. The same pertains to the rights of the community as a whole.

B. ESTABLISHING TITLE TO PROPERTY

1. ESTABLISHING TITLE THROUGH USUCAPTION: Three years of utilization of a property establishes the presumptive right of ownership to the property, provided there is an explicit claim to that effect, accompanied by successful demonstration of a claim should it be opposed.

2. TRANSFERRING REAL ESTATE AND MOVABLES THROUGH SALE: WHAT IS INCLUDED IN THE TRANSACTION? It is taken for granted that what is essential to that which is sold is included in the transaction, but what is not essential and is not explicitly included is not covered by the sale, e.g., a permanent mortar but not a movable one. But if the language is used, "It and everything which is in it," lo, all of them are sold. The same goes for a cistern, the water goes with.

C. CONDITIONS OF IRREVOCABLE TRANSFER OF GOODS

1. BOTH PARTIES TO A TRANSACTION HAVE THE RIGHT TO A FAIR DEAL: If one has sold good wheat and it turns out to be bad, the purchaser has the power to retract. If one has sold bad wheat and it turns out to be good, the seller has the power to retract. If he has claimed to sell bad wheat, and it turns out to be bad, or if he claimed to sell good wheat and it turns out to be good, neither one of them has the power to retract.

2. UNSTATED STIPULATIONS GOVERN IN ACCORD WITH REASONABLE EXPECTATIONS: The buyer assumes some of what he buys will be rotten. Customary usage governs.

The requirement of the Halakhah that measures be kept clean and accurate is explicit in Scripture:

> "You shall do no wrong in judgment, in measures of length or weight or quantity. You shall have just balances, just weights, a just ephah, and a just hin: I am the Lord your God who brought you out of the land of Egypt" (Lev. 19:35-36).

Dt. 25:13ff. goes over the same matter.

D. INHERITANCES, WILLS, AND OTHER LEGAL DOCUMENTS

1. RULES OF INHERITANCE: There are those who inherit and bequeath, there are those who inherit but do not bequeath, bequeath but do not inherit, do not inherit and do not bequeath. These inherit and bequeath: the father as to the sons, the sons as to the father; and brothers from the same father but a different mother, as to one another inherit from and bequeath to one another. The man as to his mother, the man as to his wife, and the sons of sisters inherit from, but do not bequeath to, one another. The woman as to her sons, the woman as to her husband, and the brothers of the mother bequeath to, but do not inherit from one another. Brothers from the same mother do not inherit from, and do not bequeath to one another. One may not stipulate an inheritance that violates the laws of the Torah, but he may divide

his property by donation. He who died and left sons and daughters—
when the estate is large, the sons inherit, and the daughters are supported [by the estate]. [If] the estate is small, the daughters are supported, and sons go begging at [people's] doors.

The right of the daughter to inherit is explicit, so too that inheritances pass through the male, not the female line, as stated in the
Mishnah's rule, cited just above:

> "If a man dies and has no son, then you shall cause his inherit-
> ance to pass to his daughter. And if he has no daughter, then you shall
> give his inheritance to his brothers. And if he has no brothers, then
> you shall give his inheritance to his father's brothers. And if his father
> has no brothers, then you shall give his inheritance to his kinsman
> that is next to him of his family, and he shall possess it" (Num. 27:8-
> 11).

Scripture, like the Halakhah of the Oral Torah, wants inheritances
to remain in the male line.

> 2.   TESTIMONY AS TO RELATIONS: One may not give unsubstantiated
> testimony as to a relationship in such wise as to affect someone else's
> property rights.
> 3.   JOINT MANAGEMENT OF AN ESTATE: [If] he left adult and minor
> sons—[if] the adults improved the value of the estate, the increase in
> value is in the middle [shared by all heirs]. If they had said, "See what
> father has left us. Lo, we are going to work it and [from that] we shall
> enjoy the usufruct," the increase in value is theirs. If brothers who jointly
> hold an estate incur public duties, the estate is charged.
> 4.   GIFTS IN CONTEMPLATION OF DEATH: A gift in contemplation of
> death may be retracted. A dying man who wrote over all his property
> to others [as a gift] but left himself a piece of land of any size what-
> ever—his gift is valid. [If] he did not leave himself a piece of land of
> any size whatever, his gift is not valid.
> 5.   PREPARING COMMERCIAL DOCUMENTS, E.G., WRITS OF DEBT, BONDS
> AND THE LIKE: If one has the power to issue such a document, it may
> be prepared in the absence of the other; but if both parties must con-
> cur, then both parties must be present when the document is prepared.

While Baba Batra encompasses a few facts of Scripture, it pursues
its own topical program. The main points are these. (1) Joint holders of a common property enjoy equal rights and equal responsibilities. (2) Title passes through usucaption, properly established. (3)
Title covers what is integral to that which is sold, not what is pe-
ripheral (encompassing C/2, reasonable expectations). (4) Inheritances pass through the male line. If I had to identify the center of it
all, it would be at C/1: both parties have a right to a fair deal, and

neither may emerge with more than he entered the transaction. Here, once more, Scripture has made its contribution of facts, but the contribution proves paltry. More to the point, the Halakhah of the Oral Torah does not emerge as a secondary expansion of that of the Written Torah, nor does it derive from a continuous exegetical process generated thereby. The Torah is perfected through not only a labor of regularization and clarification and harmonization, but a work of fresh initiative throughout.

vi. *Is Scripture the Source of the Halakhah of the Oral Torah?*

The answer for the Civil Law code is, yes and no, but mostly no. The issue is not quantity but generative source. First, where Scripture's laws intersect with the program of the framers of the code of civil law, those laws take a critical position in the code. But, second, Scripture simply does not define the organization or the category-formations of the code, let alone its problematic. The real question is, whence have sages derived their program, the source of the questions, in respect to the topics that they treat, that they deem urgent? The answer is, the Oral Torah as recorded in the Halakhah founded in the Mishnah brings to bear its own problems, its own theory and its own conception of matters. The Oral Torah does not merely fill in gaps of the Written one, nor does it only organize and systematize and regularize by topics the heritage of the Written one. At its deepest structures, the Oral Torah makes an original statement of its own and stands as an autonomous, correlative component of the one whole Torah of Moses, our rabbi.

What lies at the foundations? The fact that the third division of the Halakhah continues the second supplies the answer. Baba Mesia flows uninterruptedly into Baba Batra, and, it follows, the issue of whether and how intentionality plays a role requires attention. But why cut off the discussion of a topic, such as is done in the jarring break from Baba Mesia chapter ten to Baba Batra chapter one? If not topical, the break then must derive from some other consideration. Since, we noted, the concluding third of Baba Mesia takes up situations in which intentionality may or may not enter into the adjudication of a case, it becomes relevant to take note that in the opening unit of Baba Batra, intentionality plays *no* role at all. That is to say, joint holders enjoy certain rights in common, and how they personally wish to arrange matters has no bearing. Custom overrides intentionality; the right of the community overrides even agreements among individuals; the rights of the other must be respected.

If we wish to make the point that certain considerations override intentionality, and certain others do not, there is, moreover, no more effective way of making such a statement than to say, even where the owner of a property has not abandoned the hope of recovering the property—even when despair has not nullified his title—he may still lose the property. His neglect of his rights speaks for itself and overrides his intentionality toward the property; actions here set aside attitude. That comes about when the owner neglects the property, so, by his action, indicates disinterest in the property.

And, finally, the private, idiosyncratic intention of the purchaser is null, if common usage is violated. The buyer may say that he assumed the sale of property encompassed various movables, but that claim is null. People conform to customary usage, including language, and cannot invent their own conditions of sale. The law does not take account of idiosyncrasy. That same matter carries us forward to C/1-2, unstated stipulations govern when all parties share the same general view; so far as nullifying a transaction, the reasonable expectations of each party are taken into account in accord with a common law. When it comes to transferring property at death, there is a way for one's intentionality to prevail, and that is through an act of donation (gift) before death; but when it comes to transferring property through the right of inheritance, then the Torah's law takes over, and personal intentionality—which we should have placed at the very center of dividing an estate—is null. So, seen from this perspective, the entire set of rules forms a sustained essay on where and how intentionality gives way before established procedures and usages.

Viewed as we have, the system of civil law put forth by the Oral Torah must be judged alone to have supplied the Torah with a system of civil law; the Written Torah did not do so. Its scattered facts fit into the system, but were not generated, and did not yield, a system, only random information, of limited utility in constructing the civil order.

vii. *How Does the Oral Torah Solve the Problem Set forth by Scripture?*

By the criterion of the Oral Torah, perfection requires constructing a cogent, encompassing system of civil law, a system that is logically set forth to respond to broad issues of a philosophical character, having to do with a pervasive concern for the role of intentionality in the articulation of the civil law. The precipitating question for the system is, when does a person's will register, and when does it make no difference? That issue is hardly peculiar to civil law; it pervades the sub-system of Purities, for one thing, and surfaces throughout Holy Things as well. But intentionality hardly demands a place on the agenda of civil law, yet proves the paramount taxonomic principle, imposing order and structure throughout. But it is not the sole generative principle. The topical program that is animated by it divides along other lines as well, specifically, restoring the social order versus maintaining it.

How so? The first half of the tractates, which, as we noted at the outset, break in the middle of Baba Mesia, focuses upon repairing damage that is done to the social order, the second half, upon preserving the balance and perfection of that same social order. Israel in its interior relationships is governed by Halakhah that establishes and maintains stasis, which signifies perfection, all things in their place, all persons possessing appropriate value in property, security in person. That goal the Halakhah accomplishes, as is clear, by righting imbalances and once they are restored, by preserving them. That dual purpose explains why the three tractates form a single, unfolding and coherent statement, half (Baba Qamma's ten chapters and the first five chapters of Baba Mesia) devoted to repairing damages done to the political economy of society by chattel and persons, the other half (the second five chapters of Baba Mesia and Baba Batra's ten chapters)[1] to maintaining the perfection of equitable relationships. To interpret that statement, we have to stand back and see

---

[1] The division into chapters is integral to the presentation of the tractates, as shown by the formal traits that define a given chapter and separate it from others, fore and aft. So form-analysis has shown. If the printers had not imposed the divisions by chapters, we should still know how to divide the several tractates and the Halakhah they set forth, since where a topic changes, the form shifts as well. This is now a well-established fact. It accounts for the analysis given in the text, which on formal-analytical bases treats the division into tractates and chapters as integral to the document and not imposed at some later point by copyists or printers.

the three tractates whole. Then the several dimensions of discourse will emerge.

When we survey the entire construction of the thirty topical chapters of the three Babas, what we see is a simple set of eight units. They move from abnormal to normal events, I-IV, then V-VIII. The whole begins with damages done by chattels or by persons, thefts and other sorts of conversion of the property of others, with special attention to how we restore to a state of normality the property and person of the injured party. Numbers I-IV run through the whole of Baba Qamma and half way through Baba Mesia, to M. B.M. 5:11. The second half of the three tractates then shifts to normal transactions, not those involving torts and damages: labor relationships, rentals and bailments, real estate transactions, inheritances and estates, units V-VIII.

Then the whole, as I said, produces two complementary constructions, first abnormal or illicit, then normal or licit transactions. That is shown by the correspondence of unit IV, illicit commercial transactions (overcharge and usury) and unit VII, licit commercial transactions, the legal transfer of goods, unstipulated conditions and how they are enforced. This plan furthermore explains why we treat bailments twice, at III.C, damages to bailments, and then at V.C, E, responsibilities of the bailee. The former fits into the larger structure of law on the restoration of the balance of the social order (here, the value possessed by parties to the transaction at the outset, equitably distributed at the end), the latter, that on the preservation of the same order.

If we look again at the snapshot of the whole given at the outset, we see a clear picture. All of Baba Qamma takes up the results of wicked intentionality, an act of will that takes the form of malice, on the one side, or flagrant neglect of one's duties, on the other. The rules of Baba Mesia address the situations in which intentionality plays a role, is excluded as irrelevant, and may or may not enter into the adjudication of a situation of conflict. And, as we have seen, the topics treated in Baba Batra in common take account of the idiosyncrasy of intentionality and exclude private interest from intervening in customary arrangements.

So we may say that the entire repertoire of topics lays itself out as a huge essay on the role of man's intentionality and consequent responsibility—his will, his private plans—in the ordering of Israel's inner life. All topics grouped by me as illicit transactions involve righting the wrongs done by people on their own account. When free will is taken into account, encompassing negligence and malice, the social order requires forceful intervention to right the balance upset by individual aggression. Some licit transactions permit individual intentionality to register, specifically, those freely entered into and fairly balanced among contracting parties. And some licit transactions leave no space for the will of the participants and their idiosyncratic plans. Considerations of fairness take over and exclude any engagement with the private and the personal. So Israel's social order takes account of intentionality, especially controlling for the damage that ill will brings about.

The first fifteen chapters then treat intentionality in the form of negligence as a critical factor in assessing damages. But normal licit transactions are carried forward in accord with those rules of balance, proportion, and coherence that yield a society that is stable and enduring, fair and trustworthy. In the second fifteen chapters, intentionality forms only one consideration in the process of preserving the status, as to value, of parties to transactions and exchanges; it may make all the difference, no difference, some difference; it may not enter into consideration at all. That underscores the judgment of the Halakhah that, when it comes to righting wrongs against chattels and persons, the malefactor has acted willfully and has therefore to be penalized in an equitable manner. By his act of will, he has diminished the property or person of the victim; he must then restore the property or person to its prior value, so far as this is possible, and may not benefit from what he has done.

viii. *Does the Halakhah of the Oral Torah Set forth in the Babas Take as its Principal Task the Exegesis of Scripture's Laws?*

Let us now recapitulate the principal concern defined by the present study: does the Halakhah of the Oral Torah set forth in the Babas take as its principal task the exegesis of the Written Torah's laws? The key is, what is principal? Certainly, I have shown, what Scripture presents episodically, the Halakhah takes over and portrays systematically. That is so in Baba Qamma. But that does not define the primary task carried out by the Oral Torah's code of civil law. Indeed, the purpose of the tractates in no way comes to realization in the articulation of the law of Scripture on the topics at hand. That is proved by the simple fact that most of Baba Mesia and Baba Batra

pursues problems to which Scripture in no way devotes even episodic rulings or remarks. So where Scripture provides topics of the
Halakhah, the Oral Torah faithfully attends to that Halakhah; but
the Oral Torah in no way limits itself to Scripture's repertoire of
topics. More to the point, the Oral Torah organizes the Halakhah
systematically, but in accord with its own system and its problematics, not in accord with the system—the order, the program—of the
Written Torah. We have, therefore, to look elsewhere for the religious program that animates the Halakhah of the Babas.

For that purpose, our mind naturally turns to the generative conviction that the one and only God created the world in justice.[2] That
conviction precipitates acute tension between divine justice and man's
fate, the claim of a perfect creation and the palpable failure of world
order to realize stasis and perfection. Stability, stasis, equity in exchange and restoration of what is inequitable—these mark perfection of the social order that the Halakhah therefore proposes to bring
about in Israel's inner existence. Then what has the restorationist
reworking of the civil order into a state of perfection and stasis to
do with Israel's interior bonds and relationships? How, specifically,
does the formation of a civil order of stable, proportionate relationships in accord with principles of justice bring about Israel's right
relationship with God? Asking the question in this way dictates the
answer. The opening unit—Baba Qamma and the first half of Baba
Mesia—takes the more difficult labor of restoring the perfection of
the social order, the closing unit, the rest of Baba Mesia and Baba
Batra, the easier one of maintaining it.

How do the Rabbinic sages accomplish their statement in the
matter of restoring order and value? They undertake to expose the
rationality upon which the social order is founded. This they do
through their exposition of Scripture's laws of injury and misappropriation. They therefore formulate their own, much more elaborate
topical program for the civil order and the resolution of conflict at
home. That is how the sages in acute detail instantiate the order
that inheres in the episodic rules of Scripture: its power of restoring
and sustaining stasis. Since, in their intellectual context, consistency, immutability, coherence mark perfection, sages affirm that in its
details the Torah's design for dealing with conflict within holy Isra-

---

[2] *The Theology of the Oral Torah. Revealing the Justice of God.* Kingston and Montreal,
1999: McGill-Queen's University Press and Ithaca, 1999: Cornell University Press.

el promises to perfect Israel's workaday world in the model set forth at Sinai. The Written Torah makes clear God's intense interest in the justice and equity of the Israelites' ordinary transactions among themselves. Israelites are to form the kingdom of priests and the holy people. Their conduct with one another—the Written Torah's civil law insists in every line—shapes God's judgment of them and therefore dictates their fate. So sages here demonstrate what a man can do actively to participate in the perfection of the social order through the results of his own and his chattels' conduct. Here the consideration of man's free will proves paramount: what man by an act of will has upset, man by an act of will must restore.

Let us then return to the topical program of the Babas, working our way from start to finish. Take first of all the Halakhah of Baba Qamma—injury and misappropriation. That comes about when we ask, what, as signified by the Halakhah of Baba Qamma, does the Halakhah ask a man to do in relationship to the exemplary social order under construction within Israel? In accord with the Halakhah of Baba Qamma man undertakes to assume responsibility for what he does, always in just proportion to causation. Within Israel's social order what God wants a man to do is take responsibility for his own actions, for the results of what he or his chattel has done—no more, no less. And that pervasive point of insistence transforms our view of the Halakhic category before us. True, it forms an exercise in restoration and stasis of the just society.

But in the details of the law is worked out a chapter of theological anthropology, an answer to the question primary to constructing the social order, what, in the formation of the just society, can a man do? For what is a man responsible? And the answer is, a man can and must take responsibility for not only what he does but also—and especially—what he brings about, the things he may not do but does cause to happen. Viewed in this way, the laws of the Babas, particularly of Baba Qamma, form a massive essay upon the interplay of causation and responsibility: what one can have prevented but through negligence (in varying measure depending on context) has allowed to take place, he is deemed in that same measure to have caused. And for that, he is held in that same measure to make amends.

Responsibility begins in right attitude. Man must form the intentionality of taking responsibility for his actions; this he must do by an act of will. That is why the whole of Baba Qamma plays itself

out as an exercise in the definition of the valid intentionality in transactions involving damage and conflict. Where one has diminished
another, he must willingly take responsibility for his deed of omis-
sion or commission (as the tractate unfolds). The message of the
Halakhah on man's taking responsibility cannot be missed in the
ringing opening words of the Mishnah-tractate. I underline the full
statement of the matter that links causality and responsibility: "What
they have in common is that they customarily do damage and taking care of them is your responsibility. And when one of them has
caused damage, the [owner] of that which causes the damage is liable to pay compensation." I cannot overstress the centrality of the
next clause for stating the purpose of the entire system: *"In the case
of anything of which I am liable to take care, I am deemed to render possible
whatever damage it may do.* If I am deemed to have rendered possible
part of the damage it may do, I am liable for compensation as if [I
have] made possible all of the damage it may do." That remarkably eloquent, decisive formulation contains the entire message of
Baba Qamma and the first half of Baba Mesia.

It follows that man in all of his dignity is portrayed through the
Halakhah of Baba Qamma as possessed (1) of free will to assume
responsibility, on the one side, and (2) of the power to take action
in consequence of responsibility, on the other. And that principle
assumes religious status in two steps. First, in the words of the Written
Torah God himself has framed the laws that link causation and responsibility—negligence and culpability, for instance. In the very
portrayal of the holy society that Israel at Sinai is commanded to
realize, God's stake in man's framing of the social order is made
explicit. And consequently, second, Israel in the workaday transactions of one person with another acts out in this-worldly terms its
governing principle of transactions with Heaven. The one in palpable terms shows the character of the other in intangible ways.

Does the Halakhah of injury and misappropriation focus upon
the link of causation and responsibility? The cited language shows
that the Halakhah states in so many words the fundamental law of
man's responsibility for the consequences of his actions. It insists upon
God's stake in the transaction by systematically working out Scripture's rules and even stating their general principle. What follows?
A catalogue that encompasses nearly the entire detailed program of
the Halakhah of the Oral Torah. Consider the topical program of
the Halakhah, and see how, start to finish, the details define a state-

ment concerning the data of the category at hand. Here is the repertoire: how compensation is to be paid; the variation in compensation by reason of Scripture's distinctions, e.g., between cases of mere accident and those of culpable negligence (attested dangers), where people should have known to take care; man's responsibility for the public interest and the general welfare of the public domain; variables in liability for oneself and one's chattels; attenuated forms of responsibility ("He who causes a fire to break out through the action of a deaf-mute, idiot, or minor, is exempt from punishment under the laws of man, but liable to punishment under the laws of heaven"); penalties for causing damages done in the three dimensions of social concern: damages done to the Land (public property, encompassing ecological considerations), damages done to persons, and damages done to private property.

And the statement that is made, *and that can best be made in connection with the topics of injury and misappropriation*, emerges in sages' sorting out of details and nuances of responsibility and consequent liability for compensation. If someone set out to teach through a concrete example the variation of responsibility by reason of variables of what is willful and foreseeable and preventable, how better to deliver the message than by distinguishing between what is (formerly) deemed harmless and what is (formerly) an attested danger? The Halakhic medium precisely matches the theological message. For once the Torah makes that distinction, the message emerges: we are responsible for all damages that we could have foreseen, but our responsibility is mitigated when the damages cannot have been foreseen, prevented, let alone wanted. And, further, responsibility is to be accepted, damages compensated—the whole in a forthright transaction among honorable men.

If we could then summarize the details of the law in a few general principles, what should we say? The Halakhah holds that we are responsible for what we do and what we cause, but we are not responsible (or not responsible in the same degree) for what we cannot control. So the law asks, how does our action or lack of action relate to the consequence of what we do or not do? If we do not know that an act has caused a result, we cannot hold responsible the person who has done the act for the consequences he has brought about. The law works out these gradations between total culpability or blame, by reason of one's forming the efficient cause without mitigating considerations, and total absolution from culpability and blame, by reason of one's bearing no responsibility whatsoever for what has happened:

(1)   responsibility for all damages done, because the event that has caused loss and damage is voluntary and foreseeable, not the result of overwhelming external force; preventable; brought about by willful action; the result of culpable knowledge; deliberate choice, not mere negligence;

(2)   responsibility for the greater part of the damages that are done, because the damage is foreseeable; not the result of overwhelming external force; preventable; thus in the event the ignorance is classified as culpable; but not voluntary;

(3)   responsibility for the lesser part of the damages that are done, because the damage is foreseeable; but the result of overwhelming external force and not preventable, thus: involuntary, but the result of culpable ignorance and negligence;

(4)   no responsibility at all, the event being involuntary, the result of overwhelming external force, not foreseeable, hence, inculpable ignorance; e.g., pure chance.

We therefore identify in the working out of the Halakhah three operative criteria—points of differentiation in the analysis of events and the actions that produce them, which form a cubic grid, with, in theory, nine gradations of blame and responsibility and consequent culpability:

(1)   an event produced by an action that is voluntary vs. involuntary;

(2)   an event that is foreseeable vs. not foreseeable, or an action the consequences of which are foreseeable vs. not;

(3)   an event that is preventable vs. not preventable; or an action that is necessary and therefore blameless, or one that is not.

Thus we may construct a grid of three dimensions, one grid formed of considerations of what is voluntary vs. involuntary, the second, of what is foreseeable vs. not foreseeable, the third, of what is preventable vs. not preventable, lines. That permits us to identify an efficient cause that is voluntary, foreseeable, and preventable; voluntary, foreseeable, and not preventable; involuntary, foreseeable, and preventable; involuntary, not foreseeable, and not preventable; and so on.

ix. *The Imperfection of the Written Torah, the Perfection of the One Whole Torah of Moses, Our Rabbi*

The power of the Oral Torah lies in its analytical re-presentation of the civil law. But Scripture has set forth the issue: responsibility and intentionality, if not in an articulated, Halakhic framework. That is, after all, what is at stake in the narrative of Eden and Adam's and Eve's loss of Paradise. The Halakhah has simply articulated the interplay of responsibility and intentionality in singularly fitting cases. It has invented nearly everything except the main thing. I dwell on this matter of responsibility because for the Babas, particularly for Baba Qamma—on the surface an exercise in the recapitulation of Scripture's own law on the same topical program—it forms the *leitmotiv* of the Halakhah, the hermeneutical crux, the exegetical provocation for the analysis of particular problems.

What, exactly, is at stake in the linkage of causation and responsibility? The religious dimension of the matter emerges when we explain why the Halakhah makes the statement that it does. That statement, set forth in a few words, holds that in a society ordered by God's justice—as Israelite society is supposed to be—man will acknowledge his responsibility and bear the consequences of his actions. The negative here makes all the difference: what will Israelite man not do? Unlike Adam in Eden, he will not deny or dissimulate. He will not blame others and take no blame himself. When he has upset the social order by diminishing the other and aggrandizing the self, he will restore the balance he has upset. Confronted with the result of his own negligence or worse, man cannot shift the burden of blame or avoid responsibility for the consequences of what he has caused. And the entire arrangement for restoring the social balance and preserving the social order builds upon that principle. The Israelite social order then forms an arena for the exercise of man's accepting responsibility for what he does. What, in Israelite context, marks that statement as critical to the religious world of the Torah?

To answer that question, we revert to the initial point at which the world order of justice—balance, order, rationality—was disrupted by an act of man. And when we take up that moment of flaw and imperfection, we must examine whether and how the consideration of accepting responsibility for the damage one has done enters in. In this context, then, we turn to beginnings. The story of man's dis-

obedience in Eden (Gen. 3:11-13) tells why man's accepting responsibility for what he causes forms the center of the Halakhah of damages and misappropriation. Here is the original version of man's
denial of responsibility:

> God: *Did you eat of the tree from which I had forbidden you to eat?*
> Man: *The woman you put at my side—she gave me of the tree and I ate*
> God: *What is this you have done?*
> Woman: *The serpent duped me and I ate.*

At the center of the story of the human condition after Eden is man's
and woman's denial of responsibility for the deed each did, and,
implicitly, rejection of responsibility for the consequent loss of Eden
that is coming.

At the heart of the Halakhah of damages and misappropriation
is the opposite: Israelite man's explicit acceptance of responsibility
for what he causes. Why so? Because if Israel wants to show God
that it is regenerate, how better to do so than act out in cases of
damages and injury the requirement to bear responsibility for what
one does and causes to happen (Adam, Eve, respectively)? Here in
its everyday conduct of the inner affairs of the community, Israel
shows how, unlike Adam and Eve, through the instruction of the
Torah, Israel has learned what it means to take responsibility for
injury and damage to others.

Within Israel's workaday life, in the very practicalities of conflict
and its resolution aimed at restoring and preserving the perfection
of the status quo, is conducted an on-going exercise. It is one of
making explicit one's responsibility for what one has caused, then
apportioning damages in proportion to one's negligence or malfeasance. What is voluntary, foreseeable, and preventable imposes
maximum liability for restoration. Man cannot blame his ox, nor in
the public way impose upon bypassers the responsibility to accommodate the obstacles he has set up. The premise of the exercise is
that Israel's inner affairs, the transactions between and among Israelites, in the most practical terms, are conducted as a test of whether regenerate man—Israelite man—can bear responsibility for his
own actions, now viewed in the broadest context of causation, and,
if so, what it means to match levels of compensation to degrees of
responsibility. No excuses ("the woman you put at my side," "the
snake duped me") exculpate when one has caused damage, because
Israelite man assumes the burden of his actions and takes responsibility so far as possible to restore the world to its original condition,

before, in the here and now, some deed or act of negligence of his has disrupted it. I can think of no more direct response to "the woman...the snake..." than the language, "In the case of anything of which I am liable to take care, I am deemed to render possible whatever damage it may do."

So much for the first of the Babas. The second and third gates complete the picture. Here the issue is sustaining the social order, and here too attitude and intentionality come into play. But that is in a different way from the approach of Baba Qamma. Sin, crime, torts and damages—these carry forward bad attitudes; differentiating types and degrees of intentionality when addressing how the social order is disrupted yields nothing of interest. By contrast, in treating ordinary exchanges and transactions, the Halakhah for the second half of the Babas, half of Baba Mesia and all of Baba Batra, turns out to form an essay on when intentionality matters and when it does not.

How is this the case? That is when it comes to restoring the perfection of society. The generative issue is, specifically, where do we take account of intentionality and where not? Intentionality or attitude matters in situations of conflict. Then the attitude of both parties makes all the difference, since to resolve conflicting claims, we have in the end to conciliate all parties to a common outcome; there, intentionality or attitude forms the critical medium for restoring and sustaining balance and order. Parties to an exchange are now responsible to one another, and they must intend the outcome to be a proportionate and equal exchange of value. Both parties must accept the outcome, that is, form at the end the same attitude toward the transaction. A claim of ownership ends in an act of despair. Responsibility is proportionate to the attitude of the bailee, that is, to the degree of accountability that he has accepted to begin with. So much for the uses of intentionality in the restoration and maintenance of the social order.

But then where do we dismiss as null all considerations of intentionality or attitude, even when parties to an exchange concur? In market transactions, by contrast, true value overrides the attitude of the players, who cannot agree to an exchange that in objective terms is deemed null. Even where all parties agree, the Torah too must approve. And, we noted, we impute to all parties the same attitude and deny the pertinence of idiosyncratic or private meanings. Broadly-held expectations govern, whether those of custom or of the written Torah's own law. In these two ways—the Torah's law, which is not relative to the will of man, and established custom, which defines the norm for man—intentionality possesses no power, because it serves no purpose in restoring or sustaining the balances of a well-ordered society.

So the thirty chapters, breaking into two halves at the end of the first fifteen, set forth a massive exercise in the applied reason and practical logic of the abstract philosophical and (here) mythic-theological categories, responsibility and intentionality. What message emerges when we move from the illicit to the licit, the abnormal to the normal? The transactions that all together form the ordinary life of inner Israel, Israel on its own, yield two matching propositions.

First, when it comes to acts that disrupt the social order, man is responsible for what he does.

But, second, when we turn to transactions that sustain the ordinary relationships within Israel, man's proper intentionality takes over.

Then man's will forms only one element in a complex transaction. Where wills clash, compromise takes over. Where the Torah imposes its own rule, intentionality is null. Publicly-accepted custom and procedure take the paramount position. In cases of negligence or malfeasance, man takes responsibility for what he has done—so much for the first half of the Babas.

And that brings us to the everyday conduct of affairs in ordinary Israelite society. Social order restored, the status quo as to value regained, what forces hold the whole together? Where responsibility prevails, man's own will and intentionality, God's will in the Torah, and the customary arrangements of a stable, just society—all these variables come into play and are to be sorted out. That is why, while single message addresses the abnormal and the illicit, the realm of torts and damages: take responsibility, a much more complex message states the requirements of maintaining matters. That message responds to the realities of the ideal society that the Halakhah makes possible.

Specifically, Israel in its interior arrangements is to hold in the balance (1) personal will, (2) the Torah's law, and (3) the long-standing customary requirements of enduring order. In the Babas, as this survey of the Halakhah has shown, these distinct and inter-related forces—man's will, God's law, and accepted public practice—are far from abstractions. In the interplay of individual will, God's ab-

solute law, and ancient, enduring custom, comes about the realization of Israel in the here and now. It is self-evident that the messages conveyed by the Halakhah of the Babas originate not in the law
of Scripture, which does not coalesce into a single coherent statement in any event. Rather the strikingly coherent structure before
us arises out of the deep layers of rationality that infuse the formation of the principles and then the details of the Halakhah of the
Oral Torah: the program and its articulation and exegesis. Scripture has defined the matrix, the Oral Torah in its Halakhah, the
particular context, and the details of the law, the text. Now the
question is, how does the Halakhic medium match the Halakhic
message? And in what way does monotheism figure in all this?

CHAPTER TWO

THE MATCH OF MESSAGE AND MEDIUM (1)
HALAKHIC

i. *Criterion of Perfection: How Better Deliver the Message than through the Selected Medium?*

The message of hierarchical classification that forms the medium of the Halakhah of the Mishnah is that many things really form a single thing, the many species a single genus, the many genera an encompassing and well-crafted, cogent whole. And the process works in the other direction as well. Every time we speciate, we affirm that position. So too, each successful labor of Halakhic exposition, of forming relationships among species, e.g., making them into a genus, or identifying the hierarchy of the species, proves it again. Not only so, but when we can show that many things are really one, or that one thing yields many (the reverse and confirmation of the former), we say in a fresh way a single immutable truth, the one of this philosophy concerning the unity of all being in an orderly composition of all things within a single taxon. Exegesis always is repetitive—and a sound exegesis of the systemic exegesis must then be equally so, everywhere explaining the same thing in the same way. What we have before us is monotheism expressed through natural philosophy, thus: philosophical monotheism. But in saying so, I have gotten ahead of my story. Let me start from the beginning.

Chapter one has shown that the Halakhah forms a dual message, the concrete one involved in the details of the law, the abstract one embodied in the concrete details. For expressing their philosophical message, given their preference for the concrete over the abstract, the Rabbinic sages cannot have chosen a more suitable medium than the Halakhah as they expose its structure. For Scripture endowed them with a massive heritage of details, awaiting systematization, extension and amplification. The sages preserved that received medium of concrete, detailed rulings. But these rulings they organized by topics. Then they made the topics bear the message of abstract principle, transcending law altogether, as we saw in the matter of the Babas with their subtext devoted to intentionality and responsibility. So the Rabbinic sages thought philosophically about law, just as, we shall see in chapters three and four, they thought theologically about religious propositions set forth in Scripture. When responding to Scripture, accordingly, the authorities who recorded the Oral Torah aimed to form of the details of the Halakhah set forth in the Mishnah a statement that stood for more than the case at hand.

But how does the dual-voice of the Halakhic exposition bear upon the issue of perfection, and what criterion of perfection do I invoke in the present context? To review the familiar answer to the second question first: a perfect piece of writing will match the message with the medium. Compelling evidence must accrue that the Rabbinic sages have chosen the best of all possible media for the expression, within the framework of the law, of the philosophical or the theological proposition they wished to convey. And the first question answers itself in that context: the Halakhic exposition through matters of well-ordered detail gives concrete and immediate expression to a critical philosophical and theological proposition, vastly transcending the particularities of the data that embody that proposition. The medium they chose embodied the message it was selected to convey, as we now shall see.

I take as the message that of monotheism, namely, the statement that one God created the world and, the ground of all being, orders all things in it. I take as the medium the Halakhic demonstration that all things flow from one thing, and one thing contains within itself everything. So the medium is ideal for conveying the philosophical, metaphysical monotheism embodied in systematic exposition of details. Rather than amplify these simple claims, let me turn to concrete evidence that supports them. At the end we shall return to the issue briefly touched on here: the message and its chosen medium.

ii. *The Halakhah as the Medium for the Exposition of Philosophical Monotheism*

Philosophical monotheism maintains that all things are not only orderly, but ordered in such wise that many things fall into one classification, and one thing may hold together many things of a diverse classifications. The category-formations of the Mishnah repeatedly show how many things are made to say one thing and one thing to yield many things. Through much of the Halakhah, as we shall see, the Mishnah claims to show that the foundations of being are unitary. One construction of all things into one, one thing forms the source of all things—a process that goes in both directions, attests to the unity of all being. The two matched and complementary propositions—many things are one, one thing encompasses many—complement each other, because, in forming matched opposites, the two provide a single, complete and final judgment of the whole of being, social, natural, supernatural alike. That outcome forms the demonstration of philosophical monotheism through the nature of being. It shows how the philosophical message of the Mishnah is matched by the philosophical medium of hierarchical classification that dominates in the Mishnah's presentation of the Halakhah.

Here is where I find that perfect match I promised to identify. Showing (1) that all things can be ordered, each thing in its taxon, all taxa in correct sequence, from least to greatest, and (2) that all orders can be set into relationship with one another, we transform taxic method into ontological message. We say the same thing about the nature of things in many ways, which is precisely how the sages set forth the Halakhah. And that one thing encompasses all things, defines the point of sages' Halakhic discourse throughout. So living the life well ordered by the law of the Torah was made into an exercise in realized monotheism. No more apt, indeed elegant, medium for the message of philosophical monotheism presents itself than the Halakhic one. That is because its concreteness exposes within itself compelling evidence of ontological monotheism.

To show how this theology yields a hermeneutics that begets a systematic mode of Halakhic exegesis, I work backward, as the Halakhah requires, from exegesis of details to hermeneutics that govern throughout to the theology that is shown embedded in the details as interpreted properly. Thus the sequence follows: from case to rule to governing principle. To begin with, I turn to the sustained effort to demonstrate how many classes of things—actions, relationships, circumstances, persons, places—are demonstrated really to form one class. Just as God, in creation, ordered all things, each in its class under its name, so in the Mishnah (and its continuation-documents of the Halakhah, that is, the Tosefta, Yerushalmi, and Bavli) the Halakhic classification works its way through the potentialities of chaos to explicit order. As in the miracle of God's creation of the world in six days, here too is classification transformed from the *how* of intellection to the *why* and the *what for* and, above all, the *what-does-it-all-mean*. Through the medium of the Halakhic labor of hierarchical classification, God is set at the apex of ontological analysis.

But speaking of God in the context of the Mishnah proves jarring, for God is not at issue. The issue concerns nature and ontology, not supernature and theology, and sorts out and sifts the everyday data of the here and the now. It will prove its points, therefore, by appeal to the palpable facts of creation, which everyone knows and can test. So recognition that one thing may fall into several categories and many things into a single one comes to expression, for the authorship of the Mishnah, in secular ways. One of the interesting ones is the analysis of the several taxa into which a single action may fall, with an account of the multiple consequences, e.g., as to sanctions that are called into play, for a single action. The right taxonomy of persons, actions, and things will show the unity of all being by finding many things in one thing, and that forms the first of the two components of what I take to be the Halakhic philosophy's teleology.

Mishnah-tractate Keritot 3:9

A. There is one who ploughs a single furrow and is liable on eight counts of violating a negative commandment:

B. [specifically, it is] he who (1) ploughs with an ox and an ass [Deut. 22:10], which are (2, 3) both Holy Things, in the case of (4) [ploughing] Mixed Seeds in a vineyard [Deut. 22:9], (5) in the Seventh Year [Lev. 25:4], (6) on a festival [Lev. 23:7] and who was both a (7) priest [Lev. 21:1] and (8) a Nazirite [Num. 6:6] [ploughing] in a grave-yard.

C. Hanania b. Hakhinai says, "Also: He is [ploughing while] wearing a garment of diverse kinds" [Lev. 19:19, Deut. 22:11].

D. They said to him, "This is not within the same class."

E. He said to them, "Also the Nazir [B8] is not within the same class [as the other transgressions]."

Here is a case in which more than a single set of flogging is called for. B's felon is liable to 312 stripes, on the listed counts. The ox is sanctified to the altar, the ass to the Temple upkeep (B2, 3). Hanania's contribution is rejected since it has nothing to do with ploughing, and sages' position is equally flawed. The main point, for our inquiry, is simple. The one action draws in its wake multiple consequences. Classifying a single thing as a mixture of many things then forms a part of the larger intellectual address to the nature of mixtures. But it yields a result that, in the analysis of an action, far transcends the metaphysical problem of mixtures, because it moves us toward the ontological solution of the unity of being.

So much for actions. How about substances? Can we say that diverse things, each in its own classification, form a single thing? Indeed so. Here is one example, among a great many candidates, taken from Mishnah-tractate Hallah. The tractate takes as its theme the dough-offering to which the framers assume Num. 15:17-21 refers: "of the first of your coarse meal you shall present a cake as an offering." The tractate deals with the definition of dough liable to the dough offering, defining the bread, the process of separating dough-offering, and the liability of mixtures.

Mishnah-tractate Hallah 1:1, 3

1:1 A. [Loaves of bread made from] five types [of grain] are subject to dough offering:

B. (1) wheat, (2) barley, (3) spelt, (4) oats, and (5) rye;

C. lo, [loaves of bread made from] these [species] are subject to dough offering,

D. and combine with each other [for the purpose of reckoning whether or not a batch of dough comprises the minimum volume subject to dough offering (M. Hal. 1:4, 2:6, M. Ed. 1:2)].

E. and products of these species are forbidden for common use until Passover under the category of new produce [produce harvested before the waving of the first sheaf (Lev. 23:14)].

F. And grasses of these species may not be reaped until the reaping of the first sheaf.

G. And if they took root prior to the waving of the first sheaf, the waving of the first sheaf releases them for common use;

H. but if they did not take root prior to the waving of the omer, they are forbidden for common use until the next omer.

1:3 A. Grain in the following categories is liable to dough-offering when made into dough but exempt from tithes:

B. Gleanings, forgotten sheaves, produce in the corner of a field, that which has been abandoned, first tithe from which heave offering of the tithe has been removed, second tithe, and that which is dedicated to the temple which has been redeemed, the left over portion of grain which was harvested for the offering of the first sheaf, and grain which has not reached a third of its anticipated growth.

C. R. Eliezer says, "Grain which has not reached one third of its growth is exempt from dough offering when made into dough."

M. Hal. 1:1 addresses the issuing of whether or not five species of grain join together to produce dough of sufficient volume to incur liability to the dough-offering. Since they share in common the trait that they are capable of being leavened (*himus*), they do. So the genus encompasses all of the species, with the result that the classification-process is neatly illustrated. "Joining together" or connection then forms a statement that these many things are one thing. M. 1:2 makes the same point about the five species. The interstitial cases at M. Hal. 1:3 are subject to ownership other than that of the farmer. But that fact does not change their status as to dough offering. We take no account of the status with regard to ownership, past or present use as another type of offering, or the stage of growth of the grain whence the dough derives. This then forms the other side of the taxonomic labor: indicators that do not register also serve to distinguish. The upshot is as I said: many things are one thing; one rule applies to a variety of classes of grains.

The real interest in demonstrating the unity of being lies not in things but in abstractions, and, among abstractions, types of actions take the center stage. So I present in evidence not episodic compositions, but the better part of a complete composite, a tractate, which, I maintain, is formulated to address the issue of method that I deem critical. For that purpose I point to Mishnah-tractate Keritot, because its governing purpose is to work out how many things are really one thing. This is accomplished by showing the end or consequence of diverse actions to be always one and the same. The issue of the tractate is the definition of occasions on which one is obligated to bring a sin-offering and a suspensive guilt-offering. The tractate lists those sins that are classified together by the differentiating criterion of intention. If one deliberately commits those sins, he is punished through extirpation. If it is done inadvertently, he brings a sin-offering. In case of doubt as to whether or not a sin has been committed (hence: inadvertently), he brings a suspensive guilt offering. Lev. 5:17-19 specifies that if one sins but does not know it, he brings a sin-offering or a guilt offering. Then if he does, a different penalty is invoked, with the suspensive guilt offering at stake as well. While we have a sustained exposition of implications of facts that Scripture has provided, the tractate also covers problems of classification of many things as one thing, in the form of a single-sin-offering for multiple sins, and that problem fills the bulk of the tractate.

MISHNAH-TRACTATE KERITOT 1:1, 2, 7, 3:2, 4

1:1 A. Thirty-six transgressions subject to extirpation are in the Torah...

1:2 A. For those [transgressions] are people liable, for deliberately doing them, to the punishment of extirpation,

B. and for accidentally doing them, to the bringing of a sin offering,

C. and for not being certain of whether or not one has done them, to a suspensive guilt offering [Lev. 5:17]—

D. "except for the one who imparts uncleanness to the sanctuary and its Holy Things,

E. "because he is subject to bringing a sliding scale offering (Lev. 5:6-7, 11)," the words of R. Meir.

F And sages say, "Also: [except for] the one who blasphemes, as it is said, 'You shall have one law for him that does anything unwittingly' (Num. 15:29)—excluding the blasphemer, who does no concrete deed."

1:7 A. The woman who is subject to a doubt concerning [the appearance of] five fluxes,

B. or the one who is subject to a doubt concerning five miscarriages

C. brings a single offering.

D. And she [then is deemed clean so that she] eats animal sacrifices.

E. And the remainder [of the offerings, A, B] are not an obligation for her.

F. [If she is subject to] five confirmed miscarriages,

G. or five confirmed fluxes,

H. she brings a single offering.

1. And she eats animal sacrifices.

J. But the rest [of the offerings, the other four] remain as an obligation for her [to bring at some later time]—

K. M'SH S: A pair of birds in Jerusalem went up in price to a golden denar.

L. Said Rabban Simeon b. Gamaliel, "By this sanctuary! I shall not rest tonight until they shall be at [silver] denars."

M. He entered the court and taught [the following law]:

N. "The woman who is subject to five confirmed miscarriages [or] five confirmed fluxes brings a single offering.

0. "And she eats animal sacrifices.

P "And the rest [of the offerings] do not remain as an obligation for her."

0. And pairs of birds stood on that very day at a quarter-denar each [one one-hundredth of the former price].

3:2 A. [If] he ate [forbidden] fat and [again ate] fat in a single spell of inadvertence, he is liable only for a single sin offering,

B. [If] he ate forbidden fat and blood and remnant and refuse [of an offering] in a single spell of inadvertence, he is liable for each and every one of them.

C. This rule is more strict in the case of many kinds [of forbidden food] than of one kind.

D. And more strict is the rule in [the case of] one kind than in many kinds:

E. For if he ate a half—olive's bulk and went and ate a half—olive's bulk of a single kind, he is liable.

F. [But if he ate two half-olive's bulks] of two [different] kinds, he is exempt.

3:4 A. There is he who carries out a single act of eating and is liable on its account for four sin offerings and one guilt offering:

B. An unclean [lay] person who ate (1) forbidden fat, and it was (2) remnant (3) of Holy Things, and (4) it was on the Day of Atonement.

C. R. Meir says, "If it was the Sabbath and he took it out [from one domain to another] in his mouth, he is liable [for another sin offering]."

D. They said to him, "That is not of the same sort [of transgression of which we have spoken heretofore since it is not caused by eating (A)]."

M. Ker. 1:7 introduces the case of classifying several incidents within a single taxon, so that one incident encompasses a variety of cases and therefore one penalty or sanction covers a variety of instances. That same conception is much more amply set forth in chapter two of the tractate. There we have lists of five who bring a single offering for many transgressions, five who bring a sliding scale offering for many incidents, and the like, so M. 2:3-6. Then M. 3:1-3 we deal with diverse situations in which a man is accused of having eaten forbidden fat and therefore of owing a sin-offering. At M. 3:1 the issue is one of disjoined testimony. Do we treat as one the evidence of two witnesses. The debate concerns whether two cases form a single category. Sages hold that the case are hardly the same, because there are differentiating traits. M. 3:2-3 show us how we differentiate or unify several acts. We have several acts of transgression in a single spell of inadvertence; we classify them all as one action for purposes of the penalty. That at stake is the problem of classification and how we invoke diverse taxic indicators is shown vividly at M. 3:2 in particular. Along these same lines are the issues of M. Ker. 3:3, 4-6: "There is he who carries out a single act of eating and is liable on its account for four sin-offerings and one guilt-offering; there is he who carries out a single act of sexual intercourse and becomes liable on its account for six sin-offerings," with the first shown at M. 3:4.

So much for the impalpable and invisible realm of classification and status. There we can conjure, but cannot touch or feel or see, the lines of structure and division. Order is imputed and imagined. What about the visible world of space? Here we can frame a question that permits a highly tangible representation of the complexity of unity and diversity, the demonstration that one thing encompasses many things, so many things form one thing. The question is asked in this way: When is a field a field, and when is it two or ten fields? That taxonomic problem of how many are one, or how one is deemed many, is addressed at Mishnah-tractate Peah, which concerns itself with giving to the poor produce abandoned at the corner of a field. Then we have to know what constitutes a field, hence the question of when one thing is many things, or when many things are one thing, framed in terms of spatial relations:

MISHNAH-TRACTATE PEAH 2:1, 5; 3:5[1]

2:1 A. And these [landmarks] establish [the boundaries of a field] for [purposes of designating] peah:

B. (1) a river, (2) pond, (3) private road, (4) public road, (5) public path, (6) private path that is in use in the hot season and in the rainy season, (7) uncultivated land, (8) newly broken land, (9) and [an area sown with] a different [type of] seed.

C. "And [as regards] one who harvests young grain [for use as fodder—the area he harvests] establishes [the boundaries of a field]," the words of R. Meir.

D. But sages say, "[The area he harvests] does not establish [the boundaries of a field], unless he has also ploughed [the stubble] under."

2:5 A. One who sows his field with [only] one type [of seed], even if he harvests [the produce] in two lots

B. designates one [portion of produce as] peah [from the entire crop].

C. If he sowed [his field] with two types [of seeds], even if he harvests [the produce] in only one lot,

D. he designates two [separate portions of produce as] peah, [one from each type of produce].

E. He who sows his field with two types of wheat—

F [if] he harvests [the wheat] in one lot, [he] designates one [portion of produce as] peah.

G. [But if he harvests the wheat in] two lots, [he] designates two [portions of produce as] peah.

3:5 A. [Two] brothers who divided [ownership of a field which previously they had jointly owned]

B. give two [separate portions of produce] as peah [each designates peah on behalf of the produce of his half of the field].

C. [If] they return to joint ownership [of the field]

D. [together] they designate one [portion of produce] as peah [on behalf of the entire field].

---

[1] Source: Roger Brooks, *Support for the Poor in the Mishnaic Law of Agriculture: Tractate Peah* (Chico, 1983: Scholars Press for Brown Judaic Studies).

E. Two [men] who [jointly] purchased a tree [together] designate one
[portion of produce] as peah [on behalf of the entire tree]—
F. But if one purchased the northern [half of the tree], and the other
purchased the southern [half of the tree],
G. the former designates peah by himself, and the latter designates
peah by himself.

The principle of division rests upon the farmer's attitude and actions toward a field. If the farmer harvests an area as a single entity, that action indicates his attitude or intentionality in regard to that
area and serves to mark it as a field. For each patch of grain the
householder reaps separately a peah-share must be designated; the
action indicates the intentionality to treat the area as a single field.
But natural barriers intervene; rivers or hills also may mark off a
fields boundaries, whatever the farmer's action and therefore a pri-
ori intentionality or attitude. So in classifying an area of ground as
a field, there is an interplay between the givens of the physical traits
and the attitude, confirmed by action, of the farmer.

M. Peah 2:5-8 provide excellent cases for the application of these
operative principles. A farmer might harvest a single field delimited
by physical barriers, or now may harvest two fields in one lot. In
both cases we ask: do the physical barriers define matters? Or does
the attitude of the farmer confirmed by his action dictate the field's
boundary? And a further issue is whether or not a field produces a
single crop. If it does, then a single portion is designated, even if
the produce is harvested on a number of different occasions. Brooks
states in his commentary to Peah, "Because the householder has
ignored the boundaries clearly established by the field's physical characteristics, his actions have no effect. A parallel problem has a tract
of land planted with different species of a single genus. Here the farmer's actions are decisive, and, consequently, his intentionality enjoys
full play. So much for the many and the one.[2] Readers will surely

---

[2] A few more examples, chosen at random, conclude the demonstration by
showing the important fact that there is no limit imposed by the character of a
topic to the demonstration that many things form one thing. As to food, a common action links diverse classes of foods. M. Yoma 8:2-3 form a standard exercise
in classification and connection. In the genus of eating fall all foods, of drinking,
all liquids; for the present purpose, therefore, everything solid joins together with
everything else solid. That is a mode of classification that appeals to the purpose
of classification, a good point in teaching the speciation of genera. That point is
made explicitly, since liquids and foods, each with its own mode of ingestion, do

stipulate that any number of other examples of the same proposition, proved in the same manner, can be adduced. The ones in hand seem to me to suffice to demonstrate that, reading the Mishnah as philosophy, the document really does say some few things in a great many ways, in the analogy to the hedgehog, not the fox, offered at the outset.

If then many things become one thing, how about the one thing that yields the many? If we can show that a single classification may be *subdivided*, then the unity of the many in the one is demonstrated from a fresh angle. If so, the systemic contention concerning the fundamental and essential unity of all being finds reinforcement. That the question is faced may be shown, as usual in so coherent a piece of writing as the Mishnah, at a variety of passages. To take only a single instance, M. Makkot 3:5, 7-9 raise a question familiar to us from Mishnah-tractate Horayot: when are many actions classified as a single action, or a single action as many. But, more to the point, let us turn immediately to a very concrete reflection on the nature of actions and differentiating among them.

Mishnah-tractate Nazir 6:4-5

6:4 A. A Nazir who was drinking wine all day long is liable only on one count.

B. [If] they said to him, "Don't drink it!" "Don't drink it!" and he continues drinking, he is liable on each and every count [of drinking].

C. [If] he was cutting his hair all day long, he is liable only on a single count.

D. [If] they said to him, "Don't cut it!" "Don't cut it!" and he continued to cut his hair, he is liable for each and every count [of cutting].

E. [If] he was contracting corpse uncleanness all day long, he is liable on only one count.

F. If they said to him, "Don't contract corpse uncleanness!" "Don't contract corpse uncleanness!" and he continued to contract corpse uncleanness, he is liable for each and every count.

---

not join together to form the requisite volume. The equally familiar consideration of classifying sequences of distinct actions—are they one or many—occupies M. 8:3, another standard and familiar exercise. As to persons, castes differentiate, but individual traits, particular to a given person, do not. At M. Gittin 2:5 the classification of persons is worked out on a new principle. If the consideration of classification is not personal, then all persons fall into a single classification, there being no basis on which to differentiate among them and compose a hierarchy. That is explained: "The confirmation of a writ of divorce is solely through the signatures of the witnesses." The same fact affects the delivery. Excluded are those who are physically or mentally incapable, as specified.

6:5 A. Three things are prohibited to a Nazir: [corpse] uncleanness, cutting the hair, and anything which goes forth from the grapevine.
B. A more strict rule applies to corpse uncleanness and haircutting than applies to that which comes forth from the grapevine.
C. For corpse uncleanness and haircutting cause the loss of the days already observed, but [violating the prohibition against] that which goes forth from the vine does not cause the loss of the days already observed.
D. A more strict rule applies to that which goes forth from the vine than applies to corpse uncleanness and haircutting.
E. For that which goes forth from the vine allows for no exception, but corpse uncleanness and haircutting allow for exceptions,
F. in the case of [cutting the hair for] a religious duty and in the case of finding a neglected corpse [with no one else to provide for burial, in which case, the Nazir is absolutely required to bury the corpse].
G. A more strict rule applies to corpse uncleanness than to haircutting.
H. For corpse uncleanness causes the loss of all the days previously observed and imposes the liability for an offering.
I. But haircutting causes the loss of only thirty days and does not impose liability for an offering.

At M. Naz. 6:4 we take up the issue of disjoined actions, for each of which one is liable, when these actions are of a single species. What distinguishes one action from another, when all are of the same species, is that one is made aware each time he does the prohibited action that he is forbidden to do so. Then each action is individual. But if not, then all of the actions form a single sustained action, for which one is liable on only one count. This interesting conception then imposes upon the differentiation of actions the consideration of intentionality: the man now knows that the particular action he is about to undertake is prohibited. Hence it seems to me a case in which we invoke intentionality in the work of the classification of actions (= counts of culpability). What is at stake in the issue? It is the application of hierarchical classification, which as we know forms the goal of the philosophy's method of classification. So we see the unity of philosophical medium and philosophical message. For M. Naz. 6:5 takes the facts of Scripture and forms of them a composition of hierarchical classification, in which the taxic indicators are laid out in accord with a single program.

I have repeatedly claimed that the recognition that one thing becomes many does not challenge the philosophy of the unity of all being, but confirms the main point. Why do I insist on that proposition? The reason is simple. If we can show that differentiation flows from within what is differentiated,—that is, from the intrinsic or inherent traits of things—then we confirm that at the heart of things is a fundamental ontological being, single, cogent, simple, that is capable of diversification, yielding complexity and diversity. The upshot is to be stated with emphasis.

That diversity in species or diversification in actions subject to speciation of a common genus follows orderly lines confirms the claim that there is that single point from which many lines come forth.

Carried out in proper order—(1) the many form one thing, and (2) one thing yields many—the demonstration then leaves no doubt as to the truth of the matter. Ideally, therefore, we shall argue from the simple to the complex, showing that the one yields the many, one thing, many things, two, four.

Mishnah-tractate Shabbat 1:1

1:1 A. [Acts of] transporting objects from one domain to another, [which violate] the Sabbath, (1) are two, which [indeed] are four [for one who is] inside, (2) and two which are four [for one who is] outside,

B. How so?

C. [If on the Sabbath] the beggar stands outside and the householder inside,

D. [and] the beggar stuck his hand inside and put [a beggar's bowl] into the hand of the householder,

E. or if he took [something] from inside it and brought it out,

F. the beggar is liable, the householder is exempt.

G. [If] the householder stuck his hand outside and put [something] into the hand of the beggar,

H. or if he took [something] from it and brought it inside,

I. the householder is liable, and the beggar is exempt.

J. [If] the beggar stuck his hand inside, and the householder took [something] from it,

K. or if [the householder] put something in it and he [the beggar] removed

L. both of them are exempt.

M. [If] the householder put his hand outside and the beggar took [something] from it,

N. or if [the beggar] put something into it and [the householder] brought it back inside,

O. both of them are exempt.

M. Shab. 1:1 classifies diverse circumstances of transporting objects from private to public domain. The purpose is to assess the rules that classify as culpable or exempt from culpability diverse arrangements. The operative point is that a prohibited action is culpable only if one and the same person commits the whole of the violation of the law. If two or more people share in the single action, neither of them is subject to punishment. At stake therefore is the conception that one thing may be many things, and if that is the case, then culpability is not incurred by any one actor.

The consequence of showing that one thing is many things is set forth with great clarity in the consideration not of the actor but of the action. One class of actions is formed by those that violate the sanctity of the Sabbath. Do these form many subdivisions, and, if so, what difference does it make? Here is a famous passage[3] that shows how a single class of actions yields multiple and complex speciation, while remaining one:

MISHNAH-TRACTATE SHABBAT 7:1-2

7:1 A. A general rule did they state concerning the Sabbath:

B. Whoever forgets the basic principle of the Sabbath and performed many acts of labor on many different Sabbath days is liable only for a single sin offering.

C. He who knows the principle of the Sabbath and performed many acts of labor on many different Sabbaths is liable for the violation of each and every Sabbath.

D. He who knows that it is the Sabbath and performed many acts of labor on many different Sabbaths is liable for the violation of each and every generative category of labor.

E. He who performs many acts of labor of a single type is liable only for a single sin offering.

7:2 A. The generative categories of acts of labor [prohibited on the Sabbath] are forty less one:

B. (1) he who sews, (2) ploughs, (3) reaps, (4) binds sheaves, (5) threshes, (6) winnows, (7) selects [fit from unfit produce or crops], (8) grinds, (9) sifts, (10) kneads, (11) bakes;

C. (12) he who shears wool, (13) washes it, (14) beats it, (15) dyes it;

D. (16) spins, (17) weaves,

E. (18) makes two loops, (19) weaves two threads, (20) separates two threads;

F (21) ties, (22) unties,

G. (23) sews two stitches, (24) tears in order to sew two stitches;

H. (25) he who traps a deer, (26) slaughters it, (27) flays it, (28) salts it, (29) cures its hide, (30) scrapes it, and (31) cuts it up;

I. (32) he who writes two letters, (33) erases two letters in order to write two letters;

---

[3] And one of my favorites, among many. In my view, the whole of the Mishnah's method, seen with great precision as philosophical in program and logic, legal in idiom and expression, is typified by this wonderful, and deservedly famous, pericope.

J. (34) he who builds, (35) tears down;

K. (36) he who puts out a fire, (37) kindles a fire;

L. (38) he who hits with a hammer; (39) he who transports an object from one domain to another—

M. lo, these are the forty generative acts of labor less one.

Now we see how the fact that one thing yields many things confirms the philosophy of the unity of all being. For the many things all really are one thing, here, the intrusion into sacred time of actions that do not belong there. M. Shab. 7:1-2 presents a parallel to the discussion, in Mishnah-tractate Sanhedrin, of how many things can be shown to be one thing and to fall under a single rule, and how one thing may be shown to be many things and to invoke multiple consequences. It is that interest at M. 7:1 which accounts for the inclusion of M. 7:2, and the exposition of M. 7:2 occupies much of the tractate that follows. Accordingly, just as at Mishnah-tractate Sanhedrin the specification of the many and diverse sins or felonies that are penalized in a given way shows us how many things are one thing and then draws in its wake the specification of those many things, so here we find a similar exercise. It is one of classification, working in two ways, then: the power of a unifying taxon, the force of a differentiating and divisive one. The list of the acts of labor then gives us the categories of work, and performing any one of these constitutes a single action in violation of the Sabbath.

How, exactly, do these things work themselves out? If one does not know that the Sabbath is incumbent upon him, then whatever he does falls into a single taxon. If he knows that the Sabbath exists and violates several Sabbath days in succession, what he does falls into another taxon. If one knows that the Sabbath exists in principle and violates it in diverse ways, e.g., through different types of prohibited acts of labor, then many things become still more differentiated. The consideration throughout, then, is how to assess whether something is a single or multiple action as to the reckoning of the consequence.

I have repeatedly pointed to the philosophical unity of mode of argument, medium of expression, and fundamental proposition. In this connection let us turn back to our consideration of the rules of speciation. These form the methodological counterpart to the proposition that one thing yields many things. Here is the consequence, in the context of the exposition of the one and the many, of the rule of sub- and super-speciation:

MISHNAH-TRACTATE SHABBAT 10:6

10:6 A. He who pares his fingernails with one another, or with his teeth,

B. so too [if he pulled out the hair of] his (1) head, (2) moustache, or (3) beard—

C. and so she who (1) dresses her hair, (2) puts on eye shadow, or (3) rouges her face—

D. R. Eliezer declares liable [for doing so on the Sabbath].

E. And sages prohibit [doing so] because of [the principle of] Sabbath rest.

E He who picks [something] from a pot that has a hole [in the bottom] is liable.

G. [If he picks something from a pot] that has no hole [in the bottom] he is exempt.

H. And R. Simeon exempts him on this account and on that account.

The interest in the classification of acts of labor draws attention, at M. 10:6, to the lesson of superspeciation. We make a distinction between a derivative of the generative categories of prohibited acts, commission of which invokes a penalty, and an act which is not to be done by reason of the general principle of "Sabbath rest," but which is not culpable under the list of thirty-nine specifically prohibited acts of labor. From superspeciation—acts that cannot be speciated but that fall into the genus of prohibited deeds—we move, in Mishnah-tractate Shabbat chapters twelve through sixteen, to the subspecies of the thirty-nine categories of prohibited acts of labor. Here we ask about the extent to which one must perform a prohibited act of labor in order to be subject to liability; chapter twelve addresses building, ploughing, writing; in chapter thirteen, we proceed to weaving and hunting (one who completes an action is liable, one who does not is exempt; one who does not intend by his action to violate the Sabbath is not liable and one who does intend to violate the Sabbath is liable; if two people together do a single act of prohibited labor, neither is liable); chapter fifteen moves on to knot-tying; chapter sixteen, to saving things from the fire even though that involves moving objects across the boundary between private and public domain.

The Sabbath-exposition appears so apt and perfect for the present proposition that readers may wonder whether the authorship of the Mishnah could accomplish that same marvel of concision of complex thought more than a single time. Joining rhetoric, logic, and specific (no longer general, methodological) proposition transforms thought into not merely expository prose but poetry. Have I given a proof consisting of one case? Quite to the contrary, the document contains a plethora of exercises of the same kind. My final demonstration of the power of speciation in demonstrating the opposite, namely, the generic unity of species and the hierarchy that orders them, derives from the treatment of oaths, to which we now turn. The basic topical program of Mishnah-tractate Shabuot responds systematically to the potpourri of subjects covered by Leviticus chapters five and six within the (to the priestly author) unifying rubric of those who bring a guilt-offering. Lev. 5:1-6 concerns oaths, an oath of testimony, and one who touches something unclean in connection with the Temple cult, and finally, one who utters a rash oath.

MISHNAH-TRACTATE SHABUOT 1:1-2, 2:1

1:1 A. Oaths are of two sorts, which yield four subdivisions.

B. Awareness of [having sinned through] uncleanness is of two sorts, which yield four subdivisions.

C. Transportation [of objects from one domain to the other] on the Sabbath is of two sorts, which yield four subdivisions.

D. The symptoms of negas are of two sorts, which yield four subdivisions.

1:2 A. In any case in which there is awareness of uncleanness at the outset and awareness [of uncleanness] at the end but unawareness in the meantime—lo, this one is subject to bringing an offering of variable value.

B . [If] there is awareness [of uncleanness] at the outset but no apprehension [of uncleanness] at the end, a goat which [yields blood to be sprinkled] within [in the Holy of Holies], and the Day of Atonement suspend [the punishment],

C. until it will be made known to the person, so that he may bring an offering of variable value.

2:1 A. Awareness of uncleanness is of two sorts, which yield four subdivisions [M. 1:1B].

B. (1) [If] one was made unclean and knew about it, then the uncleanness left his mind, but he knew [that the food he had eaten was] Holy Things,

C. (2) the fact that the food he had eaten was Holy Things left his mind, but he knew about [his having contracted] uncleanness,

D. (3) both this and that left his mind, but he ate Holy Things without knowing it and after he ate them, he realized it—

E. lo, this one is liable to bring an offering of variable value.

F. (1) [If] he was made unclean and knew about it, and the uncleanness left his mind, but he remembered that he was in the sanctuary;

G. (2) the fact that he was in the sanctuary left his mind, but he remembered that he was unclean,

H. (3) both this and that left his mind, and he entered the sanctuary without realizing it, and then when he had left the sanctuary, he realized it—lo, this one is liable to bring an offering of variable value.

M. Shabuot 1:1-7, 2:1-5 accomplish the speciation of oaths, on the one side, and uncleanness in regard to the cult, on the other. That work of speciation then joins two utterly disparate subjects, oaths and uncleanness, so showing a unity of structure that forms a metaphysical argument for the systemic proposition on the unity of being. We do so in a way that is now to be predicted. It is by showing that many things are one thing, now, as I said, oaths, uncleanness. When the priestly author joined the same subjects, it was because a single offering was involved for diverse and distinct sins or crimes. When the Mishnaic author does, it is because a single inner structure sustains these same diverse and distinct sins or crimes. Comparing the priestly with the Mishnah's strategy of exposition underlines the remarkable shift accomplished by our philosophers. Their power of formulation—rhetoric, logic together—of course, works to demonstrate through the medium the message that these enormously diverse subjects in fact can be classified within a simple taxonomic principle. It is that there are two species to a genus, and two subspecies to each species, and these are readily determined by appeal to fixed taxic indicators. An abstract statement of the rule of classification (and, it must follow, also hierarchization) will have yielded less useful intellectual experience than the remarkably well balanced concrete exemplification of the rule, and that is precisely what we have in Mishnah-tractate Shabuot chapters one and two.

The main point of differentiation—the taxic indicator—derives from the intersecting issues of a divided sequence of time-frames and of awareness. If one knows something at one point in a differentiated process ("the outset," "the meantime," "the end") but (having become oblivious or distracted) does not know that thing at some other point, then we have a grid in two dimensions: sequence of time, sequence of spells of awareness or unawareness. And then the taxic indicators are in place, so the process of speciation and subspeciation is routine. At stake is the power of the taxic indicator. What is stunning is that the same process of speciation and subspeciation is explicitly applied to utterly unrelated matters, which demonstrates for all to see that the foundations of knowledge lie in method, which makes sense of chaos, and method means correct knowledge of the classification of things and the ability to identify the taxic indicators that make classification possible. All of this prepares the way for the treatment of oaths, Mishnah-tractate Shabuot 3:1-8:6, that is, the entire tractate.

And that process of speciation and subspeciation is where the uniformity of oaths is established, with the consequence, given our starting point, that many things are really one thing, for, as we see at the outset, they come from one thing.

MISHNAH-TRACTATE SHABUOT 3:1-2, 8-9, 11

3:1 A. Oaths are of two sorts, which yield four subdivisions [M. 1:lA].

B. (1) "I swear I shall eat," and (2) "...I shall not eat,"

C. (3) "...that I ate," and (4) "...that I didn't eat."

D. "[If one said], 'I swear I won't eat,' and he ate anything [in any volume] whatsoever, he is liable," the words of R. Aqiba.

E. They said to R. Aqiba, "Where have we found that someone who eats anything in any negligible volume is liable, that this one should be deemed liable?"

F. Said to them R. Aqiba, "And where have we found that one who merely speaks has to bring an offering?"

G. "I swear that I won't eat," and he ate and drank—he is liable on only one count.

H. "I swear that I won't eat and drink," and he ate and drank—he is liable on two counts.

3:2 A. "I swear I won't eat,"—

B. and he ate a piece of bread made of wheat, a piece of bread made of barley, and a piece of bread made of spelt, he is liable on one count only.

C. "I swear that I won't eat a piece of bread made of wheat, a piece of bread made of barley, and a piece of bread made of spelt," and he ate—

D. he is liable on each and every count.

3:8 A. What is a vain oath?

B. [If] one has taken an oath to differ from what is well known to people.

C. If he said (1) concerning a pillar of stone that it is made of gold,

D. (2) concerning a man that he is a woman,

E. (3) concerning a woman that she is a man—

F [if] one has taken an oath concerning something which is impossible—

G. (1) "...if I did not see a camel flying in the air ...'"

H. (2) "...if I did not see a snake as thick as the beam of an olive press ..."

I. (3) [if] he said to witnesses, "Come and bear witness of me,"

J. [and they said to him,] "We swear that we shall not bear witness for you" —

K. [if] he took an oath to nullify a commandment—
L. (1) not to build a Sukkah, (2) not to take lulab and (3) not to put on phylacteries—
M. this is a vain oath,
N. on account of the deliberate making of which one is liable for flogging, and on account of the inadvertent making of which one is exempt [from all punishment]—
3:9 A. "I swear that I shall eat this loaf of bread," "I swear that I shall not eat it"—
B. the first statement is a rash oath, and the second is a vain oath.
C. [If] he ate it, he has violated a vain oath.
D. [If] he did not eat it, he has violated a rash oath.
3:11 11 A. [The law governing] a vain oath applies (1) to men and women, (2) to those who are not related and to those who are related, (3) to those who are suitable [to bear witness] and to those who are not suitable [to bear witness],
B. (4) before a court and not before a court.
C. (5) [But it must be stated] by a man out of his own mouth.
D. And they are liable for deliberately taking such an oath to flogging, and for inadvertently taking such an oath, one is exempt [from all punishment].
E. All the same are this oath and that oath:
F he who was subjected to an oath by others is liable.
G. How so?
H. [If] one said, "I did not eat today, and I did not put on phylacteries today,"
I. [and his friend said,] "I impose an oath on you [that that is so],"
J. and he said, "Amen,"
K. he is liable.

The speciation and subspeciation of oaths occupies the rest of the tractate. Not only so, but we now find out what is at stake in the matter. It has to do with the number of counts for which one is liable, which is to say, the division of a given action or statement into its components and the identification of each completed action or statement, which is to say, the number of counts of liability. All of this is entirely familiar. It is the point at which we started.

But here, that point emerges in the analysis of the language one has used in the oath at hand. Since one has taken one oath, there is one point of liability. But since he has in the oath specified two or more actions, he is liable for violating the oath as to each of those actions. Thus at Mishnah-tractate Shabuot 3:1ff., we have the speciation of oaths into four types, then the demonstration of the subspeciation of a given type by appeal to the language that is used.

M. 3:1-6 go over oaths in general. M. 3:2 shows how one thing yields many things. M. 3:7-11 deals with the vain oath, differentiating that from the rash oath. These show us the model that is followed, with variations required by the subject-matter, for the rest.

The model applies throughout, so joining diverse data in a single pattern. Mishnah-tractate Shabuot 4:1-13 goes over the oath of testimony and specifies who is subject to such an oath, where it is taken (in court, not in court), examples of how it may be violated. M. 5:1-5 go over the oath of bailment: to whom it applies, an example, several claims of bailment and a single false oath, and the like. M. 6:1-7, 7:1-8 go over the oath imposed by judges: to what it applies, who takes it, to what matters it does not apply, and the like. Then come concluding exercises, M. 8:1-6, in which oaths and bailments are speciated: the unpaid bailiff and the cases in which he takes an oath, the borrower, the paid bailiff and the renter; this then is illustrated in a long taxonomic exercise, M. 8:2-6, which illustrates the proposition that a false oath that does not save a person from liability is not punishable, but one that serves to lighten one's burden is punishable. I cannot imagine a more logical or comprehensive treatment of any topic.

The medium for the Halakhic message has shown that any topic allows for the same demonstration of the same proposition in a single way, and that means everything really does fall into one simple pattern. The very diversity of the topical program of the Mishnah then forms on its own an argument in behalf of the philosophy's single proposition. For if one wants to show that many things are really one, and that one thing yields many things, the best way to do it is to show that you can say the same thing about many things—the more, the better. So the species point to the genus, all classes to one class, all taxa properly hierarchized then rise to the top of the structure and the system forming one taxon. So all things ascend to, reach one thing. All that remains is for the theologian to define that one thing: God—God in the form, God in the order, God in the structure, God in the heights, God at the head of the great chain of well-ordered being, social and cosmic, in its proper hierarchy. True, God is premise, scarcely mentioned. But it is because God's name does not have to be mentioned when the whole of the order of being says that name. That is what I mean by the Halakhah as the most perfect medium for philosophical monotheism.

iii. *Philosophical Monotheism: The Halakhic Method of Hierarchical*
Classification in the Context of Philosophy

Now that I have argued that a particular medium bears the message of the Halakhah, I wish to underscore not only the singularity
of that medium but its affinity with other media employed to deliver a comparable method of (1) the hierarchical classification of all
things in (2) an exercise of ontological ordering, in the Judaic and
Christian frameworks, meant to express philosophical monotheism.
That affinity underscores difference and argues for the uniqueness
of that perfect medium—Halakhah properly ordered—employed by
the Rabbinic sages for their message. What we shall see is that the
sages conveyed inductively and in remarkably concrete manner some
pertinent chapters of abstract philosophy. This they did through their
concrete re-presentation of the principles of monotheist ontology,
their recapitulation of the principle the diversity is transcended in
the unity of being. The Rabbinic sages' disciples learned through
the concrete presentation of the Halakhah elements of the Aristotelian method of natural philosophy and the neo-Platonic message of
the unity of being.

Let us concentrate first on Aristotelian method concretized in the
Halakhic medium. Classification and hierarchization of what is classified forms the method of natural philosophy associated with the
name of Aristotle. We begin with the simple observation that the
distinction between genus and species lies at the foundation of all
knowledge. Adkins states the matter in the most accessible way,
"Aristotle, a systematic biologist, uses his method of classification by
genera and species, itself developed from the classificatory interests
of the later Plato, to place man among other animals...The classification must be based on the final development of the creature...."[4]

But to classify, we have to take as our premise that things are
subject to classification, and that means that they have traits that
are essential and indicative, on the one side, but also shared with
other things, on the other. The point of direct contact and intersec-
tion between the Judaism's philosophy of hierarchical classification
and the natural philosophy of Aristotle lies in the shared, and criti-

---

[4] A. W. H. Adkins, *From the Many to the One. A Study of Personality and Views of*
Human Nature in the Context of Ancient Greek Society, Values, and Beliefs (Ithaca, 1970:
Cornell University Press)., pp. 170-171.

cal, conviction concerning the true nature or character of things. Both parties concur that there *is* such a true definition—a commonplace for philosophers, generative of interesting problems, e.g., about Ideas, or Form and Substance, Actual and Potential, and the like—of what things really are. Rabbinic sages and Aristotelian philosophers concur that objects are not random but fall into classes and so may be described, analyzed, and explained by appeal to general traits or rules. A single example in two cases of the formation of Halakhic issues around the conflict of the actual and the potential is readily selected:

> MISHNAH-TRACTATE UQSIN 3:8, 11
> 3:8 A. Fish—from what point do they receive uncleanness?
> B. The House of Shammai say, "When they are caught."
> C. And the House of Hillel say, "When they die."
> 3:11 A. Honeycombs—from what point are they susceptible to uncleanness as liquid?
> B. The House of Shammai say, "When one will smoke out [the bees therefrom]."
> C. And the House of Hillel say, "When one will have broken [the honeycombs to remove the honey] ."

Fish are susceptible to uncleanness as food only when they die. Do we identify that point from when they are caught, at which moment, while not dead, they are certainly going to die? Or is it when they actually have died, whatever the potentiality? Honeycombs are susceptible to uncleanness as liquid from the point at which the honey flows (no longer being solid or contained). Is this when one signifies the intentionality of taking the honey, as the House of Shammai say? Or is it when by an action one has confirmed the intentionality and realized it? The issue of whether what is potential is assumed to come to realization is articulated in accord with the debate on whether one's intentionality serves as the criterion of classification, or whether the action that realizes the intentionality or potentiality is taken. These trivial examples of the interplay of the potential and the actual, the intention and the action, find counterparts in every classification of the Halakhah.

My contention is more specific than merely the claim that hierarchical classification yields the rules in that govern in the Halakhic analytical process as much as in natural philosophy. The particular component of Aristotelianism that pertains here is "the use of deductive reasoning proceeding from self-evident principles or discovered general truths to conclusions of a more limited import; and syllogistic forms of demonstrative or persuasive arguments."[5] The goal is the classification of things, which is to say, the discovery of general rules that apply to discrete data or instances. Minio-Paluello states,

> "In epistemology...Aristotelianism includes a concentration on knowledge accessible by natural means or accountable for by reason; an inductive, analytical empiricism, or stress on experience in the study of nature...leading from the perception of contingent individual occurrences to the discovery of permanent, universal patterns; and the primacy of the universal, that which is expressed by common or general terms. In metaphysics, or the theory of Being, Aristotelianism involves belief in the primacy of the individual in the realm of existence; in correlated conceptions allowing an articulate account of reality (e.g., 10 categories; genus-species-individual, matter-form, potentiality-actuality, essential-accidental; the four material elements and their basic qualities; and the four causes-formal, material, efficient and final); in the soul as the inseparable form of each living body in the vegetable and animal kingdoms; in activity as the essence of things; and in the primacy of speculative over practical activity."

The manner in which we accomplish this work is to establish categories of traits, and these will yield the besought rules or generalizations that make possible both classification, and, in the nature of things, therefore also hierarchization.

While, as a matter of fact, "the world is composed of individuals, no two of whom are precisely alike,"[6] the correlated categories, matter and form allow us to establish categories that encompass individual or distinct items. Allan states:

> The wood which is potentially a table is also the matter upon which the carpenter will impress the form of a table...Matter and form are relative terms, in the sense that a thing which has some degree of form may serve as the matter upon which a new form is imposed...It is Form..which imparts structural unity to a single individual. Various materials are required in order to build a house...what holds them together is the Form of the house... Form... tends to unity of design, matter to plurality..[7]

---

[5] Minio-Paluello, Lorenzo, "Aristotelianism," *Encyclopaedia Britannica* 1:1155-1161, p. 1155.

[6] Allan, D. J., *The Philosophy of Aristotle* (London, New York, Toronto, 1952: Oxford University Press/Geoffrey Cumberlege), p. 42.

[7] *op. cit.*, p. 39.

On the matter of form and matter, G. H. Parker further explains, ""The Matter is the basic stuff which makes it possible for the Form to have existence at all."[8] The Form represents what is particular to a given instance. Parker proceeds, "Coupled with the concept of Matter and Form in every substance we find that other typically Aristotelian pair, Actual and Potential." Parker continues:

> "Typically Aristotelian" because it is here we see the outlook of one deeply immersed in Natural History, of one who has studied with minute care the development of living organisms from embryo to old age, of one who attempts to oppose a dynamic to a static view of things.... Matter is potential, embryo is actual; the embryo in turn is potential, the baby is actual... The Potential is eternally moving, eternally changing into the Actual. Equally, Matter is eternally moved into Form.[9]

What Aristotle seeks to know is causes: "to know that something happens is mere shallowness unless one probes deeper and reveals the reason why." The answer to the question of why derives from the famous "four causes."

Taking as the question, what has "caused" the famous status of Zeus in his temple at Olympia, "made of ivory and gold on a core of wood by Phidias, the foremost sculptor of his time...placed in the central shrine of Olympia...," we have these four causes in play:

1. The material Cause: the gold, the ivory, and the wood.
2. The efficient cause: the hands and tools of Phidias.
3. The formal cause: what the thing represents; in this case the figure of Zeus.
4. The final cause: the purpose and meaning of the thing; in this case the greater glory of Zeus and the improvement of man.

We may draw these four causes into relationship with the issue— happily, familiar in the discourses of the Mishnah—of the potential and the actual: "The whole end and purpose of an acorn is to grow into an oak; the form taken by an acorn as it so develops is that of an oak; and the efficient cause, that which gave an acorn the opportunity of taking on the form of an oak, was a parent oak....Each cause plays its part in the process which makes a thing become what it is."

So much for method. What about message? Here the Rabbinic sages go their own way, the Aristotelian method serving a monotheist message. Aristotle's goal and that of the Mishnah's philoso-

---

[8] Parker, G. F., *A Short Account of Greek Philosophy from Thales to Epicurus* (Edward Arnold Publishers Ltd)

[9] Parker, p. 142.

phers simply do not relate, for while the former is aiming at dis-
covering the final causes of things, their purpose and the source of
their movement and change, the latter have a different objective in
mind. For Aristotle, the aim of science "is to produce a body of judg-
ments which, in their connection with each other, reflect the necessary connections between substances and properties in the real
world."[10] For the philosophy of the Mishnah the aim of science, that
is to say, learning, is quite different. The following summary of what
is at stake for Aristotle appeals to the methods shared by Aristotle
and the philosophers of the Mishnah to reach a conclusion that simply
has no bearing upon the interests of the latter:

> The primary immobile movement that Aristotle has in mind is evi-
> dently enough the soul of the outermost heaven. Any animated thing,
> plant or animal, is a self-movement, and its soul originates motion.
> Such perishable self-movements, however, require a higher and im-
> perishable efficient cause to account for the eternal series of genera-
> tions and passings-away. The operative notion in the Aristotelian
> demonstration of the primary efficient cause is therefore the eternity
> of the cosmic processes. The first efficient cause is necessary, not to
> explain the existence of things, but to account for the eternal charac-
> ter of their motion. The argument is based clearly upon the eternity
> of cosmic motion and of time. Without that basis it is no longer the
> Aristotelian proof.[11]

If I may now specify the point at which the Mishnah in its first principles takes its leave from Aristotle's philosophy, it is not merely in
the subject-matter, even in the level of abstraction and generalization characteristic of Aristotle, though such a mode of mathemati-
cal thought seems to me unimagined by the philosophers of the
Mishnah. The difference is that the goal of Aristotle's system, the
teleological argument in favor of the unmoved mover, and the goal
of Judaism's system, the demonstration of the unity of being, are
essentially contradictory, marking utterly opposed positions on the
fundamental character of God and the traits of the created world
that carries us upward to God. Aristotle's God attained through teleological demonstration accomplished through the right classification of all things and the Mishnah's God, whose workings in the world
derive from the demonstration of the ontological unity of all things,
cannot recognize one another.

---

[10] Allan, p. 147.
[11] Owens, p. 317.

iv. *Why the Halakhah Serves as the Best Possible Medium for the Message of Philosophical Monotheism Deriving from Scripture: The Unity of All Being, Systematically Demonstrated through Concrete Cases*

The Mishnah's paramount proposition runs along the lines of important fundamentals of the philosophy that came to full expression in the writings of Plotinus (204-270) in the name of Plato, and to that message we have now to turn.[12] The principal proposition of the Mishnah, concerning the ontological unity of being, with many things forming one thing, and one thing yielding many things, proves entirely congruent with one important conception of Middle Platonism, neo-Platonism, and Plotinus, concerning the unity of all being. Let us begin with the most difficult point, deriving from a general description of Middle, or Neo-Platonism. When we speak of ontological unity, we find ourselves at home:

> We can conceive of a unity that increases to the point where the parts of a being fuse and become almost inseparable. For instance, we cannot speak in the same sense of the parts of a living body and of the parts of a science; in a living body the parts are solitary but are locally separated, whereas in a science a part is a theorem and each theorem contains potentially every other theorem. Thus we see how an additional degree of unification takes us from the corporeal to the spiritual.[13]

---

[12] On Middle Platonism and Plotinus I consulted the following works:

Armstrong, A. Hilary, *Plotinian and Christian Studies* (London, 1979: Variorum Reprints).

Armstrong, A. H., *The Architecture of the Intelligible Universe in the Philosophy of Plotinus. An Analytical and Historical Study* (Amsterdam, 1967: Adolf M. Hakkert, Publisher).

Bréhier, Émile, *The Philosophy of Plotinus.* Translated by Joseph Thomas (Chicago, 1958: University of Chicago Press).

Dillon, J. M., and A. A. Long, *The Question of "Eclecticism." Studies in Later Greek Philosophy* (Los Angeles and Berkeley, 1988: University of California Press).

Katz, Joseph, *The Philosophy of Plotinus. Representative Books from the Enneads. Selected and Translated with an Introduction* (N.Y., 1950: Appleton-Century-Crofts, Inc.)

O'Brien, Elmer, *The Essential Plotinus. Representative Treatises from the Enneads* (Repr., 1975: Hackett Publishing Co., Inc.)

Rist, J. M., *Plotinus: The Road to Reality* (Cambridge, 1967: Cambridge University Press).

Sambursky, Samuel, *The Concept of Place in Late Neoplatonism* (Jerusalem, 1982: Israel Academy of Arts and Sciences).

Sambursky, Samuel, and S. Pines, *The Concept of Time in Late Neoplatonism* (Jerusalem, 1971: Israel Academy of Arts and Sciences).

Turnbull, Grace H., *The Essence of Plotinus. Extracts from the Six Enneads and Porphyry's Life of Plotinus.* Based on the Translation by Stephen Mackenna. (N.Y., 1948: Oxford University Press).

[13] Ibid., pp. 184.

Here we see, in abstraction, considerations that we locate in very concrete terms in the progress from classification of things to their hierarchization and finally to their unification, shown in the fact that as one thing is made up of—holds together in unity—many things, so many things emerge from one thing. And that, in abstract language, forms the centerpiece of the Mishnaic interest in classification.

So too, as Émile Bréhier says, "But every imperfect reality or union of parts implies a more complete unity beyond itself...In the absence of the higher unity, everything disperses, crumbles and loses its being. Nothing is other than through the One." As to method, what is at hand is "explaining a particular aspect of reality by relating it to a more perfect unity." What we find in the Mishnah is the distinctive definition of those components of reality that are to be taken up in the quest for ontological unity: the this and that of the every day and the here and now, precisely what Plotinus finds of no consequence whatsoever, but what Aristotle in his scientific writings took as the focus of analytical interest.

Specifically, Plotinus in the name of Plato set forth a doctrine of the hierarchical order of being, in which many things are subsumed within one thing, and one thing yields many things, from the lowest order, which is diverse, to the highest, which is unified. The doctrine of the One in Plotinus may be best summarized as follows:

> The One is infinite, the others finite; the One is creator, the others creatures; the One is entirely itself, entirely infinite, the others are both finite and infinite...the One has no otherness, the others are other than the One. It is not the case that while the Forms exist, the One does not. Rather the One exists in an infinite way, the others finitely....[14]

The centerpiece of the system then is the conception of the One, and, as we shall now see, the fundamental hierarchical unity of being in the orderly world that descends from the One.

Accordingly, moving from Aristotle to neo-Platonism opens the way to the rough and ready comparison between the philosophical message of a critical and paramount philosophical system, that which came to full expression only after the closure of the Mishnah, with Plotinus in the middle of the third century, and the philosophical message of the Mishnah, at the end of the second century or begin-

---

[14] J. M. Rist, *Plotinus: The Road to Reality* (Cambridge, 1967: Cambridge University Press), p. 37.

ning of the third. Let me proceed with a simple definition of "Platonism and neo-Platonism," that supplied by A. H. Armstrong, as follows (with the pertinent points I wish to emphasize given in italics, supplied by me):

> Neoplatonism, the form of Platonism developed by Plotinus in the third century A.D., contains among its leading ideas the following:
>
> 1.   *There is plurality of spheres of being, arranged in hierarchical descending order, the last and lowest comprising the universe, which exists in time and space and is perceptible to the senses.*

I take it the descent through the hierarchy is from simple to complex, from one to many, along the lines of the Halakhic proof that a single action encompasses many sub-actions (ascent from the many to the one) and from a single action, many sub-actions are to be derived (descent from the one to the many).

> 2.   Each sphere of being is derived from its superior, a derivation that is not a process in time or space.
>
> 3.   Each derived being is established in its own reality by turning back toward its superior in a movement of contemplative desire, which is implicit in the original creative impulse of outgoing that it receives from its superior....
>
> 4.   Each sphere of being is an image or expression on a lower level of the sphere above it.
>
> 5.   *Degrees of being are also degrees of unity; in each subsequent sphere of being there is greater multiplicity, more separateness, and increasing limitation,— till the atomic individualization of the spatio-temporal world is reached.*

Here I find the notion that the ultimate unity of being is embodied in the One (who for the Rabbinic sages can only be God), the perfection of ontological unity. This is articulated at principles No. 6 and 7:

> 6.   The supreme sphere of being, and through it all of what in any sense exists, derives from the ultimate principle, which is absolutely free from determinations and limitations and utterly transcends any conceivable reality, so that it may be said to be 'being.' As it has no limitations, so it has no division, attributes, or qualifications; it cannot really be named but may be called 'the One' to designate its complete simplicity. It may also be called 'the Good' as the source of all perfections and the ultimate goal of return; for the impulse of outgoing and return that constitutes the hierarchy of derived reality comes from and leads back to the Good.
>
> 7.   Since this supreme principle is absolutely simple and undetermined (or devoid of specific traits), man's knowledge of it must be

radically different from any other kind of knowledge: it is not an object (a separate, determined, limited thing) and no predicates can be applied to it; hence it can be known only if it raises the mind to an immediate union with itself, which cannot be imagined or described. [15]

Central to our problem is the conviction of a hierarchical order of being, in which, as one ascends, one moves ever toward a more unified realm of being.

This conception here is expressed in the reverse order: as one descends, things become more complex, so the one yields the many. The differences in detail—as any scholar of Middle Platonism must remind us—are stupefying. But I see no fundamental difference between the two positions on the unity of being and subordinated matters I should classify as ontological. Armstrong's points 1 and 5 thus appear to me to coincide with the Mishnah's fundamental and repeatedly demonstrated proposition about the unity of being, attained through the hierarchical classification of all things. Bréhier states the matter in the simplest possible way:

> ... the universe appears as a series of forms each of which depends hierarchically on the preceding, and the universe can be the object of rational thought.[16]

Exactly how this is demonstrated is hardly our problem, since Plotinus's way of showing the ordered hierarchy of being is not the same as Aristotle's, and as to mode of thought it is Aristotle's and not Plotinus's that served our philosophers.

It is the proposition of the One that matters, and here I find an identity of viewpoint between the two philosophies, the pagan and the Judaic. A. H. Armstrong's account of the One[17] leaves no doubt of the complexity of what is at stake for Plotinus in thought about that fundamental subject. But the basic point serves our purpose full well: the first aspect of the One" is "as conclusion of the metaphys-

---

[15] Armstrong, A. H., "Platoism and Neoplatonism," *Encyclopaedia Britannica* (Chicago, 1975) 14:539-545

[16] Bréhier, *Plotinus*, p. 43.

[17] A. H. Armstrong, *The Architecture of the Intelligible Universe in the Philosophy of Plotinus. An Analytical and Historical Study* (Amsterdam, 1967: Adolf M. Hakkert, Publisher), pp. 1-48. Armstrong maintains that "Behind this stands the systematic theology of Aristotle," and he finds in the Metaphysics and De Anima influences on the Enneads: "This transcendent self-sufficing God, pure and self-directed Act, the supreme object of desire but himself desiring nothing but himself, appears in philosophy before Plotinus only in Aristotle and in the Platonic literature of the Imperial period."

ical and religious search for a primary reality which can act as explanation of the universe." The One of course is transcendent and absolute. The One is "not only self-thinking but self-willing and self-loving." Then what is at stake? Once more the answer is the same, but now in greater specificity. It is the proposition that "above this multiple unity, which constitutes the intelligible world, we must posit...the absolute One without distinction and without variety,"[18] that I find pertinent to the simple case at hand. And, I add, that alone.

For while Plotinus set forth a way of life, not only a doctrine, and the way of life posited by the philosophers of the Mishnah contained their doctrine too, the respective ways of life bore nothing in common. To live by the Halakhah was to realize in concrete ways a well-ordered embodiment of ontological monotheism: to classify things and act out the rules of the classification. The Rabbinic sages should not be represented as pretend-philosophers, and I hardly need say that the sages of Judaic philosophy were not precursors of Plotinus's mystics, portrayed as living in "the solitude of the sage who is alone with the supreme principle which he has attained because he has successively abandoned all finite and definite reality."[19]

On the contrary, the more we examine the concept of the unity of all being as expressed in the Mishnah's hierarchical ordering of all things, the less Middle or Neo-Platonic the Mishnah's ontological system appears in detail to be. The main point is the only point: systems that center upon ontological unity are deemed philosophical when put forth within Middle- and Neo-Platonism and by Plotinus, and therefore the Mishnah system of ontological unity also is to be classified as philosophical. All I allege is that the one and the many of the philosophy of the Mishnah portrays a proposition strikingly congruent with the unity of being set forth by Middle Platonism.

Yet having set in a prominent place the obvious and fundamental differences, let me turn to a brief component of Bréhier's moving account and see how far apart the two systems really are:

> To think, for Plotinus, is then to comprehend the unity of a composition of which sensations acquaint us only with the dispersed elements—the intention of the dancer in the multiplicity of movements

---

[18] Ibid., p. 45.
[19] Bréhier, *Plotinus*, p. 5.

in a dance figure, the living unity of the circular course of a star across
the infinity of positions it occupies successively. It is to proceed
toward a reality which, from losing anything of the richness of sensa-
tion, quite to the contrary goes beyond it and uncovers its depth.[20]

Here, I would claim, the Judaic philosophers would indeed concur
even in detail. They express the counterpart to the multiplicity of
movements in a dance figure, the infinity of positions the star occupies, yielding the possibility that Israel on earth will match the astral realm in the regularity and order of its movements too.

In the Halakhah I cannot find an explicit exercise of astral correspondence, but in the Aggadah I can. A statement of how Israel's
being corresponds with the movement of the heavenly bodies derives from Pesiqta deRab Kahana, an Aggadic document. Chosen
for a focus in that exegetical construction are those passages of Scripture that speak to liturgical occasions set by the passage of the moon
and the solar seasons in the heavens. And the sequence and sense
of coherence then derive from the lunar-solar calendar, that alone.
Pesiqta deRab Kahana therefore forms an exercise in correlating
Israel's affairs on earth with the movement of the heavenly bodies.
Israel's history, linear and sequential, no longer governs. Now exemplary moments, chosen out of time and not arranged in tempo-
ral sequence, define matters. Hence—history set aside, its sequence
no longer pertinent—the natural, seasonal passage of the moon in
the heavens signals paradigmatic moments in Israel's life on earth.
Israel on earth responds—and corresponds—to the heavenly bodies above. Pesiqta deRab Kahana sets forth an exercise in astral
religion,

To return to the present matter: this movement from detail, within
detail, through detail, toward the sense of the unity of things—the
rule, the order—in my judgment is gained by the philosophy of the
Mishnah in a way different from the way that it is gained in Plotinus's thought as Bréhier interprets it. For he says:

> The contemplation of the intelligible proceeds along the same line
> as the contemplation of the sensible. It extends contemplation of the
> sensible directly without passing in any way through the intermediary
> of logically connected ideas; for it is not through reasoning and in-

---

[20] Ibid., p. 11.
[21] Ibid., p. 11.

duction that one ascends from the first to the second but only through a more collected and intense contemplation.[21]

Here our sages would have to part company. For they remain wholly within the limits of the sensible world, encompassing the heavenly bodies to be sure, uncovering what is intelligible within what is sensible, there alone. There is no bypassing of reasoning and induction, but rather a focus upon the reasoning of classification and the induction of hierarchization of what is classified, that alone. But that observation only confirms my proposition, which is that the method is that of Aristotle, in behalf of the proposition important to Plotinus, among Middle Platonism overall.

What then can we say of that proposition concerning the ontological unity of being? Here we turn again to Bréhier's exposition, which emphasizes how Plotinus joined religious problems to Greek philosophizing:[22]

> True to the tradition of Plato, adopted by the Neo-Pythagoreans, the One is in Plotinus the ultimate condition of the spiritual life, the principles thanks to which Intelligence provides itself with objects and contemplates them...[23]
> ...for Plotinus, there is never any intellectual knowledge without spiritual life. The soul, for example, is aware of Intelligence only in uniting with it. True realities are not inert objects of knowledge but subjective spiritual attitudes.[24]

Having come this far, I may say very simply that not a single category or concept in the foregoing, and the vast structure to which Bréhier alludes, finds a counterpart in the philosophy of the Mishnah.

And yet, if in detail, we find ourselves far from the Mishnah, whether in method or medium or message, in the main point we are entirely at home; as Bréhier says in a stunning generalization of his own:

> A true philosophical reform, such as that of a Socrates or of a Descartes, always takes for its point of departure a confrontation of the needs of human nature with the representation the mind forms of reality. It is the sense of a lack of correspondence between these needs and this representation which, in exceptionally endowed minds, awakens the philosophical vocation. Thus, little by little, philosophy reveals man

---

[22] Bréhier, p. 19.
[23] Bréhier, p. 141.
[24] Ibid, p. 148.

to himself. It is the reality of his own needs, of his own inclinations, which forms the basis of living philosophical thought. A philosophy which does not give the impression of being indispensable to the period in which it appears is merely a vain and futile curiosity.[25]

By that definition, I should claim, the philosophy of the Mishnah indeed is a philosophy: it reveals "that correspondence between the givens of the everyday and their representation in the ordered rules by which they are placed into hierarchy that for those to whom the philosophers meant to speak formed reality: in proportion, in balance, in proper place: the reality of Israel's own needs and inclinations."[26] And that draws us to the end of this inquiry into the philosophical classification that encompasses the Mishnah.

The fundamental argument in favor of the unity of God in the philosophy of the Halakhah through the category-formations of the Mishnah is by showing the hierarchical order, therefore the unity, of the world. The world therefore is made to testify to the unity of being, and—to say the obvious with very heavy emphasis—*the power of the philosophy derives from its capacity for hierarchical classification.*

The comparison of the Judaic, Christian, and pagan systems of Middle Platonism seems to me made possible, in a very preliminary way to be sure, by Armstrong:

> The difference here between pagans and Christians...is a difference about the degree of religious relevance of the material cosmos, and, closely connected with this, about the relative importance of general, natural, and special, supernatural, divine self-manifestation and self-communication. On the one side, the pagan, there is the conviction that a multiple self-communication and self-revelation of divinity takes place always and everywhere in the world, and that good and wise men everywhere...have been able to find the way to God and the truth about God in and through rational reflection on themselves and on the world, not only the heavens but the earth, and the living unity of the whole. On the other side, the Christian, there is indeed a readiness to see the goodness and beauty of the visible cosmos as a testimony to God's creation...but the religious emphasis lies elsewhere. Saving truth and the self-communication of the life of God come through the Incarnation of God as a man and through the human...society of

---

[25] Ibid., pp. 183-4.

[26] The comparison of the Judaic, Christian, and pagan systems of Middle Platonism seems to me made possible, in a very preliminary way to be sure, by Armstrong in his "Man in the Cosmos," Armstrong, A. Hilary, *Plotinian and Christian Studies* (London, 1979: Variorum Reprints) No. XVII, p. 11.

which the God-Man is the head, the Church...It is only in the Church
that material things become means of revelation and salvation through
being understood in the light of Scripture and Church tradition and
used by God's human ministers in the celebration of the Church's
sacraments. It is the ecclesiastical cosmos, not the natural cosmos, which
appears to be of primary religious importance for the Christian.[27]

If God is revealed in the artifacts of the world, then, so pagans in
general considered, God must be multiple. No, the philosophy of
the Mishnah is here seen to respond. Here we find a Judaic argument, within the premises of paganism, against paganism. To state
with emphasis what I conceive to be that argument: *the very artifacts
that* appear *multiple in fact form classes of things, and, moreover, these classes themselves are subject to a reasoned ordering, by appeal to this-worldly characteristics signified by properties and indicative traits.*

Monotheism hence is to be demonstrated by appeal to those very
same data that for paganism prove the opposite. The medium of
hierarchical classification, which is Aristotle's, conveys the message
of the unity of being, which is Plato's and Plotinus's, in the this-
worldly mode of discourse formed by the framers of the Mishnah.
The way to one God, ground of being and ontological unity of the
world, lies through "rational reflection on themselves and on the
world," this world, which yields a living unity encompassing the
whole. That claim, conducted in an argument covering overwhelming
detail in the Mishnah, directly faces the issue as framed by paganism. Immanent in its medium, it is transcendent in its message. And
I hardly need spell out the simple reasons, self-evident in Armstrong's
words, for dismissing as irrelevant to their interests the Christian
reading of the cosmos. To the Mishnah's sages, it is not (merely)
wrong, it is insufficient.

And yet, that is not the whole story. For the Mishnah's sages reach
into Scripture for their generative categories, and, in doing so, they
address head-on a Christianity that Armstrong centers, with entire
soundness, upon the life of the Church of Jesus Christ, God-Man.
We do well here to review Armstrong's language: "It is only in the
Church that material things become means of revelation and salvation through being understood in the light of Scripture and Church

---

[27] "Man in the Cosmos," Armstrong, A. Hilary, *Plotinian and Christian Studies*
(London, 1979: Variorum Reprints) No. XVII, p. 11.

tradition and used by God's human ministers in the celebration of the Church's sacraments."

The framers of the Mishnah will have responded, *"It is in the Torah that material things are identified and set forth as a means of revelation."*

Again Armstrong: "It is the ecclesiastical cosmos, not the natural cosmos, which appears to be of primary religious importance for the Christian."

To this the philosophers responsible for the system set forth in the Mishnah reply, *"It is the scriptural account of the cosmos that forms our generative categories, which, by the power of intellect, we show to constitute an ordered, hierarchical unity of being."*

So the power of this identification of "the ecclesiastical cosmos" is revealed when we frame the cosmos of the Mishnah by appeal to its persistent response to the classifications and categories of Scripture. If the Church as Armstrong portrays matters worked out an ecclesiastical cosmos, only later on producing the Bible as it did, for its part the philosophy of the Mishnah framed a scriptural cosmos,— and then read it philosophically in the way in which I have explained matters. We may therefore identify three distinct positions on the reading of the natural world: the pagan, the Christian, and the Judaic. The one reads nature as a source of revelation. The other two insist on a medium of mediation between nature and intellect. For Christianity it is, as Armstrong says, ecclesiastical, and, as I claim, for the Mishnah, the medium of mediation of nature lies through revelation, the Torah.

Given their circumstance, the philosophers' search, for the many things that they would show are really one, in Scripture's entire practical program, as worked out in Exodus, Leviticus, Numbers, and Deuteronomy, is not only indicative. It also is to be predicted. But that is not for "traditional" or merely cultural reasons. There is a philosophical reason. By not merely appealing to the authority of Scripture, but by themselves analyzing the revealed truths of Scripture, the Rabbinic sages accomplished their purposes. By themselves showing the order and unity inherent within Scripture's ad hoc and occasional exposition of episodic topics, the philosophers on their own power meant to penetrate into the ground of being as God has revealed matters. This they did by working their way back from the epiphenomena of creation to the phenomenon of Creation—then to the numinous, that is, the Creator. That self-assigned challenge forms an intellectual vocation worthy of a particular kind of philosopher, an Israelite one. And, in my view, it explains also why in the Mishnah philosophers produced their philosophy in the form that they chose: the perfect medium for the selected message of philosophical monotheism.

CHAPTER THREE

THE THEOLOGICAL STRUCTURE

i. *The Problem Scripture Presents: The Case of Qohelet and Song of Songs*

The theological structure of the one whole Torah of Moses, our Rabbi, rested heavily on Scripture and took as its task the regularization and ordering of not only Scripture's episodic theological data—sayings and stories severally—but its entire corpus of narrative and prophecy viewed jointly, as a coherent and continuous account.[1] Given the power of the Rabbinic sages to contemplate Scripture not only in bits and pieces but whole and complete, we should find special interest in how they took up entire books of Scripture. Some of those books contained details that contradicted the governing theological structure. Others at their foundations proved anomalous. These the sages perfected by accommodating the books' messages, respectively, to their own theological reconstruction of the whole. How were Aggadic-theological components of Scripture to be taken over whole within the system put forth by the complete Torah written and oral alike? The answer to that question defines the meaning of perfection in theological structure for the perfect Torah.

To answer that question, we address not episodic verses and their ad hoc rationalization within the prevailing system but two entire books that by the Rabbinic sages' own judgment posed fundamental problems of a theological order. Here is their own designation of imperfection and exercise in perfection. Chief among the anomalous books of Scripture the Rabbinic sages themselves identified Song of Songs and Qohelet. The former gives the appearance of a set of secular love songs. How it belongs in the Written Torah ob-

---

[1] See *The Theology of the Oral Torah. Revealing the Justice of God.* Kingston and Montreal, 1999: McGill-Queen's University Press and Ithaca, 1999: Cornell University Press, and *The Theology of the Halakhah.* Leiden, 2001: Brill. BRILL REFERENCE LIBRARY OF ANCIENT JUDAISM.

viously requires explanation. The latter, Qohelet, delivers a despairing message of cynicism and ennui. Its aged author declares that nothing matters, everyone, righteous and wicked, ends up in the grave. Both books of Scripture, each for its own reason, challenged theological convictions of the Rabbinic sages, the one by its celebration of bodily love alone, the other by its nihilism. And as entire books, they could not be dismissed with an ad hoc exegesis of a passage. A hermeneutical solution yielding detailed exegesis was required for the theological problem they posed. And for the Torah to be perfect, the hermeneutics had to derive from the Torah's theological structure, whole and complete.

Mishnah-tractate Yadayim 3:5 defines the Halakhic setting in which sages took up the Song of Songs and Qohelet. The issue was, which documents are regarded as holy, among the received canon of ancient Israel? The specific problem focuses upon Qohelet ("Ecclesiastes") and the Song of Songs. That the two scriptural books formed enormous flaws in the otherwise perfect Torah thus is made explicit by the Rabbinic sages themselves. Here is how they addressed the canonical status of Song of Songs and Qohelet, in deciding whether, like the other components of the Torah, they enjoy the protection afforded by being declared a source of cultic uncleanness, therefore requiring special attention:

MISHNAH-TRACTATE YADAYIM 3:5

G. All sacred scriptures impart uncleanness to hands.

H. The Song of Songs and Qohelet [belong to the category of sacred scriptures and therefore] impart uncleanness to hands.

I. R. Judah says, "The Song of Songs imparts uncleanness to hands, but as to Qohelet there is dispute."

J. R. Yosé says, "Qohelet does not impart uncleanness to hands, but as to Song of Songs there is dispute."

K. R. Simeon says, "Qohelet is among the lenient rulings of the House of Shammai and strict rulings of the House of Hillel."

L. Said R. Simeon b. Azzai, "I have a tradition from the testimony of the seventy-two elders,

M. "on the day on which they seated R. Eleazar b. Azariah in the session,

N. "that the Song of Songs and Qohelet do impart uncleanness to hands."

O. Said R. Aqiba, "Heaven forbid! No Israelite man ever disputed concerning Song of Songs that it imparts uncleanness to hands.

P. "For the entire age is not so worthy as the day on which the Song of Songs was given to Israel.

Q.   "For all the scriptures are holy, but the Song of Songs is holiest of all.
R.   "And if they disputed, they disputed only concerning Qohelet."
S.   Said R. Yohanan b. Joshua the son of R. Aqiba's father-in-law, according to the words of Ben Azzai, "Indeed did they dispute, and indeed did they come to a decision."

The terms of the issue derive from the matter of uncleanness. For our purpose it suffices to know that if a document is holy, then it is held to be unclean. Accordingly, if one touches the document, he has to undergo a process of purification before he could eat food in a certain status of sanctification (the details are unimportant here) or, when the Temple stood, before he could go to the Temple. What that meant in practice is, people were to be quite cautious about handling such sacred documents, which then will be regarded as subject to special protection. So when sages declare that a parchment or hide on which certain words are written imparts uncleanness to hands, they mean to say, those words, and the object on which they are written, must be handled reverently and thoughtfully.

ii. *The Oral Torah's Program for Qohelet. In the Matter of Leviticus Rabbah*

Why is Qohelet a problem? Its author, the aged Solomon, sees as vain and empty all effort to achieve something lasting, while the one whole Torah of Moses, our rabbi, ultimately promises resurrection and life eternal. These solutions to the monotheist problem—how can an all-powerful, just God permit the righteous to suffer, the wicked to prosper—lie beyond the imagination of the Solomon of Qohelet. Within the dual Torah's system for the sanctification of Israel, by contrast, much that people do makes a difference. Above all there is a judge, there is judgment, and justice prevails in God's plan. Humanity has the hope of resurrection, life beyond the grave. A common fate does not await all, whatever the singular record of any one. Actions sanctify. The one whole Torah of Moses our rabbi founds its theological structure upon the eschatological vindication of monotheism.

So much for the problem of the text and its theology. But the context of Qohelet and its focus of all discourse, with its stress on the radically isolated individual, presented a still more severe contrast with that of the Torah as the Rabbinic sages mediated it. The

Rabbinic system speaks of Israel and Israelites within the framework of God's active engagement with the moral entity of Israel, uniquely transcending the limits of individuality. Qohelet for his part speaks of individuals on their own. It addresses private persons, not speaking to the community formed by Israelites as Israel. When the Oral Torah says, "All Israel has a portion in the world to come," it speaks of "Israel" as well as of "Israelites," and Solomon's Qohelet addresses neither. In his anomie, as well as hopelessness and denial of justice, Qohelet challenged much of the rest of Scripture and blatantly disrupted the Rabbinic recapitulation of Scripture.

First, let me provide evidence that the Rabbinic sages found Qohelet to form a flaw in the Written Torah, one that required repair. This is stated explicitly, and the remedy is provided in so many words, in the following:

LEVITICUS RABBAH PARASHAH TWENTY-EIGHT
XXVIII:I
1.   A.   "[When you come into the land which I give you and reap its harvest,] you shall bring the sheaf of the first fruits of your harvest to the priest" (Lev. 23:10).
B.   "What does man gain by all the toil at which he toils under the sun? [A generation goes, and a generation comes, but the earth remains forever]" (Qoh.1:3).
C.   Said R. Benjamin b. R. Levi, "Sages proposed to hide away the scroll of Qohelet, for they found in it[s teachings] matters that tended toward heresy.
D.   "They said, 'Lo, is this the whole of Solomon's wisdom, which he came along to teach: "What does man gain by all the toil at which he toils under the sun?" May one then suppose that that is the case even for the [man's] toil over Torah?'
E.   "They retracted and ruled, 'He did not phrase matters as "all the toil" but "all the toil for his own benefit." [The meaning of Solomon therefore must be] for the toil that pertains to oneself, he does not profit, thus [implying] one does profit from the toil that pertains to the Torah.'"
2.   A.   Said R. Samuel b. R. Isaac, "Sages proposed to hide away the scroll of Qohelet, for they found in it[s teachings] matters that tended toward heresy.
B.   "They said, 'Lo, is this the whole of Solomon's wisdom, which he came along to teach: "Rejoice, O young man, in your youth, and let your heart cheer you in the days of your youth; walk in the ways of your heart and the sight of your eyes. [But know that for all these things, God will bring you into judgment]'" (Qoh. 11:9)?
C.   "Moses stated, '...not to follow after your own heart and your own eyes, [which you are inclined to go after wantonly]' [Num. 15:39],

and yet [Solomon] has said, 'Walk in the ways of your heart and the sight of your eyes!'

D.   "'[Accordingly, he would imply] there is neither justice nor a Judge, so the penalty of flogging has been annulled!'

E.   "But when [Solomon further] stated, 'But know that for all these things, God will bring you judgment' (Qoh. 11:9), they stated, 'Well has Solomon spoken.'"

3.   A.   [With regard to the statement, "What does man gain by all the toil at which he toils under the sun?" (Qoh. 1:3)], R. Huna and R. Aha in the name of R. Ilpai: "[Solomon means] one toils under the sun but lays up treasures *above* the sun [in Heaven]."

B.   R. Yudan said, "[He means the toil that one does in study of Torah only] under the sun [after sunrise] does not [yield gain], but [what he studies] before the sun [has risen] does yield [gain]."

The issue of No. 1 is that nothing is of enduring worth, and even study of the Torah does not yield anything of transcendent value, an obvious heresy. So 2.E makes a distinction that solves the problem, between what one does for oneself and what he does for the Torah. No. 2 wants to know whether Solomon denies justice, judge, and judgment, such as are givens in the Rabbinic system, and the sages prove that that is not his position. No. 3 goes through the same matter. The importance of the passage cannot be missed: Solomon's meditations on the surface contain heretical implications, which must be removed. The perfection effected by the Rabbinic sages, which we shall see in some detail, situates Solomon's writing squarely within the Rabbinic theological system and structure, which perfect the Torah by realizing its inner logic.

How then to perfect the Torah in the matter of the entire book? In the Rabbinic system, focused on the perfect justice of God, active and optimistic as it is, Qohelet's aimless cynicism found no natural home. His extravagant, lugubrious ennui contradicted the vital and constructive philosophy of life characteristic of the system of Torah-study and practice of commandments, sanctification now, salvation at the end, put forth in the perfected Torah, oral and written, of Rabbi Moses at Sinai.

To understand how the Rabbinic sages reworked Qohelet so that it would fit naturally into the dual Torah, we have to understand a particularity of Rabbinic Midrash, best instantiated for the present purpose by Leviticus Rabbah. That compilation, ca. 450 C.E., involved not the systematic exegesis of verse after verse of a given book, e.g., the book of Leviticus. Rather, Scripture was made the basis for the formation of a large-scale proposition, set forth through the selection and arrangement of Midrash-exegeses of unrelated verses of Scripture, all of which provide facts in behalf of a given, rather abstract proposition. The propositional composition exhibits a surface of exegesis of verses, but at its depths it conveys a particular point. In form, it involves the use of verses from a variety of books of Scripture to illuminate a given verse of the book of Scripture under analysis. That procedure rests on the preface of a cogent, unitary divine statement, best understood with the whole of Scripture in hand. Here is what it means to read Scripture at the end, all parts in conversation with all other parts, demanding a reciprocal process of harmonious clarification throughout. Every allegation, every verse, then serves equally well to clarify any other allegation and verse. The procedure envelops the parts within the entirety of Scripture and allows—indeed, requires—that the components be situated within the structure of the whole.

What follows? The imported verses are subjected to analysis, then introduced into the reading of the verse of Leviticus that is subject to analysis. That is how that "whole" is made to infuse the part, in this case, the verse deriving from some other book of Scripture imparts its context and meaning on the verse deriving from the book of Leviticus that is subject to analysis. And with what result? That verse chosen from some other book now sheds light on the generative verse—and vice versa. I call the components the base-verse and the intersecting verse. The base-verse/intersecting-verse compositions predominate in Leviticus Rabbah and its companion, Pesiqta deRab Kahana, and are important in Genesis Rabbah and some other compilations of the fourth and fifth centuries.

How does this exegetical program pertain to Qohelet? In the construction at hand, a verse of Leviticus is cited as the exegetical foundation for a composition (hence: base-verse), and then another verse, chosen from such books as Job, Proverbs, Qohelet, or Psalms, is cited for exegesis (hence: intersecting verse). That systematic reading of the whole of Scripture into the intersecting verse takes place first in its own terms, then in the context of the base-verse. As I shall show, Qohelet supplies a considerable proportion of the intersecting verses of Leviticus Rabbah. I estimate that approximately a third of the propositional composites built on base-verses of the book of Leviticus in Leviticus Rabbah are precipitated by analysis of intersecting verses of Qohelet. How they emerge in this construction supplies the key to the Rabbinization of Qohelet, its accommodation in the perfected Torah of Sinai.

The intersecting verse, not the base verse, is subjected to detailed and systematic exegesis. But the exegetical exercise ends up by leading the intersecting verse back to the base-verse and reading the latter in terms of the former. In such an exercise, what in fact does the exegete do? It is to read one thing in terms of something else. To begin with, it is the base-verse in terms of the intersecting verse. But it also is the intersecting verse in other terms as well, yielding a multi-layered construction of analogy and parable. The intersecting verse's elements always turn out to stand for, to signify, to speak of, something other than that to which they openly refer. If in the case of Leviticus Rabbah water stands for Torah, the skin disease of Leviticus 13-14 for gossip or evil speech, the reference to something for some other thing entirely, then the mode of thought at hand is simple. One thing symbolizes another, speaks not of itself but of some other thing entirely. I can think of no more effective way of removing a verse from its context and imposing upon it tasks of meaning and proof deriving from another context.

Note the upshot, which we shall see in detail: the subversion of Qohelet, the transformation of the despondency and depression into testimonies of Torah. On the surface, Qohelet imposes its meaning on Leviticus. In fact, it is the other way around: Qohelet serves as a medium for the messages that the whole Torah infuses into Leviticus, as we shall see in some detail. The Rabbinic sages refer to "the whole Torah," and, it should be clear, by "whole" I understand, the Torah *read whole into the parts*. What results is the statement of the entirety of Scripture, as reconstructed by the Rabbinic sages, read into, made to infuse and permeate, all of the parts: the wholeness attained, the parts perfected. And that labor of systematic recapitulation of the whole within the parts, which I call, a work of "rabbinization," is how the imperfection of Qohelet is removed and bits and pieces of Qohelet are set forth as part of the dual Torah as conveyed by Leviticus in Leviticus Rabbah.

In what follows I survey the intersecting-verse/base-verse compositions of Leviticus Rabbah in which Qohelet supplies the intersecting verse. I omit citations of Qohelet that do not function in the generative framework of the intersecting-verse/base-verse constructions, and I also omit glosses and intruded material.

LEVITICUS RABBAH PARASHAH THREE

III:I

1. A. "When anyone brings a cereal offering as an offering to the Lord, [his offering shall be of fine flour; he shall pour oil upon it and put frankincense on it and bring it to Aaron's sons the priests. And he shall take from it a handful of fine flour...]" (Lev. 2:1-2).

B. R. Isaac opened [discourse by citing the following verse]: "'Better is a handful of gratification than two fistfuls of labor which is pursuit of wind. [And I have noted this further futility under the sun, the case of the man who is alone]'" (Qoh. 4:6).

C. "Better is the one who [learns by] repeating [and memorizing] two divisions [of the Mishnah] and is at home in them than the one who [learns by] repeating [a great many] laws, but is not at home in them.

D. "'which is pursuit of wind—he wants to be called a legal authority [which is why he has tried to learn more than he is able to accomplish].

E. "[Along these same lines], better is the one who [learns by] repeating [and memorizing] laws and is at home in them than the one who [learns by] repeating [and memorizing] both laws and exegetical principles but is not in home at them.

F. "'which is pursuit of wind—he wants to be called a master of exegesis [of the law, through its overriding principles].

G. "Better is the one who [learns by] repeating [and memorizing] laws and exegetical principles and is at home in them than the one who [learns by] repeating [and memorizing] laws, exegetical principles, and Talmud, but is not at home at them.

H. "'which is pursuit of wind—he wants to be called a master of learning [and expert in the Talmud, so able to give practical decisions].

I. "Better is one who has [a total capital of only] ten gold coins, but who does business with them and earns his living with them [maintaining a rapid velocity of capital circulation], than one who goes and borrows [additional capital] on usurious rates.

K. "'which is pursuit of wind—for he wants to be known as a successful entrepreneur.

L. "Better is the one who goes and works and gives charity from what he has earned than the one who goes and steals and seizes other people's property by violence and then gives to charity out of what in fact belongs to other people.

N. "'which is pursuit of wind—for he wants to be known as a charitable person.

O. "Better is the one who has a vegetable patch and who fertilizes it and hoes it and makes a living from it than one goes and undertakes to share-crop the plot of [a great many] others for half the harvest.

Q. "'Desire of the spirit'—he wants to be known as a big landowner."

2. A. Said R. Berekhiah [commenting on 'a handful of quietness' and reading the Hebrew, *kaf nahat* to mean, footfall], "Better is one

footstep that the Holy One, blessed be He, took in the land of Egypt,

B.   "in line with the following verse of Scripture: 'And I shall pass through the land of Egypt' (Ex. 12:12),

C.   "than the two handfuls of furnace-ash [thrown] by Moses and Aaron.

D.   "Why? Because with the former came redemption, and with the latter came no redemption."

3.   A.   Said R. Hiyya bar Abba, "'Better is a handful of gratification' (Qoh. 4:6)—this refers to the Sabbath-day.

B.   "'Than two fistfuls of labor, which is pursuit of wind'—this refers to the six days of work.

C.   "'...the desire of the spirit'—one wants to work on [the six days of labor].

D.   "You should know that that is the case, for Israel will be redeemed only on the Sabbath.

E.   "That is in line with the following verse of Scripture: 'Through repentance (SWBH) and repose you will be saved' (Is. 30:15) [and that is on the Sabbath day] [meaning], in Sabbath repose you will be saved."

4.   A.   Said R. Jacob bar Qorshai, "'Better is a handful of gratification' (Qoh. 4:6)—this refers to the world to come.

B.   "'Than two fistfuls of labor, which is pursuit of wind'—this refers to this world.

C.   "'which is pursuit of wind—Bad people want to do whatever they want in this world and to have the penalty exacted from them in the world to come."

D.   That [statement of Jacob bar Qorshai] is in line with the following passage, which we have learned in the Mishnah: "[Jacob] would say, 'Better is a single hour spent in repentance and good deeds in this world than the whole of the world to come. Better is one hour of serenity in the world to come than the whole of the life of this world' (Abot 4:17)."

5.   A.   R. Isaac interpreted the cited verse [Qoh. 4:6] to refer to the tribes of Reuben and Gad: "When the tribes of Reuben and Gad came into the land and saw how rich was the potential for sowing and planting there, they said, 'Better is a handful of gratification' in the [holy] Land 'than both hands full' in Transjordan.

B.   "'which is pursuit of wind—It is what we want.

C.   "That is in line with the following verse of Scripture: 'Let this land be given to your servants as a possession' (Num. 32:5).

D.   "Then they went and said, 'Did we not choose [Transjordan] for ourselves? [So we cannot retract.]"

6.   A.   Another possibility [for interpreting Qoh. 4:6]: "Better is a handful of gratification"—this refers to the handful of cereal offering brought as a freewill offering by a poor person, [the handful of cereal sufficing].

B.   "...than two fistfuls of labor, which is pursuit of wind"—this refers to the finely ground incense of spices [Lev. 16:12] brought by the community as a whole.

C. [How so?] Said the Holy One, blessed be He, "I prefer the handful of cereal offering brought as a freewill offering by a poor person
than the two hands full of finely ground incense of spices brought by
the community as a whole,

D. "for the former bears with it expiation [for sin] while the latter
does not bear with it expiation [for sin]."

E. And what is [the measure of the handful of cereal offering]? It is
a tenth of an *ephah.*

F. "When anyone brings a cereal offering..." (Lev. 2:1).

The intersecting verse "Better is a handful of gratification than two
fistfuls of labor, which is pursuit of wind" in context underscores the
futility of effort; "it is better to be satisfied with a little than work
hard, which is for nothing." The passage then proceeds to "this further futility under the sun." That standard view of Qohelet is Rabbinized by transposition to the case of Torah-study. It is better to
master a portion of the Mishnah rather than superficially learn a
great many laws, and in the latter case, one would be motivated by
a desire for honor. And the matter unfolds along these same lines,
C-D being replicated at E-F, G-H, I-K, L-N, O-Q. In all these cases
excellence in a small undertaking is better than mediocrity in a large
one—which lesson scarcely intersects with the clear meaning of the
intersecting verse that is cited at the outset. No. 2 proceeds to a different context altogether, now Israel in Egypt, the Sabbath day, then
this world and the world to come, and so forth. The base verse is
reached at No. 6. From our perspective what has happened to the
intersecting verse is at issue: the verse is translated willy-nilly into
the category-formations of the Rabbinic system. It is no longer a statement of despair. It is now sound counsel on solid achievement in a
variety of contexts dictated by the dual Torah: a little well done,
rather than much poorly executed, in any of the several cited contexts.

But No. 6 is then very jarring, because the message of the intersecting verse is set aside. Now what is better is the modest cereal
offering as a freewill offering than the expensive incense offering for
expiation of sin. It is the point at which the interests of Leviticus
take over. Both Nos. 1-5 and No. 6, however, bear the same implications for the Oral Torah's disposition of the documentary message of Qohelet.

LEVITICUS RABBAH PARASHAH FOUR

IV:I.

1. A.   "[And the Lord said to Moses, 'Say to the people of Israel,] 'If [any one] soul sins [unwittingly in any of the things which the Lord has commanded not to be done and does any one of them...]'" (Lev. 4:1-2).

B.   "And moreover I saw under the sun, in the place of justice, wickedness was there, and in the place of righteousness, wickedness was there" (Qoh. 3:16).

C.   R. Eliezer and R. Joshua:

D.   R. Eliezer said, "'In the place of justice, wickedness was there'— in the place in which the great Sanhedrin of Israel was in session, deciding the legislation of Israel, 'wickedness was there'—there: 'All the princes of the king of Babylonia came in and sat in the middle gate' [Jer. 39:3].

F.   "And the Holy Spirit cries out, saying, 'In the place of righteousness, wickedness was there'—in a place concerning which is written, 'Righteousness lodged in her' [Is. 1:21].

G.   "'But now murderers' [Is. 1:21]—lo, they commit murder. There they killed Zechariah and Uriah."

H.   R. Joshua said, "'In the place of justice there was wickedness' [speaks of] the place in which the attribute of justice [showed itself, namely,] in the matter of the Golden Calf,

I.   "As it is written, 'Go to and fro, from gate to gate' [Ex. 32:27].

J.   "'There was wickedness,' for it is said, 'The Lord smote the people because they had made the calf' [Ex. 32:35].

K.   "And the Holy Spirit cries out, saying, 'In the place of righteousness, wickedness was there'—in the place in which I vindicated them and called them God-like, [saying,] 'I said, "You are God-like beings, and all of you are children of the Most High"' [Ps. 82:6],

L.   "'There was wickedness there'—there they went and said to the gold calf, 'This is your god, O Israel'" (Ex. 32:4).

2. A.   [The verse, "In the place of justice, wickedness was there, and in the place of righteousness wickedness was there" (Qoh. 3:16)] speaks of the generation of the Flood.

B.   "In the place of justice, wickedness was there"—in the place in which the attribute of justice was carried out, namely, in regard to the generation of the wilderness,

C.   as we have learned in the Mishnah, "As to the generation of the wilderness, they have no share in the world to come and they will not stand in judgment" (M. San. 10:3),

D.   there: "He blotted out every living thing" (Gen. 7:23).

E.   And the Holy Spirit cries out, saying "'In the place of righteousness, wickedness was there'—in the place in which I vindicated them, and wrote concerning them, 'Their houses are safe, without fear, and no rod of God is upon them' [Job 21:9],

F.   "'There was wickedness'—there: 'They say to God, Depart from us. We do not desire the knowledge of your ways. What is the Almighty, that we should serve him? And what profit do we get if we pray to him?'" (Job 21:14-15).

3.   A.   [Qoh. 3:16] speaks of the Sodomites.

B.   "In the place of justice, wickedness was there"—in the place in which the attribute of justice was carried out, namely, against the Sodomites,

C.   as we have learned in the Mishnah, "The men of Sodom have no share in the world to come, but they will stand in justice" (M. San. 10:3),

D.   "There is wickedness"—there: "Then the Lord made brimstone and fire rain upon Sodom and Gomorrah" (Gen. 19:24).

E.   And the Holy Spirit cries out, saying, "'In the place of righteousness, wickedness was there'—in the place in which I vindicated them and wrote concerning their land, 'A land from which bread comes forth and underneath it, it is turned up as if by fire, the stones thereof are the place of sapphires, and it has dust of gold' [Job 28:5-6].

F.   (They say, When one of them [in Sodom] went to a truck gardener and said to him, "Give me an issar's worth of vegetables," he would give them over, and the purchaser would shake the vegetables and find gold in the dust of the roots, so illustrating what Scripture says, "It has dust of gold.")

G.   "'There is wickedness'—there they said, 'Let us go and wipe out the rule [of hospitality] from among us.'

H.   "'She did not strengthen the hand of the poor and needy'" (Ez. 16:49).

4.   A.   R. Judah b. R. Simon interpreted the cited verse to speak of the incident at Shittim:

B.   "'In the place of justice, wickedness was there'—in the place in which the attribute of justice was carried out, namely, in regard to the incident at Shittim,

C.   "for it is written, 'Take the chiefs of the people and hang them up' [Num. 25:4].

D.   "'There was wickedness'—there: 'And those who died in the plague [were twenty-four thousand]' [Num. 25:9].

E.   "And the Holy Spirit cries out, saying, 'In the place of righteousness, there is wickedness'—in the place in which I vindicated them from Balaam's curse and turned the curses into blessings for them, as it is written, 'And the Lord your God turned the curse into a blessing for you' [Deut. 23:6]—

F.   "'There is evil'—there: 'While Israel dwelt in Shittim [the people began to play the harlot with the daughters of Moab]'" (Num. 25:1).

The context of Qoh. 3:16 is established at 3:17: "I mused, 'God will doom both righteous and wicked, for there is a time for every experience and for every happening. So I decided, as regards men, to dissociate them from the divine beings and to face the fact that they are beasts...as the one dies so does the other..." So the sense is, where there is justice, there also is wickedness, and vice versa. The abstract existentialism of the verse is countered by a concrete instantiation out of Scripture's own record, and the meaning is completely revised.

It is IV:I.1 that commences and revises the matter: where the Sanhedrin was located, there were the princes of the king of Babylonia, and where there was righteousness, murder; or refers to the attribute of justice corrupted by the Golden Calf. No. 2 moves on to the generation of the flood, the generation of the wilderness. No. 3 introduces the Sodomites; No. 4, the incident at Shittim. Once more, the hopeless confusion of justice and wickedness to which Qohelet refers is rendered in terms of the Torah's own data: where God has established justice, there, paradoxically, wickedness reigns. Existence is no longer aimless, there is a record of God's justice, which ultimately reigns.

LEVITICUS RABBAH PARASHAH FOUR

IV:II.

1. A. "All of man's earning is for the sake of his mouth, yet his gullet is not sated. [What advantage then has the wise man over the fool, what advantage has the pauper who knows how to get on in life? Is the feasting of the eyes more important than the pursuit of desire? That too is futility and pursuit of wind" (Qoh. 6:7-9).

B. Said R. Samuel b. R. Ammi, "Whatever a man accomplishes in the doing of religious duties and good deeds does not suffice [to compensate] for the breath [of gossip] that goes forth from his mouth."

I cite only part of this next item, which shows the same exegetical program: translate into particular, Israelite terms the cosmopolitan, existential categories of Qohelet. Where Solomon says, however hard you work, it is for food, of which you never have enough, the Rabbinic sage hears a reference to religious duties and good deeds, which never suffice to compensate for gossip—a standard Rabbinic shibboleth.

LEVITICUS RABBAH PARASHAH FOURTEEN

XIV:VII

1. A. "[Send our bread forth upon the waters, for after many days you will find it.] Distribute portions to seven or even to eight, for you cannot know what misfortune may occur on earth" (Qoh. 11:2).

B. "Give a portion to seven" refers to the seven days of a woman's menstrual period.

C. "And also to eight"—this refers to the eight days prior to circumcision.

D. Said the Holy One, blessed be he, "If a woman observes the days of her menstrual period [without having sexual relations during that time], I shall give you a son, and you will get to circumcise him on the eighth day.

E. "And on the eighth day the flesh of his foreskin shall be circumcised" (Lev. 12:3).

The detail of Qohelet is now Rabbinized, read in the context of the Torah's numerology.

LEVITICUS RABBAH PARASHAH SIXTEEN
XVI:V.

1. A. "Let not your mouth lead your flesh into sin" (Qoh. 5:5).

B. R. Joshua b. Levi applied the verse to speak of those who promise in public to give charity and then fail to do so:

C. "Let not your mouth lead your flesh into sin"—do not give the power to one of your limbs to lead all of your limbs into sin. "Your mouth will lead your entire body into sin."

D. "'And do not say before the messenger [that it was a mistake; why should God be angry at your voice and destroy the work of your hands?]' [Qoh. 5:5]..

E. "The messenger is the leader of the community [who collects charity funds].

F. "'That it was an error.' 'I made a pledge but I did not make a pledge.'

G. "'Why should God be angry at your voice'—at that very voice that made a pledge but did not pay it up.

H. "'And destroy the work of your hands.' Even the little property that you have, you will bring into disarray."

2. A. R. Benjamin interpreted the verse to speak of those who misinterpret the Torah:

B. "'Let your mouth not lead your flesh into sin'—

C. "Do not give the power to one of your limbs to lead all of your limbs into sin. Your mouth will lead your entire body into sin.

D. "'Do not say before the messenger'—this [refers to] the master.

E. "'That it was a mistake.' He pretended that he had studied Scripture, but he had never studied; [he pretended he] had repeated Mishnah traditions but had never repeated them.

F. "'Why should God be angry at your voice?'

G. "At that very voice that misinterpreted the words of Torah [by pretending to know things that the person really did not know].

H. "'And destroy the work of your hands'—even the few tractates that you actually do know, you bring into disarray."

3.   A.   R. Hananiah interpreted the verse to speak of those who gossip.

B.   "'Do not let your mouth lead your flesh into sin'—do not give the power to one of your limbs to lead all of your limbs into sin. Your mouth will lead your entire body into sin.

C.   "'Do not say before the messenger'—this [refers to] the messenger who oversees the body.

D.   "'That it was a mistake.' 'I gossiped and yet I did not gossip.'

E.   "'Why should God be angry at your voice?'

F.   "At that very voice that expressed gossip.

G.   "'And destroy the work of your hands'—even the few limbs that you have in your body you will bring into disarray [through leprosy]."

4.   A.   R. Mani interpreted the verse to speak of vowing:

B.   "'Do not let your mouth lead your flesh into sin'—do not give the power to one of your limbs to lead all of your limbs into sin. Your mouth will lead your entire body into sin.

C.   "'Do not say before the messenger'—this [refers to] the elder [who has the power to examine the vow and release it].

D.   "'That was an error.' 'I vowed but I did not vow.'

E.   "'Why should God be angry at your voice?'—at that very voice that took a vow but did not pay it.

F.   "'And destroy the work of your hands'—even those few religious duties that you have to your credit you bring into disarray."

5.   A.   Rabbis for their part interpret the verse to speak of Miriam:

B.   "'Let not your mouth lead your flesh into sin'—

C.   "Do not give the power to one of your limbs to lead all of your limbs into sin. Your mouth will lead your entire body into sin.

D.   "'Do not say before the messenger'—[this refers] to Moses.

E.   ("That is in line with the following verse of Scripture: 'And he sent forth a messenger and took us out of Egypt' (Num. 20:16).)

F.   "'That it was an error.' 'For we have done foolishly and we have sinned' [Num. 12:11].

G.   "'Why should God be angry at your voice?' At that voice: 'And the Lord was angry at them and he departed' [Num. 12:9].

H.   "'And destroy the work of your hands.'"

I.   Said R. Yohanan, "Miriam sinned with her mouth, but all the rest of her limbs [also] were smitten.

J.   "That is in line with the following verse of Scripture: 'And when the cloud removed from over the tent, behold, Miriam was leprous, as white as snow'" (Num. 12:10).

The context that is provided for Qoh. 5:5 is first the communal philanthropic arrangements: don't pledge and fail to pay up. That is the least particular reading. Next we interpret the mouth's leading the flesh to sin to pertain to those who misinterpret the Torah, pretending to know things one does not know; the third referent is the familiar concern with gossip; the fourth type of verbal sin is vowing and not keeping the vow; and, reverting to the matter of gossip, the rabbis introduce the scriptural figure of Miriam.

LEVITICUS RABBAH PARASHAH EIGHTEEN

XVIII:I

1.   A.   "[The Lord said to Moses and Aaron, 'Say to the people of Israel,] "When any man has a discharge from his body, [his discharge is unclean]"'" (Lev. 15:1-2).

B.   "Remember your creator in the days of your youth" (Qoh. 12:1).

C.   We have learned in the Mishnah (M. Abot 3:1): "Aqabiah b. Mehalalel says, 'Contemplate three things, and you will not come to commit a transgression. Know whence you have come, from a fetid drop; and where you are going, to worms and corruption; and before whom you are going to have to give a full accounting of yourself, before the King of kings of kings, the Holy One, blessed be he.'"

2.   A.   "In the days of your youth" (Qoh. 12:1) means in the days when you are young, while your strength is yet with you.

B.   "[Remember your Creator in the days of your youth,] before the evil days come" (Qoh. 12:1)—this refers to the time of old age.

C.   "When the years draw near, when you will say, 'I have no pleasure in them' (Qoh. 12:1). This refers to the time of the coming of the Messiah, at which there will no longer be consideration either of merit or of liability."

Translating "years draw near...," into "the days of the coming of the Messiah" provides a fine example of transforming an account of individual existence into a comment on Israel's corporate destiny. But Nos. 4-10 systematically explain the plain sense of Qohelet's account of the infirmities of age. I give only a piece of that exegesis, which shows that, where Qohelet does not present a jarring message, one that contradicts the Rabbinic structure overall, there the Rabbinic sages simply amplify his meaning in his own frame of reference.

4.   A.   "In the day when the keepers of the house tremble, and the strong men are bent, and the grinders of grain cease because they are few, and those that look through the wind blows are dimmed" (Qoh. 12:3).

B.   "In the day when the keepers of the house tremble" refers to one's knees.

C.   "And the strong men are bent" refers to one's ribs.

D.   R. Hiyya b. R. Nehemiah says, "This refers to his arms."

E.   "And the grinders of grain cease" refers to the stomach.

F.   "For they are few" refers to the teeth.

G.   "And those that look through the wind blows are dimmed" refers to the eyes.

H. R. Hiyya b. R. Nehemiah says, "This refers to the laps of the lungs, from which sound comes forth."

Here is the point at which Qohelet is made to expound the Rabbinic doctrine of resurrection, judgment, and the restoration of Israel to the Land, humanity to Eden; and once more, at the end, No. 15, the composite jars, since the sense imputed to Qohelet is now joined with the statement of Moses in Leviticus 15:2.

> 11. A. "Because man goes to his eternal home" (Qoh. 12:5).
> B. Said R. Simeon b. Laqish, "This teaches that each and every righteous person has an eternal home [designated for him in particular].
> C. "[The matter may be compared] to the case of a king who came into a town, with his generals, hyparchs, and soldiers. Even though the entire unit enters by the same gate, each unit is encamped in accord with its standing.
> D. "Likewise even though every individual tastes the flavor of death, every righteous person has an eternal home [designated for him in particular]."
> 15. A. All of these matters (Qoh. 12:1-7) pertain to the time of a person's old age. But as to one's youth, if a person sins, he is smitten with a flux (Lev. 15:1) or with leprosy.
> B. Therefore Moses admonished Israel, saying to them, "When any man has a discharge from his body, his discharge is unclean" (Lev. 15:2).

Remembering one's creator, 2.H, means, specifically, the King of kings of kings. I see little distance between the allegations of the intersecting verses, Qoh. 12:1ff., and the interpretation accorded to them. Most of the composite pertains to the frailties of age, though 2.C reminds us of the larger context. I have not reproduced the systematic exposition of the ailments of old age. No. 4 typifies the whole. No. 11B, D introduces a Rabbinic motif that corrects the impression of the reading of the intersecting verses that all is hopeless. The righteous surpass old age and death. The reversion to the base verse at No. 15 hardly taxes the exegete's skills. In true Rabbinic fashion, he invokes divine justice: what happens in old age comes about by reason of one's sin, so too, in youth there are other penalties, as specified at Lev. 15:2.

LEVITICUS RABBAH PARASHAH NINETEEN
XIX:IV.
1. A. R. Kohen opened [discourse by citing the following verse]: "'Through sloth [restraint] the roof sinks in, [and through indolence the house leaks]' [Qoh. 10:18].

The intersecting verse, dealing with sloth/restraint, is now made to refer to events in Israel's encounter with God. What was individual is made corporate, what was a private vice is made a public virtue ("restraint"). Here is an extreme transformation of meaning, but it is what is required to naturalize Qohelet's statements into the whole Torah. In this case the house is the house of Israel, not of a particular Israelite, as in Qohelet's exposition of the results of neglect.

> B. "[Through sloth]"—"Because the Israelites were restrained from encamping in separate divisions before Mount Sinai [but camped as a unified group, see 9:9],
> C. "'The roof sank down:' 'The Lord came down on to Mount Sinai' [Ex. 19:20]. 'He bowed the heavens and came down' (Ps. 18:10).
> D. "'And through indolence:' through Israel's distaste for making camp in separate divisions before Mount Sinai,
> E. "'The house leaks:' 'Also the clouds dripped water'" (Jud. 5:4). [The Torah was revealed only to a unified nation.]
> 2. A. Another interpretation: "Through sloth [the roof sinks in]:"
> B. Because the Israelites were slothful about repenting in the time of Jeremiah,
> C. "The roof sinks in:" "And the covering of Judah was laid bare: [Is. 22:8], [referring to] the uncovering of [secrets] that had been covered.
> D. "Through indolence [the house leaks]:" Because the Israelites were indolent about repenting in the time of Jeremiah,
> E. "The house leaks:" "For behold, the Lord has commanded, and the great house will be smitten into splinters, and the small house into chips" (Amos 6:11).
> F. The two [the great house: the kingdom of Israel, the ten tribes, and the small house: Judah] are not equivalent to one another. [The great house was demolished, the small one merely damaged.]

But the personal aspect of the intersecting verse registers as well, as the following indicates. No. 4 then matches the public to the personal.

> 3. A. Another interpretation: "Through sloth the roof sinks in:" Because a person is slothful about covering his head as is appropriate,
> B. "the roof sinks in:" lo, he becomes rheumatic.
> C. "Through indolence:" Because a person is indolent about drying his body as is appropriate,
> D. "the house leaks:" his body produces open sores.
> 4. A. R. Kohen interpreted the cited verse to speak of a woman:
> B. "'Through sloth the roof sinks in:' Because a woman is slothful about covering herself as is appropriate,
> C. "'the roof sinks in:' 'and he shall uncover her nakedness he has

made naked her fountain, [and she has uncovered the fountain of her blood—both of them shall be cut off from among their people]' [Lev. 20:18].

D.   "'And through indolence:' Because this woman is indolent about examining herself during her menstrual period, she menstruates a great deal [and her period is prolonged]:

E.   [Thus] "'If a woman has a discharge of blood for many days, [not at the time of her impurity]'" (Lev. 15:25).

The rabbinization of Qohelet extends to finding theological reference-points in perfectly secular observations of King Solomon. Wisdom about maintaining the house becomes a reprise of Israel's encounter with God. The sense of the verse shifts from "sloth" to "restraint," yielding 1.B-C, the Israelites unified at Sinai, so God came down, repeated at D-E. No. 2 reverts to the more obvious sense, sloth, thus 2.B-C, repeated at D-E, because the Israelites were indolent about repenting in the time of Jeremiah, the secrets were revealed. No. 3 then brings the reference-point back to the life of an individual Israelite, bringing the intersecting verse home to the base verse at No. 4. The main point of interest, then, is at Nos. 1-2, with their introduction, into the reading of Qohelet, of chapters in the relationship of Israel and God.

LEVITICUS RABBAH PARASHAH TWENTY

XX:I.

1.   A.   "[The Lord spoke to Moses] after the death of the two sons of Aaron, [when they drew near before the Lord and died]" (Lev. 16:1).

B.   R. Simeon b. R. Abbayye opened [discourse by citing the following verse of Scripture]: "'Since one fate comes to all, to the righteous and the wicked, [to the good (supply: and the evil), to the clean and the unclean, to him who sacrifices and him who does not sacrifice]' [Qoh. 9:2].

Qohelet clearly means by "one fate" that everyone ends up in the grave. But by finding a different common fate for pairs of righteous and wicked, that obvious sense is set aside, and the observation of Qohelet is made to pertain to not death but some other indicative experience, e.g., the condition in which Noah and Pharaoh died, what was common to Moses, Aaron, and the spies, and the like.

C.   "'The righteous' refers to Noah: 'And Noah was righteous'" (Gen. 6:9).

E.   (Simeon continues:) "And 'to the wicked' refers to Pharaoh Necho [2 Kgs. 23:29].

F.   "When he wanted to sit in Solomon's throne, he did not know how it worked, and a snake bit him and a lion maimed him. So this one [Noah] died [maimed in a condition of frailty], and that one [Necho] died [maimed in a condition of frailty]. Is it not so, then, that 'one fate comes to all?'"

2. A. "To the good [and the evil], to the clean and the unclean" (Qoh. 9:2).

B. "The good" refers to Moses, for it is said, "And she looked at him, for he was good" (Ex. 2:2).

D. "The clean [or pacifier]" refers to Aaron, who was responsible for the (cultic purification) of Israel, as it is said, "He walked with me in peace and uprightness [and did turn many away from iniquity]" (Mal. 2:6).

E. "And to the unclean" refers to the spies. These [Moses and Aaron] reported good things about the land of Israel, and those reported bad things about the land of Israel. These did not enter the land of Israel, but those also did not enter the land of Israel.

F. Is it not so, then, that "one fate comes to the good and to the clean and to the unclean"?

3. A. "To him who sacrifices [and him who does not sacrifice]" (Qoh. 9:2)]. "[To him who sacrifices]" refers to Josiah: "And Josiah sacrificed of the flock, lambs and kids" (2 Chron. 35:7).

B. "And to the one who does not sacrifice" (Qoh. 9:2) refers to Ahab, who brought about the cessation of sacrifices from the altar.

C. That is in line with the following verse of Scripture: "And Ahab sacrificed for himself an abundance of animals from the flock and herd" (2 Chron. 18:2). The reference to "for himself" indicates that it was for himself that he made the sacrifice, and he did not sacrifice offerings [to God].

D. Now this one died in a hail of arrows, and that one died in a hail of arrows.

E. Is it not so, then, that "one fate comes to him who sacrifices and to him who does not sacrifice"?

4. A. "As to the good man, so is the sinner [and he who swears is as he who shuns an oath]" (Qoh. 9:2).

B. "As to the good man" refers to David: "And he sent and brought him, and he was ruddy, with a lovely face, and good appearance" (1 Sam. 16:12).

C. Said R. Isaac, "'He was of good appearance' in knowledge of the law, for whoever looked upon him would remember what he had learned."

D. "So is the sinner" refers to Nebuchadnezzar: "Break off your sin through righteousness" (Dan. 4:24).

E. This one [David] built the house of the sanctuary and ruled for forty years, while that one destroyed it and ruled for forty-five years.

F. Is it not the case of a single fate['s affecting them both]?

5. A. ["And he who swears is as he who shuns an oath" (Qoh. 9:2).]

"He who swears" refers to Zedekiah: "And he also rebelled against King Nebuchadnezzar" (2 Chron. 36:13).

B. "As he who shuns an oath" (Qoh. 9:3) refers to Samson: "And Samson said to them, 'You take an oath to me'" (Jud. 15:12).

C. This one died with his eyes having been put out, and that one died with his eyes having been put out.

D. Is it not the case of a single fate's affecting them both?

6. A. Another interpretation of the verse, "Since one fate comes to all, to the righteous and to the wicked" (Qoh., 9:2).

B. "The righteous" refers to [supply: the sons of] Aaron, concerning whom it is written, "He walked with me in peace and uprightness [and did turn many away from iniquity]" (Mal. 2:6).

C. "And to the wicked" refers to the congregation of Korach, concerning whom it is written, "Depart, please, [from the tents of these wicked men]" (Num. 16:26).

D. The latter went in to make an offering when they were divided by contentiousness, and they ended up burned. And these went in to make an offering not divided by contentiousness, and they too ended up burned.

E. That is in line with the following verse of Scripture: "After the death of the two sons of Aaron" (Lev. 16:1).

Once more the hopeless cynicism of Qohelet is completely revised through a process of particularization. Then Qohelet is not talking of all humanity and death in general, but of specific cases of Israel's life and chapters that intersect. Then the one fate comes to Noah and Pharaoh, that is, 1.F, both maimed; No. 2 has Moses and Aaron versus the spies, and the common fate is, neither group entered the promised land. No. 3 proceeds to the next clause of the intersecting verse, the equivalence of sacrificing and not sacrificing, pertaining to Josiah who did, Ahab who did not, sacrifice; yet both died in a hail of arrows. So in all three cases, the common fate is not the self-evident one, death. No. 4 then proceeds to the explicit reference to the good man and the sinner: David vs. Nebuchadnezzar, the one who built the Temple, the other who destroyed it, yet both ruled for a long time. Then, No. 5, comes swearing and not swearing, Zedekiah and Samson, with the common fate of blindness. Finally comes the base-verse, the sons of Aaron and the congregation of Korach, and their common fate, yielding a context for the text, Lev. 16:1. The negative effect is, no one any longer claims a common fate, the grave, awaits all. Here is an acute rabbinization of a plainly-blasphemous sense of King Solomon's legacy, that there is no Judge, no judgment, and no justice. The Rabbinic sages who accepted Qohelet into the canon can have had in mind precisely an exercise in the present model.

LEVITICUS RABBAH PARASHAH TWENTY

XX:III

1.   A.   Abba b. R. Kahana opened [his discourse by citing the following verse of Scripture:] 'I said of laughter, "It is mad," [and of pleasure, "What use is it"]' (Qoh. 2:2).

B.   "If joy is only mixed, then what use is rejoicing?"

C.   There was the case of one of the great lords of Kabul, who married off his son. On the fourth day [of the week of rejoicing], he invited guests to his house.

D.   After they had eaten and drunk and made merry, he said to his son, "Go up and bring us a jug of wine from the upper room."

E.   When he got up there, a snake bit him and he died.

F.   He waited for him to come down, but he did not come down. He said, "Shall I not go up and see what's going on with my son?"

G.   He went up and found that a snake had bitten him and he had died, and he was sprawled out between the jugs.

H.   He waited until the guests had finished their meal.

I.   He said to them, "My lords, is it not to say a blessing for my son as a groom that you have come? Say a blessing for him as mourners. Is it not to bring my son into the marriage canopy that you have come? Rather, bring him to his grave."

J.   R. Zakkai from Kabul gave a eulogy for him, "'I said of laughter, It is mad'" (Qoh. 2:2).

Here the intersecting verse of Qohelet serves no base-verse, and there is no effort at rabbinizing it, nor any need. The sentiment is that unalloyed joy invites tragedy, a matter of attitude, not theological instruction, with which the Rabbinic system can find an accommodation. It is constructive, but not foolish.

LEVITICUS RABBAH PARASHAH TWENTY-TWO

XXII:I

1.   A.   "If any man of the house of Israel kills [an ox or a lamb or a goat in the camp, or kills it outside the camp, and does not bring it to the door of the tent of meeting, to offer it as a gift to the Lord before the tabernacle of the Lord, blood-guilt shall be imputed to that man; he has shed blood; and that man shall be cut off from among his people. This is to the end that the people of Israel may bring their sacrifices which they slay in the open field, that they may bring them to the Lord, to the priest at the door of the tent of meeting, and slay them as sacrifices of peace offerings to the Lord]" (Lev. 17:3-5).

B.   "For the superfluities of the land are among all of them [and a king makes himself servant to the field]" (Qoh. 5:8). [JPS: "If you see in a province oppression of the poor and suppression of right and justice, don't wonder at that fact; for one high official is protected by a higher one, and both of them by still higher ones. Thus the greatest advantage in all the land is his: he controls a field that is cultivated, A lover of money never has his fill of money" (Qoh. 5:7-10)]:

C. R. Judah and R. Nehemiah:

D. R. Judah said, "Even things that you regard as superfluous [are 'for a profit'] for the world, for example, bast for making ropes, twigs for a hedge for a vineyard. So even they serve for the benefit of the world.

E. "'A king makes himself servant to a field.' Even a king who rules from one end of the world to the other 'makes himself servant to a field.' If the earth yields a crop, he can do something, but if the earth does not yield a crop, he cannot do anything.

F. "Therefore: 'He who loves silver will not be satisfied with silver' [Qoh. 5:9]. If one loves money, he will not find satisfaction in money. For whoever covets and is greedy for money but has no real estate— what enjoyment does he have [in his capital]?"

3. A. R. Nehemiah said, "'For the superfluities of the land are among all of them.' Even things that you may regard as superfluities in the revelation of the Torah, for example, show fringes, phylacteries, and amulets for the doorpost, even they fall into the category of the revelation of the Torah [although laws concerning them are not spelled out]."

5. A. "A king makes himself servant to a field" (Qoh. 5:8).

B. R. Judah and R. Huna:

C. R. Judah said, "'King' refers to a master of the Talmud. 'Makes himself servant to a field' refers to a master of the Mishnah, who arranges the law before him [the master of the Talmud]."

D. R. Huna said, "'A king' refers to the master of the Mishnah. 'Makes himself servant to a field' refers to a master of Talmud, who readies the law before [the master of the Mishnah]."

6. A. Therefore, "He who loves money will not be satisfied with money" (Qoh. 5:10). He who loves Torah will not be satisfied with Torah.

B. For whoever covets and is greedy for teachings of Torah but has no disciple—of what benefit to him is his learning?

C. R. Eleazar b. R. Abina said in the name of R. Aha: "If one has studied but not taught, you have no greater waste [vanity] than that!"

XXII:II

1. A. And rabbis say, "'And the superfluities of the earth' [Qoh. 5:8] [is to be interpreted as follows:] 'Even things that you regard as superfluous in the world, such as flies, fleas, and gnats, also belong [within] the [purposeful] creation of the world.

B. "For it is written, 'And the heavens and the earth were finished [and all the host of them,' compassing flies, fleas, and gnats]'" (Gen. 2:1).

2.   A.   "A king is made servant to the field" (Qoh. 5:8).

B.   "A king" refers to the Holy One, blessed be he, concerning whom it is written, "The Lord is king, he is clothed in majesty" (Ps. 93:1) [God is servant to Zion].

C.   "Is made servant to the field" refers to Zion, concerning which it is written, "Zion will be ploughed like a field" (Mic. 3:12).

3.   A.   Therefore: "One who loves silver will not be satisfied with silver" (Qoh. 5:9): One who loves religious duties will not be satisfied with religious duties [successfully accomplished].

B.   For whoever covets and is greedy for religious duties but does not have to his credit a religious duty [performed as he does] set up for coming generations—what pleasure does he have?

C.   You may know that this is the case, for lo, in the case of Moses, how many acts of religious duty and of righteousness did he carry out, and how many good deeds were to his credit. But he performed one religious duty as a model established for coming generations [and that is the important one for him].

D.   That is in line with the following verse of Scripture: "Then Moses separated [three cities on the other side of the Jordan]" (Deut. 4:41).

The notion that nothing in creation is superfluous presents no challenge to the Rabbinic system, which concurs. That accounts for the interest only in a recapitulation of the sentiment of the intersecting verse, No. 1. The point is now a clause by clause reading: what is superfluous has a use. The king depends on the crop, as much as does the farmer. Real estate is more desirable than ready cash. The three sentiments are discreet, one from the other. No. 3 finds a Rabbinic framework for the naturalistic observations dealt with at No. 1. The superfluities are details of the Torah but integral thereto.

Then No. 5 takes a completely different route, simply reading the intersecting verse in the context of Torah-study, a familiar initiative. XXII:II continues the foregoing, No. 1 making the familiar point that everything in creation has its purpose. No. 2 is read disjunctively, as before, now taking the daring route of having "the king servant to the field" refer to God and Zion.

The secularity of the observation about the never-sated miser is set aside, as No. 3 carries us to the base verse, now translating the passage into a reference to religious duty, one who loves religious duties will not be satisfied with those already accomplished, but will want to carry out more of them. Moses's most important religious duty was the one that affecting coming generations. I cannot imagine a more successful reworking of a secular observation into a theological reading. If the whole hardly flows from item to item, then the parts serve quite well on their own.

LEVITICUS RABBAH PARASHAH TWENTY-TWO

XXII:III

1. A. "And the superfluities of the earth with all" (Qoh. 5:8).

B. Said the Holy One, blessed be he, to the prophets, "If you do not carry out my mission, I shall have no messengers."

C. Said R. Aha, "With anything at all does the Holy One, blessed be he, carry out his mission, even with a snake, a scorpion, a frog, or a gnat."

LEVITICUS RABBAH PARASHAH TWENTY-TWO

XXII:IV

1. A. Another interpretation of "And the superfluities of the earth."

B. R. Tanhuma said [what follows], so too R. Menahama, R. Berekhiah, R. Helbo, and R. Aha repeated the story:

C. There was a man who was standing on the bank of a river and saw a frog carrying a scorpion across the river. He said, "This [frog] is appointed to carry out its mission."

D. The frog carried it across the river and went its way and then [when the scorpion had] carried out its mission, [the frog] came and brought it back to its place.

XXII:III-IV set forth a routine extension of the foregoing, a sequence of stories that illustrate the same point. These are affecting but do not extend the argument.

LEVITICUS RABBAH PARASHAH TWENTY-FIVE

XXV:IV

1. A. R. Joshua of Sikhnin in the name of R. Levi opened [discourse by citing the following verse]: "'I made great works; I built houses [and planted vineyards] for myself; [I made myself gardens and parks and planted in them all kinds of fruit trees]' [Qoh. 2:4].

B. "'I made great works:' Said the Holy one, blessed be he, to Moses, 'Go and say to the original patriarchs, "I made great works. I have done great things for your children, in line with everything to which I stipulated with you."'

C. "'I built houses:' 'Houses filled with every good thing' [Deut. 6:11].

D. "'I planted vineyards for myself:' 'Vineyards and olive trees that you did not plant' [Deut. 6:11].

E. "'I made myself pools [from which to water the forest of growing trees]' [Qoh. 2:6]: 'And fully dug wells, which you did not dig' [Deut. 6:11].

F. "'Fountains and depths' [Qoh. 8:7], 'from which to water the forest of growing trees' [Qoh. 2:6].

G. Said R. Levi, "Not even reeds for arrows did the Land of Israel lack."

H.   "'I made myself gardens and parks:' 'A land of wheat and barley' [Deut.8:8].
I.   "'I planted in them all kinds of fruit trees:' 'When you come into the land, you will plant [all kinds of trees for food]'" (Lev. 19:23).

The sense of the verse is, "I built…I planted…I constructed…then my thoughts turned to all the fortune my hands had built up, to the wealth I had acquired and won, and oh, it was all futile and pursuit of wind; there was no value under the sun" (Qoh. 2:11, JPS). To remove that message, the value of the works has to be affirmed, not denied, and that is accomplished by having Solomon speak for God: "I, God, made great works," now refers to what God did for Israel: houses filled with every good thing and the like, that is, reading Qoh. 2:4 in light of Dt. 2:11). That then leads directly to the base-verse, Lev. 19:23, and the message of Qoh. 2:11 is simply bypassed by the formation of a different context for Qoh. 2:4, and a different speaker from Solomon, namely, God reviewing his ruling on how to use the orchards he has provided. I can think of no more characteristic a Rabbinic reading than this, and we shall see much more elaborate results in Song of Songs Rabbah.

Leviticus Rabbah Parashah Twenty-Seven
XXVII:IV

1.   A.   "That which is already has been, [that which is to be already has been. God seeks that which is pursued]" (Qoh. 3:15).
B.   R. Judah and R. Nehemiah:
C.   R. Judah says, "If someone should say to you that had the first Adam not sinned and eaten from that tree, he would have lived and endured even to this very day, tell him, 'It already has been.' Elijah lives and endures forever.
D.   "'That which is to be already has been:' If someone should tell to you, it is possible that the Holy One, blessed be he, in the future is going to resurrect the dead, say to him, 'It already has been.' He has already resurrected the dead through Elijah, Elisha, and Ezekiel in the valley of Dura."
E.   R. Nehemiah says, "If someone should say to you that it is possible that to begin with the world was entirely made up of water in water, say to him, 'It already has been,' for the ocean is full of diverse water.
F.   "'That which is to be already has been:' If someone should say to you, the Holy One, blessed be he, is going to dry [the sea] up, say to him, 'It already has been.' 'And the children of Israel walked on dry land through the sea'" (Ex. 15:19).
2.   A.   R. Aha in the name of R. Simeon b. Halapta: "Whatever the Holy One, blessed be he, is destined to do in the age to come already

has he shown to [humanity] in this world.

B.   "That he is going to resurrect the dead: he has already resurrected the dead through Elijah, Elisha, and Ezekiel.

C.   "That he is going to bring [people] through water on to dry land: 'When you pass through water, I am with you' (Is. 43:2). He has already brought Israel through [water] with Moses: 'And the children of Israel walked on dry land through the sea' [Ex. 15:19].

D.   "'And through rivers they shall not overwhelm you' [Is. 43:2]. This he has already accomplished through Joshua: 'On dry land the Israelites crossed the Jordan' [Josh. 4:22].

E.   "'When you walk through fire you shall not be burned' [Is. 43:2]. This he has already accomplished through Hananiah, Mishael, and Azariah.

F.   "'And the flame shall not consume you' [Is. 43:2]. This he has already accomplished: '[The fire had not had any power over the bodies of those men...] no smell of fire had come upon them' [Dan. 3:27].

G.   "That God will sweeten bitter water, he has already accomplished through Moses: 'The Lord showed him a tree, and he threw it into the water, and the water became sweet' [Ex. 15:25].

H.   "That God will sweeten what is bitter through something bitter, he has already accomplished through Elisha: 'Then he went to the spring of water and threw salt into it and said, Thus says the Lord, I have made this water wholesome' [2 Kgs. 2:21].

I.   "That God blesses what is little [and makes it much], he already has accomplished through Elijah and Elisha: 'For thus says the Lord, the God of Israel, "The jar of meal shall not be spent, and the cruse of oil shall not fail, [until the day that the Lord sends rain upon the earth]"' [1 Kgs. 17:14].

J.   "That God visits barren women, he has already accomplished through Sarah, Rebecca, Rachel, and Hannah.

K.   "'The wolf and the lamb will pasture together,' [Is. 65:25], he has already accomplished through Hezekiah: 'The wolf shall dwell with the lamb' [Is. 11:6].

L.   "'And kings will be your tutor' [Is. 49:23] he has already accomplished through Daniel: 'Then the king Nebuchadnezzar fell upon his face and worshipped Daniel' [Dan. 2:46].

The reference-point of Qoh. 3:15 is no longer the fatigued observation that there is nothing new, but rather the specific claim that, when Solomon says, "What is was, and what will be is, and there is nothing new," he means, the eschatological program is adumbrated in this age—a completely different, and profoundly Rabbinic judgment. For Rabbinic theology identifies as its focus not linear history but a paradigm of the story of humanity that repeats itself. In the present instance, it is a pattern of repetition of a given paradigm, first at the beginning, then at the end. Thus the matches join the restoration of Israel to the Land, Adam and Eve to Eden, and finds the end-time in the beginnings. No. 1 then compares Adam and Elijah, the one who sinned and died, but had he not sinned, he would have lived for ever, and Elijah, who never sinned and lives for ever, thus 1.C-D. Then No. 2 makes the general proposition explicit, for resurrection, 2.A-B, for bringing the people through water to dry land, C, through fire, E-F, and so on. The elaborate set of examples sustains the basic proposition, which imparts to the cited verse of Qohelet a completely fresh sense, and a constructive, optimistic one at that.

Leviticus Rabbah Parashah Twenty-Seven
XXVII:V
1. A. "God seeks what has been driven away" (Qoh. 3:15).
B. R. Huna in the name of R. Joseph said, "It is always the case that 'God seeks what has been driven away' [favoring the victim].
C. "You find when a righteous man pursues a righteous man, 'God seeks what has been driven away.'
D. "When a wicked man pursues a wicked man, 'God seeks what has been driven away.'
E. "All the more so when a wicked man pursues a righteous man, 'God seeks what has been driven away.'
F. "[The same principle applies] even when you come around to a case in which a righteous man pursues a wicked man, 'God seeks what has been driven away.'"

The observation that God favors the pursued over the pursuer is made, ultimately, to explain the selection of beasts for the altar. But the beasts that are chosen then stand for Abel over Cain, Noah over his contemporaries, Abraham over Nimrod, and the like. Then the Temple's procedures embody a moral lesson, which is now articulated:

2. A. R. Yosé b. R. Yudan in the name of R. Yosé b. R. Nehorai says, "It is always the case that the Holy One, blessed be he, demands an accounting for the blood of those who have been pursued from the hand of the pursuer.
B. "Abel was pursued by Cain, and God sought [an accounting for] the pursued: 'And the Lord looked [favorably] upon Abel and his meal offering' [Gen. 4:4].
C. "Noah was pursued by his generation, and God sought [an accounting for] the pursued: 'You and all your household shall come into the ark' [Gen. 7:1]. And it says, 'For this is like the days of Noah to me, as I swore [that the waters of Noah should no more go over the earth]' [Is. 54:9].

D. "Abraham was pursued by Nimrod, 'and God seeks what has been driven away:' 'You are the Lord, the God who chose Abram and brought him out of Ur' [Neh. 9:7].

E. "Isaac was pursued by Ishmael, 'and God seeks what has been driven away:' 'For through Isaac will seed be called for you' [Gen. 21:12].

F. "Jacob was pursued by Esau, 'and God seeks what has been driven away:' 'For the Lord has chosen Jacob, Israel for his prized possession' [Ps. 135:4].

G. "Moses was pursued by Pharaoh, 'and God seeks what has been driven away:' 'Had not Moses His chosen stood in the breach before Him' [Ps. 106:23].

H. "David was pursued by Saul, 'and God seeks what has been driven away:' 'And he chose David, his servant' [Ps. 78:70].

I. "Israel was pursued by the nations, 'and God seeks what has been driven away:' 'And you has the Lord chosen to be a people to him' [Deut. 14:2].

J. "And the rule applies also to the matter of offerings. A bull is pursued by a lion, a sheep is pursued by a wolf, a goat is pursued by a leopard.

K. "Therefore the Holy One, blessed be he, has said, 'Do not make offerings before me from those animals that pursue, but from those that are pursued: 'When a bull, a sheep, or a goat is born'" (Lev. 22:27).

The existential observation is given concrete instantiation in Israel's experience, thus we move from the general paradigm, pursued/pursuer, to Abel, Noah, Abraham, Isaac, Jacob, Moses, David, Israel—then to the offerings on the altar, K. The effect is to compare Israel to the sacrifices offered to God and to invoke Israel's subordinate status among the nations as a cause of God's favor.

LEVITICUS RABBAH PARASHAH THIRTY-TWO
XXXII:II

1. A. "Even in your thought do not curse the king, nor in your bedchamber curse the rich; [for a bird of the air will carry your voice, or some winged creature tell the matter]" (Qoh. 10:20).

B. Said R. Abin, "[God says,] 'You should not curse and blaspheme before me with that very capacity for thought that I gave you beyond [what I gave] to domesticated beasts, wild animals, and fowl.

C. "'For you I created two eyes and for them two eyes, for you two ears and for them two ears. I made you like them. [Yet] to him [namely, to man] they must keep silent.'

D. "'He is like the beasts that keep silent' [Ps. 49:21]. [God speaks], 'I have silenced them on account of the honor owing to you.'

E. "'How many favors have I done for you, and yet you do not understand.' 'Man in his honor does not understand' [Ps. 49:20]."

2. A. Another interpretation: "Even in your thought do not curse the king" (Qoh. 10:20). Do not curse the king who came before you.

B. "Nor in your bed-chamber curse the rich." Do not curse the rich man who came before you.

C. "For a bird of the air will carry your voice" (Qoh. 10:20).

D. Said R. Jeremiah bar Eleazar, "This refers to a raven and the art of bird divination."

E. "Or some winged creature will tell the matter" (Qoh. 10:20).

F. R. Levi said, "The wall has ears, the road along the ground has ears."

3. A. Another interpretation: "Even in your thought do not curse the king" (Qoh. 10:20). Do not curse the king [who rules] in your own generation.

B. "Nor in your bed-chamber curse the rich." Do not curse the rich man [who thrives] in your own generation.

C. "For a bird of the air will carry your voice" (Qoh. 10:20).

4. A. Another interpretation: "Even in your thought do not curse the king" (Qoh. 10:20):

B. The King of the world you should not curse.

C. "Nor in your bed-chamber curse the rich" (Qoh. 10:20): The Rich One of the world you should not curse.

D. "For a bird of the air will carry your voice" (Qoh. 10:20).

5. A. Another matter: "Even in your thought do not curse the king" (Qoh. 10:20). This refers to Moses, concerning whom it is written, "And there will be a king in Jeshurun" (Deut. 33:8).

B. "Nor in your bed-chamber curse the rich" (Qoh. 10:20). This refers to Moses.

F. "And that time Moses said, 'The blessing of the Lord is what makes one rich'" (Prov. 10:22).

G. "For a bird of the air will carry your voice" (Qoh. 10:20), for he flew like a bird and goes up to heaven.

H. "Or some winged creature [= God himself] tell the matter" (Qoh. 10:20): for it was told to Moses from Sinai, "Bring forth him that cursed outside the camp" (Lev. 24:14).

The context of Qoh. 10:20 is defined: God is the king not to be cursed. This is expressed at No. 1 in Abin's comment: do not even think to curse God, for your very capacity for thought, which distinguishes man from beast, I gave you. The same sentiment is treated in a this-worldly framework at No. 2, and No. 3 reverts to the focus on God. No. 4 is still better focused on God. and No. 5, introduces Moses and God. The effect is to transform political counsel into theological imperative.

LEVITICUS RABBAH PARASHAH THIRTY-SEVEN
XXXVII:I

1. A. "It is better that you not vow than that you vow and not pay" (Qoh. 5:5).

B.   R. Meir and R. Judah:

C.   R. Meir said, "'It is better that you should not vow' but better still is he who vows and pays"

D.   "What is the proof text? 'Vow and pay to the Lord your God'" (Ps. 76:12).

E.   R. Judah says, "'It is better that you should not vow' but better still is he who does not vow at all.

F.   "But one brings his lamb to the Temple court [not in advance making a vow to do so], and [only] there he declares it to be consecrated and slaughters it as an offering [without prior commitments, which he may not be able to carry out].

G.   "What is the proof text? 'But if you forbear to vow, it will be no sin against you'" (Deut. 23:23).

6.   A.   Said R. Simeon b. Yohai, "Just as in the case of vows, one [who delays] violates the commandment not to break one's word and not to defer to pay it [Num. 30:3; Qoh. 5:3], so the same considerations apply to pledges of one's value."

B.   Therefore Moses admonishes Israel, saying to him, "When a person makes a special vow of persons to the Lord at your valuation" (Lev. 27:2).

I see little more than a recapitulation of the sense of Qoh. 5:3 in the context of Num. 30:3, all for the reinforcement of Lev. 27:2.

The upshot is, Leviticus Rabbah has built a fair number of its systematic propositional composites around the rereading, within the theological structure of Scripture as read whole by the Rabbinic sages, of the detailed verses of Qohelet. Then Qohelet has been dismantled and some of its principal parts have been reassembled in the framework of not so much Leviticus in particular as the whole repertoire of Scripture's events and saints in general. That is the one way in which the Rabbinic sages perfected Scripture. The other is to reread the whole wholly within a hermeneutic deriving from the entirety of Scripture, as we shall now see. Here there is no selection and focus on bits and pieces, as with Qohelet, but a systematic reconstruction of the entirety of the anomalous book of Scripture, Song of Songs. The difference, as we shall see, is that while specific allegations of Solomon in Qohelet jarred, the entirety of the Song of Songs demanded a Rabbinic recapitulation in the Rabbinic framework of the entirety of the Torah. No one detail sufficed.

iii. *The Oral Torah's Program for Song of Songs. In the Matter of Song of Songs Rabbah*

Clearly, the Mishnah-passage, Yadayim 3:5, cited above records a point at which the status of the Song of Songs is in doubt. By the time of the compilation of Song of Songs Rabbah, that question had been settled. Everybody took for granted that our document is holy for the reason given.

The Song of Songs finds a place in the Torah because the collection of love-songs in fact speaks about the relationship between the lovers, God and Israel. The intent of the compilers of Song of Songs Rabbah is to justify that reading. In the present instance Midrash-exegesis turns to everyday experience—the love of husband and wife—for a metaphor of God's love for Israel and Israel's love for God. Then, when Solomon's song says, "O that you would kiss me with the kisses of your mouth! For your love is better than wine," (Song 1:2), the Rabbinic sages think of how God kissed Israel. Reading the Song of Songs as a metaphor, the Rabbinic sages state in a systematic and orderly way their entire structure and system. What they accomplished for Qohelet in an episodic way they did for Song of Songs in a systematic fashion.

The transformation of love poems to theological metaphors took place through revising the sense of language throughout. No longer used in an ordinary, this-worldly way, the words of the Song of Songs were given a different reference-point from the one that a superficial reading yielded. Sages read the language of Song of Songs—its long sequences of similes and metaphors—as a repertoire of opaque symbols. They set forth catalogues of words that connote meanings, elicit emotions, stand for events, form the verbal equivalent of pictures or music or dance or poetry. Through the repertoire of these verbal-symbols and their arrangement and rearrangement, the message the authors wish to convey emerges.

Sages chose for their compilation a very brief list of items among many possible candidates, a restricted vocabulary. They therefore determined to appeal to a highly limited list of implicit meanings, calling upon some very few events or persons, repeatedly identifying these as the expressions of God's profound affection for Israel, and Israel's deep love for God. The message of the document comes not so much from stories of what happened or did not happen, assertions of truth or denials of error, but rather from the repetitious rehearsal of sets of symbols.

In reading the love-songs of the Song of Songs as the story of the love affair of God and Israel, sages identify implicit meanings that are always few and invariably self-evident; no serious effort goes into demonstrating the fact that God speaks, or Israel speaks; the point of departure is the message and meaning the One or the other means to convey. To take one instance, time and again we shall be told that a certain expression of love in the poetry of the Song of Songs is God's speaking to Israel about (1) the Sea, (2) Sinai, and (3) the world to come; or (1) the first redemption, the one from Egypt; (2) the second redemption, the one from Babylonia; and (3) the third redemption, the one at the end of days. The catalogue of reference-points then is highly focused.

When in Song of Songs Rabbah we have a sequence of items alleged to form a taxon, that is, a set of things that share a common taxic indicator, what we have is a list. The list presents diverse matters that all together share, and therefore also set forth, a single fact or rule or phenomenon. That is why we can list them, in all their distinctive character and specificity, in a common catalogue of "other things" that pertain all together to one thing.

An introductory exercise is called for. What do the compilers say through their readings of the metaphor of—to take one interesting example—the nut-tree for Israel? First, Israel prospers when it gives scarce resources for the study of the Torah or for carrying out religious duties; second, Israel sins but atones, and Torah is the medium of atonement; third, Israel is identified through carrying out its religious duties, e.g., circumcision; fourth, Israel's leaders had best watch their step; fifth, Israel may be nothing well-balanced but will be in glory in the coming age; sixth, Israel has plenty of room for outsiders but cannot afford to lose a single member. What we have is a repertoire of fundamentals, dealing with Torah and Torah-study, the moral life and atonement, Israel and its holy way of life, Israel and its coming salvation. A sustained survey of these composites shows the contradictory facts that the several composites are heterogeneous, but the components of the composites derive from a rather limited list, essentially scriptural events and personalities, on the one side, and virtues of the Torah's holy way of life, on the other. Here is a selection of the Scriptural data that are collected to form lists that produce a given attitude, emotion, or occasionally, proposition:

patriarchs as against princes, offerings as against merit, and Israel as against the nations; those who love the king, proselytes, martyrs, penitents;

first, Israel at Sinai; then Israel's loss of God's presence on account of the golden calf; then God's favoring Israel by treating Israel not in accord with the requirements of justice but with mercy;

Dathan and Abiram, the spies, Jeroboam, Solomon's marriage to Pharaoh's daughter, Ahab, Jezebel, Zedekiah;

Israel is feminine, the enemy (Egypt) masculine, but God the father saves Israel the daughter;

the spoil at the Sea = the Exodus, the Torah, the Tabernacle, the ark;

the patriarchs, Abraham, Isaac, Jacob, then Israel in Egypt, Israel's atonement and God's forgiveness;

the Temple where God and Israel are joined, the Temple is God's resting place, the Temple is the source of Israel's fecundity;

Israel in Egypt, at the Sea, at Sinai, and subjugated by the gentile kingdoms, and how the redemption will come;

fire above, fire below, meaning heavenly and altar fires; Torah in writing, Torah in memory; fire of Abraham, Moriah, bush, Elijah, Hananiah, Mishael, and Azariah;

the Exodus, the conquest of the Land, the redemption and restoration of Israel to Zion after the destruction of the first Temple, and the final and ultimate salvation;

Israel at the sea and forgiveness for sins effected through their passing through the sea; Israel at Sinai; the war with Midian; the crossing of the Jordan and entry into the Land; the house of the sanctuary; the priestly watches; the offerings in the Temple; the sanhedrin; the Day of Atonement;

the return to Zion in the time of Ezra, the Exodus from Egypt in the time of Moses;

the patriarchs were with Israel in Egypt, at the Sea, and then before Sinai;

Abraham in the fiery furnace and Shadrach Meshach and Abednego, the Exile in Babylonia, well-balanced with reference to the return to Zion

The point is to show that many different things really do belong on the same list. That yields not a proposition that the list syllogistically demonstrates. The list yields only itself, but, to be sure,—but then the list invites our exegesis; the connections among these items require exegesis. What this adds up to, then, is not argument for proposition, hence comparison and contrast and rule-making of a philosophical order, but rather a theological structure—comprising well-defined attitudes. Because of the character of Song of Songs

Rabbah, the topical program of the document is best portrayed through the actual workings of the "another matter-"compositions, some of which are portrayed in the sample given below.

SONG OF SONGS RABBAH TO SONG 1:1

I:i.1 A. "The song of songs:"

B. This is in line with that which Scripture said through Solomon: "Do you see a man who is diligent in his business? He will stand before kings, he will not stand before mean men" (Prov. 22:29).

C. "Do you see a man who is diligent in his business:"

D. This refers to Joseph: "But one day, when he went into the house to do his work [and none of the men of the house was there in the house, she caught him by his garment, saying, 'Lie with me.' But he left his garment in her hand and fled and got out of the house]" (Gen. 39:10-13).

E. R. Judah and R. Nehemiah:

F. R. Judah said, "[Following Gen. R; LXXXVII:VII:] It was a festival day for the Nile. [Everybody went to see it, but he went to the household to take up his master's account-books]."

G. R. Nehemiah said, "It was a day of theater. Everybody went to see it, but he went to the household to take up his master's account-books."

2. A. R. Phineas says in the name of R. Samuel bar Abba, "Whoever serves his master properly goes forth to freedom.

B. "Whence do we learn that fact? From the case of Joseph.

C. "It was because he served his master properly that he went forth to freedom."

3. A. "He will stand before kings:"

B. this refers to Pharaoh: "Then Pharaoh sent and called Joseph and they brought him hastily from the dungeon" (Gen. 41:14).

4. A. "he will not stand before mean men:"

B. this refers to Potiphar, whose eyes the Holy One blessed be he darkened [the word for 'darkened' and 'mean men' share the same consonants], and whom he castrated.

5. A. Another interpretation of the verse, "Do you see a man who is diligent in his business" (Prov. 22:29):

B. this refers to our lord, Moses, in the making of the work of the tabernacle.

C. Therefore: "He will stand before kings."

D. this refers to Pharaoh: ""Rise up early in the morning and stand before Pharaoh" (Ex. 8:16).

E. "he will not stand before mean men:"

F. this refers to Jethro.

G. Said R. Nehemiah, "[In identifying the king with Pharaoh,] you have made the holy profane.

H. "Rather, 'He will stand before kings:' this refers to the King of kings of kings, the Holy One, blessed be he: 'And he was there with the Lord forty days' (Ex. 34:28).

I.   "'he will not stand before mean men:' this refers to Pharaoh: 'And there was thick darkness' (Ex. 10:22)."

6. A.   Another interpretation of the verse, "Do you see a man who is diligent in his business" (Prov. 22:29):

B.   this refers to those righteous persons who are occupied with the work of the Holy One, blessed be he.

C.   Therefore: "He will stand before kings."

D.   this refers to "for they stand firm in the Torah:" "By me kings rule" (Prov. 8:15).

E.   "he will not stand before mean men:"

F.   this refers to the wicked: "And their works are in the dark" (Is. 29:15); "Let their way be dark and slippery" (Ps. 35:6).

7. A.   Another interpretation of the verse, "Do you see a man who is diligent in his business" (Prov. 22:29):

B.   this refers to R. Hanina.

8. A.   They say:

B.   One time he saw people of his village bringing whole offerings and peace offerings up [on a pilgrimage to the Temple].

C.   He said, "All of them are bringing peace offerings to Jerusalem, but I am not bringing up a thing! What shall I do?"

D.   Forthwith he went out to the open fields of his town, the unoccupied area of his town, and there he found a stone. He went and plastered it and polished it and painted it and said, "Lo, I accept upon myself the vow to bring it up to Jerusalem."

E.   He sought to hire day-workers, saying to them, "Will you bring this stone up to Jerusalem for me?"

F.   They said to him, "Pay us our wage, a hundred gold pieces, and we'll be glad to carry your stone up to Jerusalem for you."

G.   He said to them, "Where in the world will I get a hundred gold pieces, or even fifty, to give you?"

H.   Since at the time he could not find the funds, they immediately went their way.

I.   Immediately the Holy One, blessed be he, arranged to have fifty angels in the form of men [meet him]. They said to him, "My lord, give us five selas [a standard coin of daily use], and we shall bring your stone to Jerusalem, on condition that you help us with the work."

J.   So he put his hand to the work with them, and they found themselves standing in Jerusalem. He wanted to pay them their wage, but he could not find them.

K.   The case came to the Chamber of the Hewn Stone [where the high court was in session]. They said to him, "It appears that in the case of our lord, ministering angels have brought the stone up to Jerusalem."

L.   Immediately he gave sages that wage for which he had hired the angels.

9. A. Another interpretation of the verse, "Do you see a man who is diligent in his business" (Prov. 22:29):

   B. this refers to Solomon son of David.

   C. "He will stand before kings."

   D. for he was diligent in building the house of the sanctuary: "So he spent seven years in building it" (1 Kgs. 6:38).

10. A. [Supply: "So he spent seven years in building it" (1 Kgs. 6:38),] but a different verse says, "And Solomon was building his own house for thirteen years" (1 Kgs. 7:1),

   B. so the building of the house of Solomon was lovelier and more elaborate than the building of the house of the sanctuary.

   C. But this is what they said:

   D. In the building of his house he was slothful, in the building of the house of the sanctuary he was diligent and not slothful.

11. A. Huna in the name of R. Joseph: "All help the king, all the more so do all help out on account of the glory of the King of kings of kings, the Holy One, blessed be he,

   B. "even spirits, demons, ministering angels."

12. A. Isaac b. R. Judah b. Ezekiel said, "'I have surely built you a house of habitation' (1 Kgs. 8:13): 'I have built what is already built.'"

13. A. R. Berekiah said, "'The house that they were building' is not what is said,

   B. "but rather, 'the house in its being built' (1 Kgs. 6:7), which is to say, it was built of itself.

   C. "'It was built of stone made ready at the quarry' (1 Kgs. 6:7):

   D. "that is says is not 'built' but 'it was built,' which is to say, the stones carried themselves and set themselves on the row."

14. A. Said Rab, "Do not find this astonishing. What is written elsewhere? 'And a stone was brought and laid upon the mouth of the den' (Dan. 6:18).

   B. "Now are there any stones in Babylonia? [No.] But from the land of Israel it was brought through flight, so that in a brief moment it came and rested on the mouth of the pit."

15. A. R. Huna in the name of R. Joseph said [concerning the verse, "And a stone was brought and laid upon the mouth of the den" (Dan. 6:18)], "An angel came down in the form of a lion made of stone and put itself at the mouth of the pit.

   B. "That is in line with this verse: 'My God has sent his angel and has shut the lions' mouths' (Dan. 6:23).

   C. "Now do not find it astonishing. If for the honor owing to that righteous man, it is written, 'a certain stone was brought' (Dan. 6:18), for the honoring of the Holy One, blessed be he, how much the more so [will stones be provided in a magical manner]."

16. A. [Resuming the discussion of 8.D:] "He will stand before kings."

   B. before the greatest authorities of the Torah he will stand.

   C. "he will not stand before mean men:"

    D.   this refers to a conspiracy of wicked men.

17. A.   Said R. Joshua b. Levi, "When they took a vote and decided, Three kings and four ordinary folk have no share in the world to come [M. San. 10:1],

    B.   "they wanted to include Solomon with them.

    C.   "But an echo came forth and said, 'Do not lay hands on my anointed ones' (Ps. 105:15)."

    D.   Said R. Judah b. R. Simon, "And not only so, but he was given the place of honor at the head of three genealogical tables: 'And Rehoboam, son of Solomon, reigned in Judah' (1 Kgs. 14:21). [Simon, p. 4: "He was placed at the head of a genealogical tree...." Simon, p. 4, n. 11: "The mention of his name here being superfluous implies that he was a founder of a royal line.]

    E.   Said R., Yudan b. R. Simon, "Not only so, but the Holy Spirit rested on him, and he said the following three books: Proverbs, the Song of Songs, and Qohelet."

While this somewhat overburdened composition hardly conforms to the required form, its basic outlines are not difficult to discern. We have an intersecting verse, Prov. 22:29, aimed at reaching the goal of Solomon, who is author of the Song of Songs, and showing him in the context of Joseph, the righteous, and Moses, four in all. The reason in both cases is the same: each one of them "stood before kings, not before mean men." Our proposed fixed formula then involves examples of the righteous, who are judged by those worthy of judging them.

The invocation of the figure of Joseph ought to carry in its wake the contrast between the impure lust of Potiphar's wife and the pure heart of Joseph, and, by extension, Solomon in the Song. But I do not see that motif present. The form is scarcely established—clause-by-clause exegesis in light of the principal's life—before it is broken by the insertion of 1.E-G, lifted whole from Gen. R. LXXXVII:VII, where it belongs. No. 2 is then parachuted down as part of the Joseph-sequence; but it does not occur in the parallel. No. 3 then resumes the broken form, and No. 4 completes it. So the first statement of the formal program is not difficult to follow. The confluence of the consonants for "mean" and "dark" accounts for the sequence of applications of the third clause to the theme of darkness.

The second exercise, with Moses, is laid out with little blemish in No. 5. No. 6 goes on to the righteous, and here too the sages' passage is worked out with no interpolations. No. 7, by contrast, provides an excuse to insert No. 8. Without No. 7, No. 8 would prove incomprehensible in this context (though entirely clear standing on its own). Finally, at No. 9, we come to Solomon. Perhaps the coming theme of the magical works performed through stones, those used in the Temple, with Daniel, persuaded the person who inserted Nos. 7-8 of the relevance of those passages; but even if they prove thematically in place, the sequence is disruptive and hardly respects the formal program that clearly has guided the framer. One may theorize, to be sure, that the break up of the initial form—three cases, disruptive insertion, then the goal and purpose of the whole—signals the advent of the central figure in the exegesis. But that would prove a viable thesis only if we should find a fair number of other instances. It is the simple fact that the Mishnah's rhetoric allows for signals of that kind, and we cannot rule out the possibility. But in the present case it seems to me we have nothing more than a rude interpolation. But that is not the only disruptive component of the passage.

No. 10 introduces the contrast of the two verses, our proof-text at No. 9 plus a contradictory one. This yields a suitable harmonization, which sustains the supplements at Nos. 11, 12, and 13. Nos. 11 and 12 are simply freestanding sentences. No. 13, with Nos. 14, 15, in its wake, by contrast is a full-scale composition, again about miracles done with stones. Hanina's passage would have found a more comfortable home here (if anywhere). Only at No. 16 are we permitted to resume our progress through the established form. No. 17 is tacked on because of the reference of 16.D to a conspiracy of wicked men; the issue then is whether Solomon belongs with them, in line with 17.A-B. 17.E forms a bridge to the sustained discussion of Ps. 45:17. But since the exposition of that verse makes no reference to the foregoing, we should regard the rather run-on sequence before us as winding down at No. 17, and, despite the rhetorical joining language of "therefore," I treat the discussion of Ps. 45:17 as autonomous. It assuredly has no formal ties to the intersecting verse on which we have been working. The whole is surely coherent in that the several components complement one another.

SONG OF SONGS RABBAH TO SONG 1:2

II:I.1   A.   "O that you would kiss me with the kisses of your mouth! [For your love is better than wine]:"

B.   In what connection was this statement made?

C.   R. Hinena b. R. Pappa said, "It was stated at the sea: '[I compare you, my love,] to a mare of Pharaoh's chariots' (Song 1:9)."

D.   R. Yuda b. R. Simon said, "It was stated at Sinai: 'The song of songs' (Song 1:1)—the song that was song by the singers: 'The singers go before, the minstrels follow after' (Ps. 68:26)."

2.   A.   It was taught on Tannaite authority in the name of R. Nathan, "The Holy One, blessed be he, in the glory of his greatness said it: 'The song of songs that is Solomon's' (Song 1:1),

   B.   "[meaning,] that belongs to the King to whom peace belongs."

3.   A.   Rabban Gamaliel says, "The ministering angels said it: 'the song of songs' (Song 1:1) —

   B.   "the song that the princes on high said."

4.   A.   R. Yohanan said, "It was said at Sinai: 'O that you would kiss me with the kisses of your mouth!' (Song 1:2)."

5.   A.   R. Meir says, "It was said in connection with the tent of meeting."

   B.   And he brings evidence from the following verse: "Awake, O north wind, and come, O south wind! Blow upon my garden, let its fragrance be wafted abroad. Let my beloved come to his garden, and eat its choicest fruits" (Song 4:16).

   C.   "Awake, O north wind:" this refers to the burnt offerings, which were slaughtered at the north side of the altar.

   D.   "and come, O south wind:" this refers to the peace offerings, which were slaughtered at the south side of the altar.

   E.   "Blow upon my garden:" this refers to the tent of meeting.

   F.   "let its fragrance be wafted abroad:" this refers to the incense offering.

   G.   "Let my beloved come to his garden:" this refers to the Presence of God.

   H.   "and eat its choicest fruits:" this refers to the offerings.

6.   A.   Rabbis say, "It was said in connection with the house of the ages [the Temple itself]."

   B.   And they bring evidence from the same verse: "Awake, O north wind, and come, O south wind! Blow upon my garden, let its fragrance by wafted abroad. Let my beloved come to his garden, and eat its choicest fruits" (Song 4:16).

   C.   "Awake, O north wind:" this refers to the burnt offerings, which were slaughtered at the north side of the altar.

   D.   "and come, O south wind:" this refers to the peace offerings, which were slaughtered at the south side of the altar.

   E.   "Blow upon my garden:" this refers to the house of the ages.

   F.   "let its fragrance be wafted abroad:" this refers to the incense offering.

   G.   "Let my beloved come to his garden:" this refers to the Presence of God.

   H.   "and eat its choicest fruits:" this refers to the offerings.

   I.   The rabbis furthermore maintain that all the other verses also refer to the house of the ages.

   J.   Said R. Aha, "The verse that refers to the Temple is the following: 'King Solomon made himself a palanquin, from the wood of Lebanon. He made its posts of silver, its back of gold, its seat of purple;

it was lovingly wrought within by the daughters of Jerusalem'(Song 3:9-10)."

K.   Rabbis treat these as the intersecting verses for the verse, 'And it came to pass on the day that Moses had made an end of setting up the tabernacle' (Num. 7:1)."

7.   A.   In the opinion of R. Hinena [1.C], who said that the verse was stated on the occasion of the Sea, [the sense of the verse, "O that you would kiss me with the kisses of your mouth"] is, "may he bring to rest upon us the Holy Spirit, so that we may say before him many songs."

B.   In the opinion of Rabban Gamaliel, who said that the verse was stated by the ministering angels, [the sense of the verse, "O that you would kiss me with the kisses of your mouth"] is, "may he give us the kisses that he gave to his sons."

C.   In the opinion of R. Meir, who said that the verse was stated in connection with the tent of meeting, [the sense of the verse, "O that you would kiss me with the kisses of your mouth"] is, "May he send fire down to us and so accept the offerings that are offered to him."

D.   In the opinion of R. Yohanan, who said that the verse was stated in connection with Sinai, [the sense of the verse, "O that you would kiss me with the kisses of your mouth"] is, "May he cause kisses to issue for us from his mouth."

E.   "That is why it is written, 'O that you would kiss me with the kisses of your mouth.'"

Our fixed list encompasses (1) Israel at the sea; (2) the ministering angels; (3) the tent of meeting; (4) the eternal house [the Temple]; (5) Sinai. This is somewhat curious, mixing as it does occasions in time, locations, the place of the cult, and the Torah. But if we hold them together, we are given the theological repertoire of suitable verbal-symbols or reference-points: the redemption from Egypt, the Temple and its cult, and the revealed Torah of Sinai. This composite then is not only complementary in a general sense, it also is explicit in a very particular sense, specifying as it does the range of suitable assignees for the authorship and occasion of the poem, and that range then encompasses the acceptable theological vocabulary of—shall we say, Judaism? the Torah? the Midrash-exegesis of our verse? I am not sure of what, but it is clear to me that we may well-balanced expect a variety of such lists, a repertoire of those topics or points that all together add up to the relationship between God and Israel that the document, the Song of Songs, portrays. Indeed, even well-balanced we may wish to propose that when we seek the theology of the Judaism of the dual Torah, we may do worse than to look in the way in which the Song of Songs is made into a metaphor for everything evocative of the relationship of God and Israel—that is to say, the subject and problematic of the theology of Judaism.

Let us attend to the specifics of the passage, if briefly. No. 7 once again shows us that our compilers are first-class editors, since they have assembled quite disparate materials and drawn them together into a cogent statement. But the subject is not our base-verse, and hence the compilers cannot have had in mind the need of a commentary of a verse-by-verse principle of conglomeration and organization. The passage as a whole refers in much more general terms to the Song of Songs, and hardly to Song 1:2 in particular. That is shown by the simple fact that various opinions invoke other verses than the one to which the whole is ultimately assigned. No. 1 serves Song 1:1, and so does No. 2. Indeed, No. 2 could have been placed in the prior assembly without any damage to its use and meaning. The same is to be said for No. 3. In fact, only Yohanan requires the verse to stand where it well-balanced does. No. 5 and No. 6 invoke Song 4:16 and do a fine job of reading that verse in light of the tent of meeting in the wilderness or the Temple in Jerusalem. Song 3:9-10 serves as an appropriate locus as well. Then the conclusion draws a variety of senses for Song 1:2 alone, and that conclusion points to the compilers of the whole for its authorship. This is once more highly sophisticated work of compilation, involving rich editorial intervention indeed.

Song of Songs Rabbah to Song 1:5

V:i.1   A.   "I am very dark, but comely, [O daughters of Jerusalem, like the tents of Kedar, like the curtains of Solomon]" (Song 1:5):

B.   "I am dark" in my deeds.

C.   "But comely" in the deeds of my forebears.

2.   A.   "I am very dark, but comely:"

B.   Said the Community of Israel, "'I am dark' in my view, 'but comely' before my Creator."

C.   For it is written, "Are you not as the children of the Ethiopians to Me, O children of Israel, says the Lord" (Amos 9:7):

D.   "as the children of the Ethiopians"—in your sight.

E.   But "to Me, O children of Israel, says the Lord."

3.   A.   Another interpretation of the verse, ""I am very dark:" in Egypt.

B.   "but comely:" in Egypt.

    C.   "I am very dark" in Egypt: "But they rebelled against me and would not hearken to me" (Ez. 20:8).

    D.   "but comely" in Egypt: with the blood of the Passover offering and circumcision, "And when I passed by you and saw you wallowing in your blood, I said to you, In your blood live" (Ez. 16:6)—in the blood of the Passover. [This verse is recited at the rite of circumcision.]

    E.   "I said to you, In your blood live" Ez. 16:6)—in the blood of the circumcision.

4.   A.   Another interpretation of the verse, "I am very dark:" at the sea, "They were rebellious at the sea, even the Red Sea" (Ps. 106:7).

    B.   "but comely:" at the sea, "This is my God and I will be comely for him" (Ex. 15:2) [following Simon's rendering of the verse].

5.   A.   "I am very dark:" at Marah, "And the people murmured against Moses, saying, What shall we drink" Ex. 15:24).

    B.   "but comely:" at Marah, "And he cried to the Lord and the Lord showed him a tree, and he cast it into the waters and the waters were made sweet" (Ex. 15:25).

6.   A.   "I am very dark:" at Rephidim, "And the name of the place was called Massah and Meribah" (Ex. 17:7).

    B.   "but comely:" at Rephidim, "And Moses built an altar and called it by the name 'the Lord is my banner'" (Ex. 17:15).

7.   A.   "I am very dark:" at Horeb, "And they made a calf at Horeb" (Ps. 106:19).

    B.   "but comely:" at Horeb, "And they said, All that the Lord has spoken we will do and obey" (Ex. 24:7).

8.   A.   "I am very dark:" in the wilderness, ""How often did they rebel against him in the wilderness" (Ps. 78:40).

    B.   "but comely:" in the wilderness at the setting up of the tabernacle, "And on the day that the tabernacle was set up" (Num. 9:15).

9.   A.   "I am very dark:" in the deed of the spies, "And they spread an evil report of the land" (Num. 13:32).

    B.   "but comely:" in the deed of Joshua and Caleb, ""Save for Caleb, the son of Jephunneh the Kenizzite" (Num. 32:12).

10.   A.   "I am very dark:" at Shittim, "And Israel abode at Shittim and the people began to commit harlotry with the daughters of Moab" (Num. 25:1).

    B.   "but comely:" at Shittim, "Then arose Phinehas and wrought judgment" (Ps. 106:30).

11.   A.   "I am very dark:" through Achan, "But the children of Israel committed a trespass concerning the devoted thing" (Josh. 7:1).

    B.   "but comely:" through Joshua, "And Joshua said to Achan, My son, give I pray you glory" (Josh. 7:19).

12. A.   "I am very dark:" through the kings of Israel.

B. "but comely:" through the kings of Judah.

C. If with my dark ones that I had, it was such that "I am comely," all the more so with my prophets.

V:ii.5.   A.   [As to the verse, "I am very dark, but comely," R. Levi b. R. Haita gave three interpretations:

B. "'I am very dark:' all the days of the week.

C. "'but comely:' on the Sabbath.

D. "'I am very dark:' all the days of the year.

E. "'but comely:' on the Day of Atonement.

F. "'I am very dark:' among the Ten Tribes.

G. "'but comely:' in the tribe of Judah and Benjamin.

H. "'I am very dark:' in this world.

I. "'but comely:' in the world to come."

The contrast of dark and comely yields a variety of applications; in all of them the same situation that is the one also is the other, and the rest follows in a wonderfully well-crafted composition. What is the repertoire of items? Dark in deeds but comely in ancestry; dark in my view but comely before God; dark when rebellious, comely when obedient, a point made at Nos. 3, for Egypt, 4, for the sea, and 5 for Marah, 6, for Massah and Meribah, 7 for Horeb, 8 for the wilderness, 9 for the spies in the Land, 10 for Shittim, 11 for Achan/Joshua and the conquest of the Land, 12 for Israel and Judah. We therefore have worked through the repertoire of events that contained the mixture of rebellion and obedience; the theological substrate of this catalogue is hardly difficult to articulate. At VII:ii.5 we have the articulation:

SONG OF SONGS RABBAH TO SONG 2:6

XXIII:i.

1   A.   "O that his left hand were under my head:"

B.   this refers to the first tablets.

C.   "and that his right hand embraced me:"

D.   this refers to the second tablets.

2.   A.   Another interpretation of the verse, "O that his left hand were under my head:"

B.   this refers to the show-fringes.

C.   "and that his right hand embraced me:"

D.   this refers to the phylacteries.

3   A.   Another interpretation of the verse, "O that his left hand were under my head:"

B.   this refers to the recitation of the *Shema*.

C.   "and that his right hand embraced me:"

D.   this refers to the Prayer.

4   A.   Another interpretation of the verse, "O that his left hand were under my head:"

B.   this refers to the tabernacle.

C.   "and that his right hand embraced me:"

D.   this refers to the cloud of the Presence of God in the world to come: "The sun shall no longer be your light by day nor for brightness will the moon give light to you" (Is. 60:19). Then what gives light to you? "The Lord shall be your everlasting light" (Is. 60:20).

Now our repertoire of reference-points is (1) the Ten Commandments; (2) the show-fringes and phylacteries; (3) the *Shema* and the Prayer; (4) the tabernacle and the cloud of the Presence of God in the world to come. Why we invoke, as our candidates for the metaphor at hand, the Ten Commandments, show-fringes and phylacteries, recitation of the Shema and the Prayer, the tabernacle and the cloud of the Presence of God, and the mezuzah, seems to me clear from the very catalogue. These reach their climax in the analogy between the home and the tabernacle, the embrace of God and the Presence of God. So the whole is meant to list those things that draw the Israelite near God and make the Israelite cleave to God, as the base-verse says, hence the right hand and the left stand for the most intimate components of the life of the individual and the home with God.

Song of Songs Rabbah to Song 3:8

XXV:i.1 A.   "The voice of my beloved! Behold he comes [leaping upon the mountains, bounding over the hills]:"

B.   R. Judah and R. Nehemiah and Rabbis:

C.   R. Judah says, "'The voice of my beloved! Behold he comes:' this refers to Moses.

D.   "When he came and said to the Israelites, 'In this month you will be redeemed,' they said to him, 'Our lord, Moses, how are we going to be redeemed? And did not the Holy One, blessed be he, say to Abraham, "And they shall work them and torment them for four hundred years" (Gen. 15:13), and well-balanced we have in hand only two hundred and ten years!'

E.   "He said to them, 'Since he wants to redeem you, he is not going to pay attention to these reckonings of yours.

F.   "'But: "leaping upon the mountains, bounding over the hills." The reference here to mountains and hills in fact alludes to calculations and specified times. "He leaps" over reckonings, calculations, and specified times.

F.   "'And in this month you are to be redeemed: "This month is the beginning of months" (Ex. 12:1).'"

2.   A.   R. Nehemiah says, "'The voice of my beloved! Behold he comes:' this refers to Moses.

        B.   "When he came and said to the Israelites, 'In this month you will be redeemed,' they said to him, 'Our lord, Moses, how are we going to be redeemed? We have no good deeds to our credit.'

        C.   "He said to them, 'Since he wants to redeem you, he is not going to pay attention to bad deeds.'

        D.   "'And to what does he pay attention? To the righteous people among you and to their deeds,

        E.   "'for example, Amram and his court.

        F.   "''leaping upon the mountains, bounding over the hills:" the word 'mountains' refers only to courts, in line with this usage: "I will depart and go down upon the mountains" (Judges 11:37).

        F.   "'And in this month you are to be redeemed: "This month is the beginning of months" (Ex. 12:1).'"

3.   A.   Rabbis say, "'The voice of my beloved! Behold he comes:' this refers to Moses.

        B.   "When he came and said to the Israelites, 'In this month you will be redeemed,' they said to him, 'Our lord, Moses, how are we going to be redeemed? And the whole of Egypt is made filthy by our own worship of idols!'

        C.   "He said to them, 'Since he wants to redeem you, he is not going to pay attention to your worship of idols.

        D.   "'Rather, "leaping upon the mountains, bounding over the hills:" mountains and hills refer only to idolatry, in line with this usage: "They sacrifice on the tops of the mountains and offer upon the hills" (Hos. 4:13).

        E.   "'And in this month you are to be redeemed: "This month is the beginning of months" (Ex. 12:1).'"

4.   A.   R. Yudan and R. Hunia:

        B.   R. Yudan in the name of R. Eliezer son of R. Yosé the Galilean, and R. Hunia in the name of R. Eliezer b. Jacob say, "'The voice of my beloved! Behold he comes:' this refers to the royal messiah.

        C.   "When he says to the Israelites, 'In this month you are to be redeemed, they will say to him, 'How are we going to be redeemed? And has not the Holy One, blessed be he, taken an oath that he would subjugate us among the seventy nations.'

        D.   "Now he will reply to them in two ways.

        E.   "He will say to them, 'If one of you is taken into exile to Barbary and one to Sarmatia, it is as though all of you had gone into exile.

        F.   "'And not only so, but this state conscripts troops from all of the world and from every nation, so that if one Samaritan or one Barbarian comes and subjugates you, it is as though his entire nation had ruled over you and as if you were subjugated by all the seventy nations.

     G. ."'In this month you are to be redeemed: "This month is the beginning of months" (Ex. 12:1).'"

Nos. 1-3 form a perfectly matched set; remove one and you lose the whole. A fixed catalogue emerges, which can be used in any number of ways to exploit available metaphors. The items go over the trilogy of the timing of redemption, the moral condition of those to be redeemed, and the past religious misdeeds of those to be redeemed. Against these three arguments Moses argues that God will redeem at God's own time, as an act of grace and forgiveness. The theological message emerges with enormous power through invoking the love of God for Israel, God "leaping upon the mountains." I cannot point to a better or more telling example of the rewards accruing to the framers of the document from their decision to work on just this part of Scripture. The obvious necessity of No. 4 to complete the message requires no comment. Any conception that first comes the individual units, then the completed composition, seems to me to take second place before the notion that the plan of the whole as a theological statement came prior to the formation of the parts. Then it hardly matters whose names are tacked on to the formally matched and perfect components. The examples suffice to show what is in play in this mode of holding together a large mass of discrete and completed materials.

iv. *How the Oral Torah Solves the Problem Set forth by Scripture*

Receiving Scripture as a coherent whole, what were sages to make of the anomalous parts they identified for special attention? The sages met the challenge in two contradictory ways. In the one case, Qohelet, they took the document apart and imposed their reading on the pieces. The upshot is to clarify the context in which Qohelet makes his statement. In the other case, Song of Songs, they read the document whole, reassembling the parts to form a composition that embodied their hermeneutics for the detailed exegesis of the entire document. The result is to impose upon the whole another set of meanings than those on the surface.

Specifically, they dismantled Qohelet, treating bits but not the whole work, to which, in the formative age, they did not devote a document of Rabbinic exegesis. That is why they did not produce in the formative age a Qohelet Rabbah comparable to Lamentations Rabbah, Esther Rabbah I, Song of Songs Rabbah, or Ruth Rabbah, devoted the other scriptural books declaimed on festival occasions along with Qohelet, each of which imposes upon every detail of its base-text a cogent proposition and a determinate perspective. Qohelet then emerged from late antiquity as the only one of the Five Scrolls singled out for synagogue declamation that was not given a systematic exegetical compilation.

By contrast to this work of dismantling, for Song of Songs they conducted an exercise of reconstruction. They read Song of Songs whole, by imposing a single meaning on all of the parts. The Rabbinic sages judged that the meaning of the love poems was, and can only have been, precisely the sense they imputed to them. On what basis did they reach that conclusion and affirm it? The entirety of Scripture is made to attest to that meaning. Read start to finish, Genesis through Kings in light of Prophecy told the story of God's search for man and election of Israel—and the consequence of God's love for Israel. Reading forward from Scripture, the Rabbinic sages found in Israel's everyday life the embodiments of the love of Israel for God. Devotion to the Torah, practice of the commandments—the whole corpus of sanctification of the material transactions of Israel sustained that reading. Reading the entirety of Scripture into Song of Songs, producing Song of Songs Rabbah—that deductive process of working from the whole to the parts permitted no other result. For placing this component of Scripture into the context of the whole of Scripture yielded the conclusion reached here. Song of Song Rabbah contributes the articulation of what is implicit in the canon of Scripture: the reason why Song of Songs belongs. It is, as Aqiba says, holiest of all.

The effect in both cases—deconstruction of the one document, recapitulation and reconstruction of the other—was to accommodate anomalous books of Scripture, regularizing them within the Rabbinic system that animated the dual Torah. The result was the perfect Torah, just as the sages represented at Mishnah-tractate Yadayim 3:5 determined. They produced works of exegesis, sustained by a coherent hermeneutics throughout. But the upshot is the realization of the theology of the whole of Scripture within the generative hermeneutics and ad hoc exegesis of the parts. By the perfect Torah, sages meant, a Torah that through all the parts sets forth one whole and complete statement of God's will and purpose. And that is precisely what God set forth to Moses, our Rabbi, at Sinai. But we have yet to encounter their preferred medium for theological discourse, which we meet not in Leviticus Rabbah nor in Song of Songs Rabbah but particularly in Lamentations Rabbah: the theological narrative.

CHAPTER FOUR

THE MATCH OF MESSAGE AND MEDIUM (2) AGGADIC

i. *Criterion of Perfection: How Better Deliver the Message than through the Selected Medium?*

How are we to define the counterpart in the Aggadic structure adumbrated in chapter three to that philosophical monotheism that animates the Halakhah, for which the Halakhah forms the ideal medium? The answer depends upon identifying the ideal medium for the Aggadic message. The generative message, monotheism, by definition defines the task: "...the Lord our God is one...." The Halakhah forms a massive, complex construction to explain the simple unity, the pure oneness of God, what it means to be "the source of all being." When we come to the Aggadah, we see that its picture of God's unity is as complex and concrete as the Halakhic one is simple and abstract. For the Aggadic compilations endow God with particular traits and distinctive qualities. God is portrayed in Aggadic theology, hermeneutics, and consequent exegesis as not only a principle attained through natural philosophy but a sentient being known through accounts of his actions and attitudes.

Showing the unity of actions and attitudes imputed by the Torah to the one and only God—that represents the paramount perplexity, and it is, so I shall now show, the one addressed by the Aggadah through the medium of narrative. In retelling Scripture's stories, the Rabbinic sages succeeded in revealing the justice and mercy of God: the rationality that animated the world he deliberately made as it is and not in some other way. In their context, that particularization of monotheism represented the paramount puzzle of. and challenge to. monotheism out of everyday experience of commonplace matters, whether political, whether personal.

Then precisely *how* the Aggadah makes its contribution to the exegetical articulation of monotheism defines the question. It is readily answered: if the Halakhah thinks philosophically, specifically, about

ontological being through the medium of natural philosophy defined
in chapter two, then the Aggadah must be said to think mythical-
ly—historically—about God's actions in time, and to record the result
in narrative. That thought about God's theological being, is carried
out hermeneutically and expressed in part exegetically through the
medium of narrative—myth—and the myth ordinarily comes to
expression in the exegesis of Scripture, already adumbrated in chapter
three. That mode of thought and medium of expression are to be
defined and instantiated here. The perfect match of message and
medium is to be instantiated in a particular kind of narrative in a
particular document, just as the Aggadic structure emerged for us
in a particular program of thought in a singular document. But before proceeding to the work of the chapter, let us define some basic
terms.

First, what do I mean by myth? By myth I understand "truth in
the form of a story." So, first, as between philosophical and mythic
monotheism, what do I mean by "mythic monotheism"? It is the
narrative mode of setting forth in detail the monotheist theology that
there is only one God, known to humanity through his self-mani-
festation in the Torah. There are elements of monotheism that in
the context of the Torah can be expressed only through mythic
narrative. Specifically, the particular traits of that one and only
God—for example, that he is all-powerful, just and merciful—do not
emerge in the Halakhic medium. They cannot, since the very power of philosophy lies in its capacity for generalization and critical
demonstration of ontology, truths about being that are always true
in the same way. That medium encompasses gross aggregates of data
to set forth a compelling account of the unity of all being.

But it is marked by reticence to speak of the traits of the ground
of that unity. Hierarchical classification by its nature speaks in generalizations and principles. It best sustains the system of monotheist
ontology. It processes all data in the same way with a consistent result
throughout. It has slight capacity to speak of the qualities of that
one God at the apex of all hierarchized classifications of things. Myth,
by contrast, has the power to speak of the particular and the unique,
the immediate and the eventful. It captures the exemplary and the
one-time outcome: determinate action, particular characteristic.
Narrative has the power to describe what God does, how God responds, and why God yearns as he does for humanity. That is why,

it is in particular in its narrative form that the Oral Torah undertakes the exercise of spelling out an important component of monotheism. The result is theology through myth: an account of who God is through what God does. The logic of mythic monotheism, then, derives from the rationality embodied in the deeds of the God who acts through Israel.

Second, can I offer an example of how the Aggadic writings of the Oral Torah set forth an account of a critical component of mythic monotheism? At the foundation of the Aggadic theology, and fundamental to Judaic monotheism, is the affirmation of God's justice and mercy. Scripture time and again tells stories of God's submission to the rule of justice, as at Genesis 18, which portrays God's negotiation with Abraham before Sodom. And it declares time and again God as the compassionate God, whether for Israel, whether for Nineveh. But how to articulate the principles of God's unity—union of justice and mercy for example? Clearly, ontological evidence scarcely intersects with the notion of God's justice, though the Halakhah, as we saw, concerns itself with the articulation of social justice. So it is implicit that the one, unique, all-powerful God at the apex of all hierarchies is just. But only in the Aggadah is the matter made explicit, and then, in the record of the Oral Torah, it is through narrative.

My probative example of the role and value of the medium of narrative to express the message of God's trait of perfect justice addresses the situation of the wife accused of unfaithfulness. There, in what is on the face of it a Halakhic exposition, we shall see constant reference to stories in Scripture that embody God's justice and instantiate it. In connection with the appeal to Aggadah for the exposition of the matter of the accused wife,[1] I address two questions. First, how does Aggadic-narrative figure in the exposition of the Halakhah, showing the working of God's justice in her regard? Second, in the matter of the ideal match of medium and message, how does God's justice emerge in the presentation of the narrative, and why could the Halakhic medium not serve, as clearly, in the Mishnah, Tosefta, and Midrash-compilations, it certainly did not?

---

[1] Deriving from Halakhic documents but Aggadic in preference for narrative over abstract law, as we shall see.

A. How Does Aggadah Figure even in a Halakhic Presentation?

The answer to the first question comes to us when we can explain how sages know that God's will is realized in the moral order of justice, involving reward and punishment. The answer is, they turned to Scripture for the pertinent facts. That is where God makes himself manifest. But of the various types of scriptural evidence—explicit commandments, stories, prophetic admonitions—that they had available to show how the moral order prevailed in all being, what type did the prefer? The one bearing the greatest probative weight derived from stories that narrate in a concrete case the exact match between sin and punishment. Here is their starting point, from which all else flows smoothly and in orderly fashion. World order, best embodied when sin is punished, merit rewarded, is conveyed by Scripture's narratives.

That body of evidence recorded human action and divine reaction, on the one side, and meritorious deed and divine response and reward, on the other. The evidence took the form of the stories told by the Written Torah. It was comprised by consequential cases, drawn from both private and public life. These sages used to insist upon the match between the personal and the public, all things subject to the same simple rule of justice. That demonstration of not only the principle but the precision of measure for measure, deriving from Scripture's own Aggadic record of God's actions, takes priority of place in the examination of the rationality of sages' universe. So what sages do in the Aggadah corresponds with what they do in the Halakhah: regularize facts, find patterns, form patterns into a coherent system. The ontological unity of God in the Halakhah then forms the model for the historical (narrative) justice of God in the Aggadah. In both cases God's unity is demonstrated by the everyday and the here and now (for the Halakhah) and the cosmic and the historical (for the Aggadah).

B. How Does God's Justice Emerge in the Presentation of Aggadic Narrative? The Implicit Narratives Evoked by the Story of the Wife Accused of Adultery

Now when sages opened Scripture to find out how, in the detail of concrete cases, the Judge of all the world bound himself by the rules of justice and systematically does justice, like philosophers in natural history they looked not for the occasional but the enduring. They sought not the singular moment but the exemplary pattern. Exegesis without a guiding hermeneutics therefore bore little appeal to them. One-shot proof-texts mattered less than governing paradigms, emerging through lists of facts joined by common indicative traits.

Sages, accordingly, were theologians before they were exegetes, and they were exegetes because they were theologians. That is, their exegesis cohered through a governing hermeneutics, given determinate shape and structure by theological principle. Here, that principle was, the one God of all creation is just and merciful. The hermeneutics translated the principle into a set of questions addressed to Scripture: how does this story show the match of virtue and reward, sin and punishment? The exegesis brought those coherent questions to bear upon specific verses or cases of Scripture and answered the questions. So proof from specific texts emerges from the exegesis of details, but hermeneutics holds details together in a single coherent whole, given proportion and balance, shape and structure, by the theology of monotheism. And the data that served throughout, as we shall see, took the form of narrative: Scripture's facts, Scripture's cases.

That is why the Rabbinic sages composed their account of the workings of the principle of measure for measure—whether for divine punishment or for divine reward—out of narrative-cases in which God does not intervene, but in which the very nature of things, the ordinary course of events, showed the workings of the principle. Justice is built into the rules of the social order, as much as hierarchical classification emerges from the data of the social order. Here in the medium of myth—Aggadah, not Halakhah—is sages' account of God's justice, which is always commensurate, both for reward and punishment, in consequence of which the present permits us to peer into the future with certainty of what is going to happen, so M. Sot. 1:7ff. What we note is sages' identification of the precision of justice, the exact match of action and reaction, each step in the sin, each step in the response, and, above all, the immediacy of God's presence in the entire transaction. The role of narrative in the account of the theological principle is blatant.

MISHNAH-TRACTATE SOTAH 1:7

A. By that same measure by which a man metes out [to others], do they mete out to him:

B. She primped herself for sin, the Omnipresent made her repulsive.

C. She exposed herself for sin, the Omnipresent exposed her.
D. With the thigh she began to sin, and afterward with the belly, therefore the thigh suffers the curse first, and afterward the belly.
E. But the rest of the body does not escape [punishment].

We begin with sages' own general observations based on the facts set forth in Scripture. The purpose here is to spell out the generalization at the outset, which is the governing principle of justice that is in play. The course of response of the woman accused of adultery to her drinking of the bitter water that is supposed to produce one result for the guilty, another for the innocent, is described in Scripture in this language: "If no man has lain with you...be free from this water of bitterness that brings the curse. But if you have gone astray...then the Lord make you an execration...when the Lord makes your thigh fall away and your body swell; may this water...pass into your bowels and make your body swell and your thigh fall away" (Num. 5:20-22). This is amplified and expanded, extended to the entire rite, where the woman is disheveled; then the order, thigh, belly, shows the perfect precision of the penalty. What Scripture treats as a case, sages transform into a generalization, so making Scripture yield governing rules.

Now narrative comes to the fore and takes over from the Halakhah the task of the exposition altogether. For the same passage proceeds to further cases, which prove the same point: where the sin begins, there the punishment also commences; but also, where an act of virtue takes its point, there divine reward focuses as well. Merely listing the following names, without spelling out details, for the cognoscenti of Scripture will have made that point: Samson, Absalom, Miriam, Joseph, and Moses. Knowing how Samson and Absalom match, also Miriam, Joseph, and Moses, would then suffice to establish the paired and matched general principles. The narrative is implicit, but ubiquitous nonetheless.

MISHNAH-TRACTATE SOTAH 1:8
A. Samson followed his eyes [where they led him], therefore the Philistines put out his eyes, since it is said, "And the Philistines laid hold on him and put out his eyes" (Judges 16:21).
B. Absalom was proud of his hair, therefore he was hung by his hair [II Sam. 14:25-26].
C. And since he had sexual relations with ten concubines of his father, therefore they thrust ten spear heads into his body, since it is said, "And ten young men that carried Jacob's armor surrounded and smote Absalom and killed him" (2 Sam. 18:15).

D. And since he stole three hearts—his father's, the court's, and the Israelites'—since it is said, "And Absalom stole the heart of the men of Israel" (2 Sam. 15:6)—therefore three darts were thrust into him, since it is said, "And he took three darts in his hand and thrust them through the heart of Absalom" (2 Sam. 18:14).

Justice requires not only punishment of the sinner or the guilty but reward of the righteous and the good, and so sages find ample, systematic evidence in Scripture for both sides of the equation of justice:

MISHNAH-TRACTATE SOTAH 1:9

A. And so is it on the good side:

B. Miriam waited a while for Moses, since it is said, "And his sister stood afar off" (Ex. 2:4), therefore, Israel waited on her seven days in the wilderness, since it is said, "And the people did not travel on until Miriam was brought in again" (Num. 12:15).

MISHNAH-TRACTATE SOTAH 1:10

A. Joseph had the merit of burying his father, and none of his brothers was greater than he, since it is said, "And Joseph went up to bury his father...and there went up with him both chariots and horsemen" (Gen. 50:7, 9).

B. We have none so great as Joseph, for only Moses took care of his [bones].

C. Moses had the merit of burying the bones of Joseph, and none in Israel was greater than he, since it is said, "And Moses took the bones of Joseph with him" (Ex. 13:19).

D. We have none so great as Moses, for only the Holy One blessed he Be took care of his [bones], since it is said, "And he buried him in the valley" (Deut. 34:6).

E. And not of Moses alone have they stated [this rule], but of all righteous people, since it is said, "And your righteousness shall go before you. The glory of the Lord shall gather you [in death]" (Is. 58:8).

Scripture's narrative provides the main probative evidence for the anticipation that when God judges, he will match the act of merit with an appropriate reward and the sin with an appropriate punishment. The proposition begins, however, with general observations as to how things are, M. 1:7, and not with specific allusions to proof-texts; the character of the law set forth in Scripture is reflected upon. The accumulated cases yield the generalization.

Before proceeding, let us recall the context: the Halakhic document, the Mishnah, here resorts to Aggadah for its theological exposition. That is because the Halakhah has no way of expressing the principle at hand with the force and the specificity that the aggadah musters. Announcing that God is just hardly compares in compelling power to proving that proposition through established facts. Where from here? Beyond the Mishnah two kinds of documents of extension and amplification take up the Mishnah's propositions and strengthen them. One pursues the passages of Scripture important in the Mishnah's exposition, here represented by Sifré to Numbers, the other, the Tosefta, carries forward the Mishnah's own method. The one is exegetical, the other propositional, and both take the Mishnah as their starting point.

In Sifré to Numbers the Mishnah's statements are brought into alignment with Scripture; verses not cited by the Mishnah are identified and shown to be paraphrased and summarized in the Mishnah. Sifré to Numbers takes up the Mishnah's proposition concerning Numbers 5:23ff., that, when God punishes, he starts with that with which the transgression commenced, which sages see as a mark of the precision of divine justice:

SIFRÉ TO NUMBERS XVIII:I.1

1. A. "And when he has made her drink the water, [then, if she has defiled herself and has acted unfaithfully against her husband, the water that brings the curse shall enter into her and cause bitter pain,] and her body shall swell, and her thigh shall fall away, [and the woman shall become an execration among her people. But if the woman has not defiled herself and is clean, then she shall be free and shall conceive children]" (Num. 5:23-28).

B. I know only that her body and thigh are affected. How do I know that that is the case for the rest of her limbs?

C. Scripture states, "...the water that brings the curse shall enter into her."

D. So I take account of the phrase, "...the water that brings the curse shall enter into her."

E. Why [if all the limbs are affected equally] then does Scripture specify her body and her thigh in particular?

F. As to her thigh, the limb with which she began to commit the transgression—from there the punishment begins.

But the sages represented by Sifré to Numbers wish to introduce their own cases in support of the same proposition, vastly generalized beyond the limits of the case:

G. Along these same lines:

H. "And he blotted out everything that sprouted from the earth, from man to beast" (Gen. 7:23.

I. From the one who began the transgression [namely Adam], the punishment begins.

Adam sinned first, therefore the flood began with Adam. Now comes a different sort of proportion: the exact match. The Sodomites are smitten with piles:

> J. Along these same lines:
> K. "and the men who were at the gate of the house they smote with piles" (Gen. 19:11).
> L. From the one who began the transgression the punishment begins.

In the third instance, Pharaoh is in the position of Adam; with him the sin began, with him the punishment starts:

> M. Along these same lines:
> N. "...and I shall be honored through Pharaoh and through all of his force" (Ex. 14:4).
> O. Pharaoh began the transgression, so from him began the punishment.
> P. Along these same lines:
> Q. "And you will most certainly smite at the edge of the sword the inhabitants of that city" (Deut. 134:15).
> R. From the one who began the transgression, the punishment begins.
> S. Along these same lines is the present case:
> T. the limb with which she began to commit the transgression—from there the punishment begins.

Here comes a point important to the system: God's mercy exceeds his justice, so the measure of reward is far greater than the measure of punishment—and, if possible, still more prompt:

> U. Now does this not yield an argument *a fortiori:*
> V. If in the case of the attribution of punishment, which is the lesser, from the limb with which she began to commit the transgression— from there the punishment begins,
> W. in the case of the attribute of bestowing good, which is the greater, how much the more so!

Punishment is rational in yet a more concrete way: it commences with the very thing that has sinned, or with the person who has sinned. So the principles of reason and good order pervade the world. We know that fact because Scripture's account of all that matters has shown it.

The second response to the Mishnah's treatment comes in the Tosefta, meaning, "supplements," that is to say, supplements to the Mishnah. Like the Mishnah, the Tosefta, sets forth free-standing propositions, not merely exegeses of verses of Scripture. True to its

role as the Mishnah's first systematic commentary and amplification
in the Mishnah's own order and style (the second and third are the
Talmuds of the Land of Israel, ca. 400 C.E., and of Babylonia, ca.
600 C.E., which take a very different form), the Tosefta contributes
further cases illustrating the exact and appropriate character of both
divine justice and divine reward. What is important here is what is
not made explicit; it concerns a question that the Mishnah does not
raise: what about the gentiles? Does the principle of world order of
justice apply to them, or are they subject to chaos? The answer giv-
en through cases here is that the same rules of justice apply to gentiles, not only Israelites such as are listed in the Mishnah's primary
statement of the principle.

   That point is made through the cases that are selected: Sennacherib, who besieged Jerusalem after destroying Israel comprised by
the northern tribes, Nebuchadnezzar, who took and destroyed Jerusalem in the time of Jeremiah. Now the sin is the single most important one, arrogance or hubris, and the penalty is swift and appropriate, the humbling of the proud by an act of humiliation:

> TOSEFTA TRACTATE SOTAH 3:18
> A. Sennacherib took pride before the Omnipresent only through an
> agent, as it is said, "By your messengers you have mocked the Lord
> and you have said, "With my many chariots I have gone up the heights
> of the mountains . . . I dug wells and drank foreign waters, and I dried
> up with the sole of my foot all the streams of Egypt" (2 Kings19:23-
> 24).
> B. So the Omnipresent, blessed be He, exacted punishment from him
> only through an agent, as it is said, "And that night the messenger of
> the Lord went forth and slew a hundred and eighty-five thousand in
> the camp of the Assyrians" (2 Kings 19:35).
> C. And all of them were kings, with their crowns bound to their heads.

> TOSEFTA TRACTATE SOTAH 3:19
> A. Nebuchadnezzar said, "The denizens of this earth are not worthy
> for me to dwell among them. I shall make for myself a little cloud and
> dwell In it," as it is said, "I will ascend above the heights of the clouds,
> I will make myself like the Most High" (Is. 14:14).
> B. Said to him the Omnipresent, blessed be He, "You said in your
> heart, 'I will ascend to heaven, above the stars of God I will set my
> throne on high'—I shall bring you down to the depths of the pit" (Is.
> 14:13, 15).
> C. What does it say? "But you are brought down to Sheol, to the depths
> of the pit" (Is. 14:15).
> D. Were you the one who said, "The denizens of this earth are not
> worthy for me to dwell among them"?

E. The king said, "Is not this great Babylon, which I have built by my mighty power as a royal residence and for the glory of my majesty? While the words were still in the king's mouth, there fell a voice from heaven, O King Nebuchadnezzar, to you it is spoken, The kingdom has departed from you, and you shall be driven from among men, and your dwelling shall be with the beasts of the field, and you shall be made to eat grass like an ox" (Dan. 4:29-32).

F. All this came upon King Nebuchadnezzar at the end of twelve months (Dan. 4:28-29).

As in the Mishnah, so here too, we wish to prove that justice governs not only to penalize sin but also to reward virtue. To this point we have shown the proportionate character of punishment to sin, the exact measure of justice. The first task in this other context is to establish the proportions, now of reward to punishment.

Is reward measured out with the same precision? Not at all, reward many times exceeds punishment. The just, compassionate God favors compassion over justice. So if the measure of retribution is exactly proportionate to the sin, the measure of reward exceeds the contrary measure by a factor of five hundred. Later on we shall see explicit argument that justice without mercy is incomplete; to have justice, mercy is the required complement. Here we address another aspect of the same matter, that if the measure of punishment precisely matches the measure of sin, when it comes to reward for merit or virtue, matters are not that way:

TOSEFTA TRACTATE SOTAH 4:1

A. I know only with regard to the measure of retribution that by that same measure by which a man metes out, they mete out to him [M. Sot. 1:7A]. How do I know that the same is so with the measure of goodness [M. Sot. 1:9A]?

B. Thus do you say:'

C. The measure of goodness is five hundred times greater than the measure of retribution.

D. With regard to the measure of retribution it is written, "Visiting the sin of the fathers on the sons and on the grandsons to the third and fourth generation" (Ex. 20:5).

E. And with regard to the measure of goodness it is written, "And doing mercy for thousands" (Ex. 20:6).

F. You must therefore conclude that the measure of goodness is five hundred times greater than the measure of retribution.

Having made that point, we revert to the specifics of cases involving mortals, not God, and here, we wish to show the simple point that reward and punishment meet in the precision of justice.

Before proceeding to the Tosefta's extension of matters in a quite unanticipated direction, let us turn to further amplifications of the basic point concerning the exact character of the punishment for a given sin. The fact is, not only does the sinner lose what he or she wanted, but the sinner also is denied what formerly he or she had possessed, a still more mordant and exact penalty indeed. At T. Sotah 4:16, the statement of the Mishnah, "Just as she is prohibited to her husband, so she is prohibited to her lover" [M. Sot. 5:1], is transformed into a generalization, which is spelled out, and then demonstrated by a list lacking all articulation; the items on the list serve to make the point. The illustrative case—the snake and Eve—is given at T. 4:17-18. The list, at T. 4:19.

Tosefta Sotah 4:16

A. Just as she is prohibited to her husband, so she is prohibited to her lover:

B. You turn out to rule in the case of an accused wife who set her eyes on someone who was not available to her:

C. What she wanted is not given to her, and what she had in hand is taken away from her.

The poetry of justice is not lost: what the sinner wanted he does not get, and what he had he loses:

Tosefta Sotah 4:17

A. "And so you find in the case of the snake of olden times, who was smarter than all the cattle and wild beasts of the field, as it is said, 'Now the serpent was smarter than any other wild creature that the Lord God had made'" (Gen. 3:1).

B. He wanted to slay Adam and to marry Eve.

C. The Omnipresent said to him, "I said that you should be king over all beasts and wild animals. Now that you did not want things that way, 'You are more cursed than all the beasts and wild animals of the field' (Gen. 3:14).

D. "I said that you should walk straight-up like man. Now that you did not want things that way, 'Upon your belly you shall go' (Gen. 3:14).

E. "I said that you should eat human food and drink human drink. Now: 'And dust you shall eat all the days of your life' (Gen. 3:14).

Tosefta Sotah 4:18

A. "You wanted to kill Adam and marry Eve? 'And I will put enmity between you and the woman' (Gen. 3:15)."

B. You turn out to rule, What he wanted was not given to him, and what he had in hand was taken away from him.

Sages' mode of thought through classification and hierarchization to uncover patterns does not require the spelling out of the consequences of the pattern through endless cases. On the contrary, sages are perfectly happy to list the other examples of the same rule, knowing that we can reconstruct the details if we know the facts of Scripture that have been shown to follow a common paradigm:

Tosefta Sotah 4:19

A. And so you find in the case of Cain, Korah, Balaam, Doeg, Ahitophel, Gahazi, Absalom, Adonijah, Uzziah, and Haman, all of whom set their eyes on what they did not have coming to them.

B. What they wanted was not given to them, and what they had in hand was taken away from them.

Were we given only T. 4:19A, a construction lacking all explanation, we should have been able to reach T. 4:19B! Here is a fine example of how a pattern signals its own details, and how knowing the native categories allows us to elaborate the pattern with little further data. But whether we should have identified as the generative message, What he wanted was not given to him, and what he had in hand was taken away from him, is not equivalently clear, and I am inclined to think that without the fully-exposed example, we could not have done what the compositor has instructed us to do: fill out the *et cetera*. What a passage of this kind underscores is sages' confidence that those who would study their writings saw the paradigm within the case and possessed minds capable of generalization and objective demonstration.

So from retributive justice and the gentiles, the discourse shifts to distributive reward, shared by the founder and his heirs later on. Reward also is governed by exact justice, the precision of the deed matched by the precision of the response:

Tosefta tractate Sotah 4:1

G. And so you find in the case of Abraham that by that same measure by which a man metes out, they mete out to him.

H. He ran before the ministering angels three times, as it is said, "When he saw them, he ran to meet them" (Gen. 18:2), "And Abraham hastened to the tent" (Gen. 18:6), "And Abraham ran to the herd" (Gen. 18:7).

1. So did the Omnipresent, blessed be He, run before his children three times, as it is said, 'The Lord came from Sinai, and dawned from Seir upon us; he shone forth from Mount Paran" (Deut. 33:2).

Justice extends beyond the limits of a single life, when the life is

Abraham's. Now justice requires that Abraham's heirs participate in the heritage of virtue that he has bequeathed. Point by point, God remembers Abraham's generous actions in favor of Abraham's children into the long future, an intimation of a doctrine involving a heritage of grace that will play a considerable role in the theological system, as we shall see in due course. Here, point by point, what Abraham does brings benefit to his heirs:

> TOSEFTA TRACTATE SOTAH 4:2
> A. Of Abraham it is said, "He bowed himself to the earth" (Gen. 18:2).
> B. So will the Omnipresent, blessed be He, respond graciously to his children in time to come, "Kings will be your foster-fathers, and their queens your nursing mothers. With their faces to the ground they shall bow down to you and lick the dust of your feet" (Is. 49:23).
> C. Of Abraham it is said, 'Let a little water be brought" (Gen. 18:4).
> D. So did the Omnipresent, blessed be He, respond graciously and give to his children a well in the wilderness, which gushed through the whole camp of Israel, as it is said, "The well which the princes dug, which the nobles of the people delved (Num. 21:18) teaching that it went over the whole south and watered the entire desert, which looks down upon the desert" (Num. 2 1 :20).
> E. Of Abraham it is said, 'And rest yourselves under the tree" (Gen. 18:4).
> F. So the Omnipresent gave his children seven glorious clouds in the wilderness, one on their right, one on their left, one before them, one behind them, one above their heads, and one as the Presence among them.

The same theme is expounded in a systematic way through the entire account; it is worth dealing with the complete statement:

> TOSEFTA TRACTATE SOTAH 4:3
> A. Of Abraham it is said, "While I fetch a morsel of bread that you may refresh yourselves" (Gen. 18:5).
> B. So did the Omnipresent, blessed be He, give them manna in the wilderness, as it is said, "The people went about and gathered it . . . and made cakes of it, and the taste of it was like the taste of cakes baked with oil" (Num. 11:8).

> TOSEFTA TRACTATE SOTAH 4:4-6
> 4:4 A. Of Abraham it is said, "And Abraham ran to the herd and took a calf, tender and good" (Gen. 18:7).
> B. So the Omnipresent, blessed be He, rained down quail from the sea for his children, as it is said, "And there went forth a wind from the Lord, and it brought quails from the sea, and let them fall beside the camp" (Num. 11:31).

4 :5 A. Of Abraham what does it say? 'And Abraham stood over them"
(Gen. I 8:8).
B. So the Omnipresent, blessed be He, watched over his children in
Egypt, as it is said, "And the Lord passed over the door" (Ex. 12:23).
4:6 A. Of Abraham what does it say? 'And Abraham went with them
to set them on their way" (Gen. 18:16).
B. So the Omnipresent, blessed be He, accompanied his children for
forty years, as it is said, "These forty years the Lord your God has
been with you" (Deut. 2:7).

The evidence is of the same character as that adduced in the Mishnah: cases of Scripture. But the power of the Tosefta's treatment of
Abraham must be felt: finding an exact counterpart in Israel's later
history to each gesture of the progenitor, Abraham, shows the match
between the deeds of the patriarchs and the destiny of their family
later on. Justice now is given dimensions we should not have anticipated, involving not only the individual but the individual's family, meaning, the entire community of holy Israel. Once more, we
note, a systematic effort focuses upon details. Justice is not a generalized expectation but a very particular fact, bread/manna, calf/
quail, and so on. There is where sages find the kind of detailed evidence that corresponds to the sort suitable in natural history. The
analytical method is one and the same for the Halakhah and the
Aggadah, only the details differ, and these match the task, whether
philosophical for the former or theological for the latter.

The focus now shifts shift from how justice applies to the actions
of named individuals—Samson, Absalom, Sennacherib and Nebuchadnezzar—to the future history of Israel, the entire sector of
humanity formed by those whom God has chosen and to whom he
will give eternal life. It is a jarring initiative. The kinds of instances
of justice that are given until that point concern sin and punishment,
or the reward of individuals for their own actions. And these cases
surely conform to the context: justice as the principle that governs
what happens to individuals in an orderly world. But now we find
ample evidence of the fundamental position in sages' system, the
generative character in their consideration of all issues that, as the
first principle of world order, that justice governs.

Now to return to the point at which we commenced: why does
narrative form the best possible medium for the particular message
of mythic monotheism involving divine justice? Enough has been said
to answer that question: philosophical monotheism had no medium
for the message that God governs justly, through mercy: its calcu-

lus made no space for paradox. Now we shall see an entire document that systematically expounds through narrative the theological response to the great challenge of monotheism: the condition,
in the framework of the Torah's account, of the people of God now
defeated and exiled.

ii. *Mythic Monotheism in the Narrative Medium: Lamentations Rabbah*

My thesis requires only a word of recapitulation: what could the
framers of Lamentations Rabbah express only through narrative, and
not through any other medium available to them? This we may find
out by describing and classifying the narratives contained in the
document—them and their messages. The theme of Lamentations
Rabbati, a systematic verse-by-verse commentary to the book of
Lamentations with an elaborate prologue as well, is Israel's relationship with God. Its message concerning Israel and God is that, with
special reference to three probative events, the destruction of the
Temple in 586 B.C.E and in 70 C.E., and to the catastrophe of Bar
Kokhba's rebellion, the stipulative covenant set forth in the Torah
governs that relationship. Therefore nothing is arbitrary, and everything that happens to Israel makes sense and bears meaning. With
the covenant to explain events, Israel is not helpless before its fate
but through its conduct controls its own destiny.

Accordingly, Lamentations Rabbah sets forth a covenantal theology, realized in history, in which Israel and God have mutually
and reciprocally agreed to bind themselves to a common law set forth
in the Torah. The rules of the relationship are such that an infrac-
tion triggers its penalty willy-nilly; but obedience to the Torah like-
wise brings the reward of redemption. The upshot is this: Israel suffers because of sin, God will respond to Israel's atonement, on the
one side, and loyalty to the covenant in the Torah, on the other.
And when Israel has attained the merit that accrues through the
Torah, God will redeem Israel. In that theological framework the
events of 586 and 70 and their counterparts make sense.

To that theological system the compilers of Lamentations Rabbah make one important contribution, defined at the very end, and
to do so resorted to authentic narrative. They could deliver their
message only through that medium, uniquely suited to express what
they wished to say.

A. What, exactly, in the Context of the Rabbinic Canon Do I
Mean by "Narrative"? The Indicative Power of the Teleological
Logic of Coherent Discourse Unique to Narrative

A narrative piece of writing in the Rabbinic corpus of late antiquity is writing that is governed by a teleological logic of coherent discourse, a matter defined presently, and all other kinds of writing in
that same corpus cohere through an other-than-teleological logic of
coherent discourse. That consideration affords a completely objective criterion for defining narrative both inclusively and exclusive-
ly. Where that logic functions, the composition qualifies as narrative, where not, not. But I hasten to qualify: the canon encompasses
pseudo-narratives, meaning, writing that resembles a story but that
coheres other than through teleological logic.

By "logic of coherent discourse" I mean, the logic by which the
writer links two or more sentences into a statement deemed to cohere, to make sense, to form a whole that exceeds the sum of the
parts as in syllogistic writing. The logic uniquely characteristic of
narrative joins two or more facts to convey a proposition through
the setting forth of happenings in a framework of inevitability, in a
sequence such that the sequence itself makes the point. In Rabbinic narrative the order of the components of the completed construction (allegations, incidents, statements) establishes not merely the facts
of what happens, but the teleology,—the purpose or goal of the facts
in necessary order—that explains those facts. Then we speak not only
of events but of their causal, consecutive relationships. This definition of matters takes on greater concreteness when we consider the
alternative logics of coherent discourse that function in the Rabbinic
canon.

Therein I discern four available logics of coherent discourse by
which two or more sentences are deemed to constitute a statement
of consequence and intelligibility. These are as follows:

(1)   the teleological logic that imparts coherence to data to yield
a coherence based on the teleology, or end-purpose, of all data, which
is different from

(2)   the propositional, syllogistic logic that imparts coherence to
data to yield a proposition and generate a syllogism, which is different from

(3)   the arbitrary logic that joins two or more statements together
on purely formal grounds, and which also is different from

(4)   the paradigmatic logic that through the juxtaposition shows

the structural coherence of two or more rules or cases, yielding a pattern, more concretely: producing (in context) jurisprudence out of laws, laws out of cases, exemplary cases out of random coincidences (such as we saw in chapters one and two).

Of the four logics that I have found to define the media of establishing coherence within pericopes of the canonical documents, two require consideration here, teleological logic and by contrast syllogistic or propositional logic.

In the teleological mode of thought that signals narrative and only narrative we link fact to fact and also prove (ordinarily implicit) propositions by appeal to the goal or end—hence, *teleological*—a logic of coherence that is implicit in the purposive sequence of *facts*. The logic of narrative establishes coherence by the principle of much historical writing of facts deemed continuous and causative, *post hoc, ergo propter hoc:* because one matter preceded another, the prior matter has caused the posterior one—hence, history or story. It follows that only at the end of the composite do all the pieces fall into place. When the goal is realized, the consequences of the combination of *this* with *that* become apparent. Then the reason, first this, then that, emerges. So by invoking the word "teleology," I mean to stress that the pieces of data cohere not by reason of their own traits but by appeal to a goal beyond themselves.

How come the goal is signaled by the very sequence of fact-bearing sentences? It is because the goal transcends, and imposes proportion, coherence, and order on, all the distinct parts of data. No datum is fixed and final until the end. Here the reader does not know what the message really is until the end of the story. In teleological discourse, therefore, the point is at the end, and not learned along the way. Stopping at any point before the end will demolish the construction and leave incoherent and senseless bits and pieces littering the path to nowhere. By contrast, in a propositional composition of a syllogistic character, each component is fully cogent in its own traits and terms, e.g., it may be constituted by an opinion that on its own bears a meaningful statement.

So what defines narrative and no other type of Rabbinic writing is a trait of mind that discerns purpose in the very order of facts, first this, then that, *therefore this led to that and explains it*. The logic that makes sequence, movement, dialectics register so that "this" coheres to "that" as I said may be roughly characterized: *post hoc, ergo propter hoc:* that happened in sequence after this, it therefore happened because of this. In more abstract language, the logic particular to narrative joins a sequence of statements of action or thought in such a way as to yield a cogent statement. By reason of their order the parts cohere into a whole that exceeds the sum of the parts. That order is taken to bear meaning and exhibit purpose or intention, and that logic I therefore call "teleological," hence "the teleological logic characteristic of and, in Rabbinic context, unique to narrative."

Now contrast teleological with syllogistic or propositional logic. By far the most important logic of coherent discourse is the philosophical logic of proposition and syllogism. By it facts and reason cohere to yield syllogisms, e.g., two facts produce a third. A way of conducting philosophical argument is the demonstration we know in general as *Listenwissenschaft,* that is, a way to classify and so establish a set of probative facts. These compel us to reach a given conclusion, one that transcends any and all of the facts but is contained within each of them. These probative facts derive from the classification of data, all of which point in one direction and not in another. Then the traits of the individual bits of data register on their own, and, seen in any order but only all together, they yield a pattern, produce a generalization, demonstrate a principle.

A catalogue of facts, for example, may be so composed that, through the regularities and indicative traits of the respective entries, that the catalogue yields a proposition affecting more facts than are catalogued, thus producing a syllogism. In the Halakhah this may or may not be articulated, but it never has to be, that is the power and art of the Mishnah, the foundation-document of the Halakhah. In the Aggadah, in the main Rabbah-compilations, Leviticus Rabbah, for example, as we saw in chapter three, the besought proposition is ordinarily articulated, outset and end, in complex composites of a syllogistic character. Accordingly, items are interchangeable. Each exemplifies a trait common to them all; that is why the list works. Therefore the order of the items rarely registers the besought proposition; the traits common to the items, in whatever sequence, make all the difference.

A list of parallel or comparable items all together points to a simple conclusion; the conclusion may or may not be given at the end of the catalogue, but the catalogue—by definition—is focused. All of the catalogued facts are taken to bear self-evident connections to one another, established by those pertinent shared traits implicit in the composition of the list. These therefore bear meaning and point through the weight of evidence to an inescapable conclusion. The discrete facts then join together because of some trait common to them all. This is a mode of classification of facts to lead to an identification of what the facts have in common and—it goes without saying, an explanation of their meaning. These and other modes of philosophical argument are entirely familiar.

How do the two logics of coherent discourse compare and contrast? Philosophical logic of coherence differs from the teleological logic characteristic of narrative for in philosophical logic, the sequencing of the facts in a philosophical construction bears no part of the burden; we can reproduce our cases in any order with the same result. By contrast, in teleological logic the manufactured sequence establishes a moral that by reason of the position of the data in some way, rather than in some other, is always blatant. Here too, it hardly matters whether or not the generalization is stated in so many words. That is because the power of well-crafted narrative is so to order the components of the construction as to make unnecessary explicitly announcing the moral. So narrative sees cogency in the necessary order of events understood as causative. Purpose, therefore cause, takes the form of a story of what happened—once upon a time, someone did something with such-and-such a consequence—because it had to happen.

Whatever the form, whether invested with the aura of story-telling or not, the presence of teleological logic marks a composition as narrative, and the absence of that logic denies it that status. If, as we shall now see in pseudo-narratives, we are told in the form of a story about what happens in the Temple on various occasions, the tale of how rites are performed, we can invoke the formal issue: does the outcome become clear only at the end, or is the sequence merely formal, a matter of a correct ordering of action, but not teleological—message-bearing, detail by detail when in fixed array.[2]

B. Pseudo-narrative

Let us take up the matter of verisimilitude as against authenticity: what about compositions that by the criterion of teleological logic do not qualify as narratives but that do convey a narrative "tone" or impression, e.g., the account of a sequence of actions and their outcomes, or a setting for a story that is not actually told except through dialogue containing ideas, no action, e.g., "they were walking along the way and he said to him…," "he said to him…" "he said to him…"—with no action but only talk that is propositional, not ordered teleologically? I call "pseudo-narratives" those compositions that adopt what looks like a narrative tone but cohere on some foundation other than the logic of teleology. In that connection I identify three special problems, all involving a described action or event, none invoking teleological logic. These bear resemblance to stories, the rhetoric corresponding to what generally characterizes narratives in Rabbinic context. But their principal parts do not cohere through the required logic of coherent discourse. They are

(1)   "conversations"[3] ("he said to him…he said to him…");
(2)   presentations of ritual conduct in the Temple (and in the court) ("he did this…he did that…"); and
(3)   the precedent or case, usually but not invariably marked *Ma'aseh*
(4)   the parable, whether exegetical or Halakhic, which translates an abstract conception into a concrete story meant as a simile.

The "conversations" construct a setting for what are, in fact, merely exchanges of principles or arguments: scripted, artificial dialogue, a pseudo-narrative setting for an analytical presentation. An example would be an account of how one day, such-and-such happened, the rabbis ruled so-and-so, and Rabbi X argued…Rabbi Y argued…through several matched exchanges, followed by "they voted and ruled…." Here is an event that yields a rule, not a narrative within the present definition.

Our task now is to identify that message that is uniquely matched by the medium of authentic narrative in the document on which we focus, Lamentations Rabbah, which is one of the two compilations in the Rabbinic canon that makes heavy and systematic use of authentic narratives to make its statement.

---

[2] I follow Ithamar Gruenwald's definition of ritual in his *Rituals and Ritual Theory in Ancient Israel*. He sees ritual as action, fixed and autonomous, without reference to the story that accompanies the action (myth).

[3] Quotation-marks signify the distinction between verbatim reports of conversations and fabrications of "conversations" out of surmise or convention, such as characterize nearly the whole of the Rabbinic canonical record of things people supposedly said to one another. In that record literary convention and artifice govern; there is nothing that remotely qualifies as a verbatim report of things really said, as a conversation that really took place on some one day in some determinate situation.

C. The Authentic Narrative in Lamentations Rabbah

Narrative is the sole selected medium for the Rabbinic sages' message concerning the destruction of the Temple, Israel's suffering and martyrdom in consequence, the coming of the Messiah, and the restoration of Israel's condition. The doctrines of theology of history and eschatological restoration take narrative shape because that is the only way—resorting necessarily to the logic of teleology—that the Rabbinic sages could articulate them with effect. Those doctrines by their nature tell a story about purpose, intentionality, and plan. These traits of God, expressed in attitude and action, may be declared, implausibly to be sure, in abstractions, but conveyed with compelling power only in stories about God and Israel.

Before any further theoretical remarks and a survey of the abbreviated data, let me give a single example of an authentic narrative set forth uniquely by Lamentations Rabbah. This example on its own suffices to meet the criterion of perfection and to illustrate the claim that there is no better medium for the message at hand than authentic narrative rendered cogent by the teleological logic of coherent discourse. Every detail finds its meaning only at the end. Later on I shall show that that is the one message for which authentic narrative serves in the document at hand.

LAMENTATIONS RABBAH XXIV.ii.

1. A. Another interpretation of the passage, "My Lord God of Hosts summoned on that day to weeping and lamenting, to tonsuring and girding with sackcloth:"

B. When the Holy One, blessed be He, considered destroying the house of the sanctuary, he said, "So long as I am within it, the nations of the world cannot lay a hand on it.

C. "I shall close my eyes to it and take an oath that I shall not become engaged with it until the time of the end."

D. Then the enemies came and destroyed it.

E. Forthwith the Holy One, blessed be He, took an oath by his right hand and put it behind him: "He has drawn back his right hand from before the enemy" (Lam. 2:3).

F. At that moment the enemies entered the sanctuary and burned it up.

G. When it had burned, the Holy One, blessed be He, said, "I do not have any dwelling on earth any more. I shall take up my presence from there and go up to my earlier dwelling."

H. That is in line with this verse: "I will go and return to my place, until they acknowledge their guilt and seek my face" (Hos. 5:15).

I. At that moment the Holy One, blessed be He, wept, saying,

"Woe is me! What have I done! I have brought my Presence to dwell below on account of the Israelites, and now that they have sinned, I have gone back to my earlier dwelling. Heaven forfend that I now become a joke to the nations and a source of ridicule among people."

J.   At that moment Metatron came, prostrated himself, and said before him, "Lord of the world, let me weep, but don't you weep!"

K.   He said to him, "If you do not let me weep now, I shall retreat to a place in which you have no right to enter, and there I shall weep."

L.   That is in line with this verse: "But if you will not hear it, my soul shall weep in secret for pride" (Jer. 13:17).

2.   A.   Said the Holy One, blessed be He, to the ministering angels, "Let's go and see what the enemies have done to my house."

B.   Forthwith the Holy One, blessed be He, and the ministering angels went forth, with Jeremiah before them.

C.   When the Holy One, blessed be He, saw the house of the sanctuary, he said, "This is certainly my house, and this is my resting place, and the enemies have come and done whatever they pleased with it!"

D.   At that moment the Holy One, blessed be He, wept, saying "Woe is me for my house! O children of mine – where are you? O priests of mine – where are you? O you who love me – where are you? What shall I do for you? I warned you, but you did not repent."

E.   Said the Holy One, blessed be He, to Jeremiah, "Today I am like a man who had an only son, who made a marriage canopy for him, and the son died under his marriage canopy. Should you not feel pain for me and for my son?

F.   "Go and call Abraham, Isaac, Jacob, and Moses from their graves, for they know how to weep."

G.   He said before him, "Lord of the world, I don't know where Moses is buried."

H.   The Holy One, blessed be He, said to him, "Go and stand at the bank of the Jordan and raise your voice and call him, 'Son of Amram, son of Amram, rise up and see your flock, which the enemy has swallowed up!'"

I.   Jeremiah immediately went to the cave of Machpelah and said to the founders of the world, "Arise, for the time has come for you to be called before the Holy One, blessed be He."

J.   They said to him, "Why?"

K.   He said to them, "I don't know," because he was afraid that they would say to him, "In your time this has come upon our children!"

L.   Jeremiah left them and went to the bank of the Jordan and cried out, "Son of Amram, son of Amram, rise up, for the time has come for you to be called before the Holy One, blessed be He."

M.   He said to him, "What makes this day so special, that I am called before the Holy One, blessed be He?"

N.   He said to them, "I don't know."

O.   Moses left him and went to the ministering angels, for he had known them from the time of the giving of the Torah. He said to them, "You who serve on high! Do you know on what account I am summoned before the Holy One, blessed be He?"

P.   They said to him, "Son of Amram! Don't you know that the house of the sanctuary has been destroyed, and the Israelites taken away into exile?"

Q.   So he cried and wept until he came to the fathers of the world. They too forthwith tore their garments and put their hands on their heads, crying and weeping, up to the gates of the house of the sanctuary.

R.   When the Holy One, blessed be He, saw them, forthwith: "My Lord God of Hosts summoned on that day to weeping and lamenting, to tonsuring and girding with sackcloth."

S.   Were it not stated explicitly in a verse of Scripture, it would not be possible to make this statement.

T.   And they went weeping from this gate to that, like a man whose deceased lies before him,

U.   and the Holy One, blessed be He, wept, lamenting, "Woe for a king who prospers in his youth and not in his old age."

3. A.   Said R. Samuel bar Nahman, "When the Temple was destroyed, Abraham came before the Holy One, blessed be He, weeping, pulling at his beard and tearing his hair, striking his face, tearing his clothes, with ashes on his head, walking about the temple, weeping and crying, saying before the Holy One, blessed be He,

B.   "'How come I am treated differently from every other nation and language, that I should be brought to such humiliation and shame!'

C.   "When the ministering angels saw him, they too [Cohen, p. 43:] composed lamentations, arranging themselves in rows, saying,

D.   "'the highways lie waste, the wayfaring man ceases' (Isa. 33:8)."

E.   "What is the meaning of the statement, 'the highways lie waste'?

F.   "Said the ministering angels before the Holy One, blessed be He, 'The highways that you paved to Jerusalem, so that the wayfarers would not cease, how have they become a desolation?'

G.   "'the wayfaring man ceases:'

H.   "Said the ministering angels before the Holy One, blessed be He, 'How have the ways become deserted, on which the Israelites would come and go for the pilgrim festivals?'

I.   "'You have broken the covenant:'

J.   "Said the ministering angels before the Holy One, blessed be He, 'Lord of the world, the covenant that was made with their father, Abraham, has been broken, the one through which the world was settled and through which you were made known in the world, that you are the most high God, the one who possesses heaven and earth.'

K.   "'He has despised the cities:'

L.   "Said the ministering angels before the Holy One, blessed be He, 'You have despised Jerusalem and Zion after you have chosen them!

M.   "Thus Scripture says, 'Have you utterly rejected Judah? Has your soul loathed Zion?' (Jer. 14:19).

N.   "'He regards not Enosh:'

O.   "Said the ministering angels before the Holy One, blessed be He, 'Even as much as the generation of Enosh, chief of all idol worshippers, you have not valued Israel!'

P.   "At that moment the Holy One, blessed be He, responded to the ministering angels, saying to them, 'How come you are composing lamentations, arranging themselves in rows, on this account?'

Q.   "They said to him, 'Lord of the world! It is on account of Abraham, who loved you, who came to your house and lamented and wept. How come you didn't pay any attention to him?'

R.   "He said to them, 'From the day on which my beloved died, going off to his eternal house, he has not come to my house, and now "what is my beloved doing in my house" (Jer. 11:15)?'

S.   "Said Abraham before the Holy One, blessed be He, 'Lord of the world! How come you have sent my children into exile and handed them over to the nations? And they have killed them with all manner of disgusting forms of death! And you have destroyed the house of the sanctuary, the place on which I offered up my son Isaac as a burnt-offering before you!?'

T.   "Said to Abraham the Holy One, blessed be He, 'Your children sinned and violated the whole Torah, transgressing the twenty-two letters that are used to write it: "Yes, all Israel have transgressed your Torah" (Dan. 9:11).'

U.   "Said Abraham before the Holy One, blessed be He, 'Lord of the world, who will give testimony against the Israelites, that they have violated your Torah?'

V.   "He said to him, 'Let the Torah come and give testimony against the Israelites.'

W.   "Forthwith the Torah came to give testimony against them.

X.   "Said Abraham to her, 'My daughter, have you come to give testimony against the Israelites that they have violated your religious duties? and are you not ashamed on my account? Remember the day on which the Holy One, blessed be He, peddled you to all the nations and languages of the world, and no one wanted to accept you, until my children came to Mount Sinai and they accepted you and honored you! And now are you coming to give testimony against them on their day of disaster?'

Y.   "When the Torah heard this, she went off to one side and did not testify against them.

Z.   "Said the Holy One, blessed be He, to Abraham, 'Then let the twenty-two letters of the alphabet come and give testimony against the Israelites.'

AA. "Forthwith the twenty-two letters of the alphabet came to give testimony against them.

BB. "The aleph came to give testimony against the Israelites, that they had violated the Torah.

CC. "Said Abraham to her, 'Aleph, you are the head of all of the letters of the alphabet, and have you now come to give testimony against the Israelites on the day of their disaster?'

DD. "'Remember the day on which the Holy One, blessed be He, revealed himself on Mount Sinai and began his discourse with you: "I [anokhi, beginning with aleph] am the Lord your God who brought you out of the Land of Egypt, out of the house of bondage" (Ex. 20:2).

EE. "'But not a single nation or language was willing to take you on, except for my children! And are you now going to give testimony against my children?'

FF. "Forthwith the aleph went off to one side and did not testify against them.

GG. "The bet came to give testimony against the Israelites.

HH. "Said Abraham to her, 'My daughter, have you come to give testimony against my children, who are meticulous about the Five Books of the Torah, at the head of which you stand, as it is said, "In the beginning [bereshit] God created..." (Gen. 1:1)?'

II. "Forthwith the bet went off to one side and did not testify against them.

JJ. "The gimel came to give testimony against the Israelites.

KK. "Said Abraham to her, 'Gimel, have you come to give testimony against my children, that they have violated the Torah? Is there any nation, besides my children, that carries out the religious duty of wearing show-fringes, at the head of which you stand, as it is said, "Twisted cords [gedelim] you shall make for yourself" (Dt. 22:12).'

LL. "Forthwith the gimel went off to one said and did not testify against them.

MM.   "Now when all of the letters of the alphabet realized that Abraham had silenced them, they were ashamed and stood off and would not testify against Israel.

NN. "Abraham forthwith commenced speaking before the Holy One, blessed be He, saying to him, 'Lord of the world, when I was a hundred years old, you gave me a son. And when he had already reached the age of volition, a boy thirty-seven years of age, you told me, "offer him up as a burnt-offering before me"!

OO. "'And I turned mean to him and had no mercy for him, but I myself tied him up. Are you not going to remember this and have mercy on my children?'

PP.   "Isaac forthwith commenced speaking before the Holy One, blessed be He, saying to him, 'Lord of the world, when father said to me, "God will see to the lamb for the offering for himself, my son"

(Gen. 22:8), I did not object to what you had said, but I was bound willingly, with all my heart, on the altar, and spread forth my neck under the knife. Are you not going to remember this and have mercy on my children!'

QQ. "Jacob forthwith commenced speaking before the Holy One, blessed be He, saying to him, 'Lord of the world, did I not remain in the house of Laban for twenty years? And when I went forth from his house, the wicked Essau met me and wanted to kill my children, and I gave myself over to death in their behalf. Now my children are handed over to their enemies like sheep for slaughter, after I raised them like fledglings of chickens. I bore on their account the anguish of raising children, for through most of my life I was pained greatly on their account. And now are you not going to remember this and have mercy on my children?'

RR. "Moses forthwith commenced speaking before the Holy One, blessed be He, saying to him, 'Lord of the world, was I not a faithful shepherd for the Israelites for forty years? I ran before them in the desert like a horse. And when the time came for them to enter the land, you issued a decree against me in the wilderness that there my bones would fall. And now that they have gone into exile, you have sent to me to mourn and weep for them.'

SS. "This is in line with the proverb people say: 'When it's good for my master, it's not good for me, but when its bad for him, it's bad for me!'

TT. "Then Moses said to Jeremiah, 'Go before me, so I may go and bring them in and see who will lay a hand on them.'

UU. "Said to him Jeremiah, 'It isn't even possible to go along the road, because of the corpses.'

VV. "He said to him, 'Nonetheless.'

WW.   "Forthwith Moses went along, with Jeremiah leading the way, until they came to the waters of Babylon.

XX. "They saw Moses and said to one another, 'Here comes the son of Amram from his grave to redeem us from the hand of our oppressors.'

YY. "An echo went forth and said, 'It is a decree from before me.'

ZZ. "Then said Moses to them, 'My children, to bring you back is not possible, for the decree has already been issued. But the Omnipresent will bring you back quickly.' Then he left them.

AAA.   "Then they raised up their voices in weeping until the sound rose on high: 'By the rivers of Babylon there we sat down, yes, we wept' (Ps. 137:1).

BBB.   "When Moses got back to the fathers of the world, they said to him, 'What have the enemies done to our children?'

CCC.   "He said to them, 'Some of them he killed, the hands of some of them he bound behind their back, some of them he put in iron chains, some of them he stripped naked, some of them died on the way, and their corpses were left for the vultures of heaven and the hyenas of the earth, some of them were left for the sun, starving and thirsting.'

DDD.   "Then they began to weep and sing dirges: 'Woe for what has happened to our children! How have you become orphans without a father! How have you had to sleep in the hot sun during the summer without clothes and covers! How have you had to walk over rocks and stones without shoes and sandals! How were you burdened with heavy bundle of sand! How were your hands bound behind your backs! How were you left unable even to swallow the spit in your mouths!'

EEE.   "Moses then said, 'Cursed are you, O sun! Why did you not grow dark when the enemy went into the house of the sanctuary?'

FFF.   "The sun answered him, 'By your life, Moses, faithful shepherd! They would not let me nor did they leave me alone, but beat me with sixty whips of fire, saying, "Go, pour out your light."'

GGG.   "Moses then said, 'Woe for your brilliance, O temple, how has it become darkened? Woe that its time has come to be destroyed, for the building to be reduced to ruins, for the school children to be killed, for their parents to go into captivity and exile and the sword!'

HHH.   "Moses then said, 'O you who have taken the captives! I impose an oath on you by your lives! If you kill, do not kill with a cruel form of death, do not exterminate them utterly, do not kill a son before his father, a daughter before her mother, for the time will come for the Lord of heaven to exact a full reckoning from you!'

III.   "The wicked Chaldeans did not do things this way, but they brought a son before his mother and said to the father, 'Go, kill him!' The mother wept, her tears flowing over him, and the father hung his head.

JJJ.   "And further Moses said before him, 'Lord of the world! You have written in your Torah, "Whether it is a cow or a ewe, you shall not kill it and its young both in one day" (Lev. 22:28).

KKK.   "'But have they not killed any number of children along with their mothers, and yet you remain silent!'

LLL.   "Then Rachel, our mother, leapt to the fray and said to the Holy One, blessed be He, 'Lord of the world! It is perfectly self-evident to you that your servant, Jacob, loved me with a mighty love, and worked for me for father for seven years, but when those seven years were fulfilled, and the time came for my wedding to my husband, father planned to substitute my sister for me in the marriage to my husband. Now that matter was very hard for me, for I knew the deceit, and I told my husband and gave him a sign by which he would know the difference between me and my sister, so that my father would not be able to trade me off. But then I regretted it and I bore my passion, and I had mercy for my sister, that she should not be shamed. So in the evening for my husband they substituted my sister for me, and I gave my sister all the signs that I had given to my husband, so that he would think that she was Rachel.

MMM.   "'And not only so, but I crawled under the bed on which he was lying with my sister, while she remained silent, and I made all the replies so that he would not discern the voice of my sister.

NNN.   "'I paid my sister only kindness, and I was not jealous of her, and I did not allow her to be shamed, and I am a mere mortal, dust and ashes. Now I had no envy of my rival, and I did not place her at risk for shame and humiliation. But you are the King, living and enduring and merciful. How come then you are jealous of idolatry, which is nothing, and so have sent my children into exile, allowed them to be killed by the sword, permitted the enemy to do whatever they wanted to them?!'

OOO.   "Forthwith the mercy of the Holy One, blessed be He, welled up, and he said, 'For Rachel I am going to bring the Israelites back to their land.'

PPP   "That is in line with this verse of Scripture: 'Thus said the Lord: A cry is heard in Ramah, wailing, bitter weeping, Rachel weeping for her children. She refuses to be comforted for her children, who are gone. Thus said the Lord, Restrain your voice from weeping, your eyes from shedding tears; for there is a reward for your labor, declares the Lord; they shall return from the enemy's land, and there is hope for your future, declares the Lord: your children shall return to their country'" (Jer. 31:15-17)."

What philosophical medium can sustain the message: God wept along with Rachel and in his tears determined to restore Israel to Zion? The Israel of Rabbinic Judaism aspired to recapitulate the second component of the pattern of exile and return set forth in Scripture. In that context I cannot imagine a more pointed or precise response to the paramount problem of the age.

Indeed, I cannot point in Midrash compilations that reached closure prior to this one to a sustained and coherent passage of the narrative ambition and power of Samuel bar Nahman's. Nor in the documents that reached closure afterward, within the limits of late antiquity, is there any. We are in a completely different literary situation when we come to so long and so carefully formed a story as this one. Now to some more general remarks about the role and task of (authentic) narrative in Lamentations Rabbah: its unique medium for its singular message within mythic monotheism. But, while the apex, the cited composition is not alone in this document.

While principally an exegetical composite, Lamentations Rabbah sets forth a vast and highly articulated corpus of authentic narrative writing. The main body of the authentic narratives of the document focuses upon the theological challenge of the exile of ancient Israel to Assyria and Babylonia, the destruction of the Second Temple, and the loss of the war led by Bar Kokhba. A cognate theme addresses Israel's relationships with the nations, and both Israel's and the nations' relationships with God, relationships defined by God's loathing of idolatry. And within the framework of theodicy, the theme of tragedy—the human suffering and sense of loss—is ever-present. Since the book of Lamentations raises all these themes, we cannot find puzzling their paramount position within its narrative component as well.

What is more striking is the selection of (authentic) narrative as the medium for exploring them. Exegesis did not fully realize the compilers' goals, nor did parable or precedent—the other two forms of narrative writing in the documents that earlier came to closure, did not accomplish their purpose, as we shall see in detail. Only telling the story, in the model of the resort to narrative by the Torah and the prophets of Scripture, served. Telling the story formed for the compilers a necessary medium for setting forth the theological message, because, as we shall see, the details of the story embody that message in exemplary, concrete terms, with a consequent power and effect that a mere statement of theological abstraction cannot hope to attain.

That explains, also, why the kind of narrative—sustained, not brief and anecdotal, realized in a fair amount of development and characterization and plot-development—devoted to the theological themes of the biblical book of Lamentations differs from the kind devoted to the theological themes of Torah-study and glorification of the sage as these are articulated in narratives throughout the Midrash-compilations and in The Fathers According to Rabbi Nathan.[4] These biographical narratives, differentiated by subject-matter, are brief, undeveloped, acted out by stick-men, with much dialogue and little action. And, it goes without saying, while Torah- and sage-stories involve only Israelites, the narratives of destruction and catastrophe that portray both the theodicy of Israel's responsibility and the tragedy that has come upon Israel introduce important gentile figures. Otherwise these classifications of players, e.g., kings and queens, rarely occur outside the framework of parables, for example. But even there it is ordinarily assumed that the king/prince/queen all are Israelites, as are all actors.

---

[4] See my *Judaism and Story: The Evidence of The Fathers According to Rabbi Nathan.* Chicago, 1992: University of Chicago Press.

Our task is now to classify the narratives by gross indicative traits of topic, theme, or proposition and narrative quality or character. What we want to find out is whether the authentic narratives fall into a single topical classification. The answer identifies the message for which narrative was found the uniquely appropriate medium. In each case, we shall therefore ask about topic and proposition, on the one side, and narrative character: short and simple or long and complex, only dialogue or action and dialogue. These taxonomic indicators bear slight weight for literary criticism, but for the religious analysis of the writing they serve quite well to differentiate types of authentic narratives. I cite only part of the narratives, which are set forth whole and complete in my analytical translation, *The Components of the Rabbinic Documents: From the Whole to the Parts*. Volume IV. *Lamentations Rabbati*.[5] In each case I focus on the main point pertinent to my analysis. I only specify the topic and proposition of the narrative and identify the narrative traits that come into play.

1.   II:i.3. Rabbi [Judah the Patriarch] would dispatch R. Assi and R. Ammi to go out and inspect the condition of the towns of the land of Israel They would go into a town and say to the people, "Bring us the guardians of the town." So the people would produce the captain of the guard and the senator and say to them, "Here are the guardians of the town. They said to them, "These are the guardians of the town? These are those who ravage the town." They said to them, "Then who are the guardians of the town? They said to them, "They are the scribes and teachers, who dwell upon, repeat, and keep the Torah day and night."

   TOPIC AND PROPOSITION: The topic is Torah-study, and the proposition is that Torah-study protects the city.
   NARRATIVE CHARACTER: We have a brief, exemplary anecdote, executed through what is said rather than sequences of actions.

2.   XXIV.ii.1. When the Holy One, blessed be He, considered destroying the house of the sanctuary, he said, "So long as I am within it, the nations of the world cannot lay a hand on it, I shall close my eyes to it and take an oath that I shall not become engaged with it until the time of the end." Then the enemies came and destroyed it. Forthwith the Holy One, blessed be He, took an oath by his right hand and put it behind him: "He has drawn back his right hand from before the enemy" (Lam. 2:3). At that moment the enemies

---

entered the sanctuary and burned it up. When it had burned, the Holy One, blessed be He, said, "I do not have any dwelling on earth any more. I shall take up my presence from there and go up to my earlier dwelling." At that moment the Holy One, blessed be He, wept, saying, "Woe is me! What have I done! I have brought my Presence to dwell below on account of the Israelites, and now that they have sinned, I have gone back to my earlier dwelling. Heaven forfend that I now become a joke to the nations and a source of ridicule among people." At that moment Metatron came, prostrated himself, and said before him, "Lord of the world, let me weep, but don't you weep!" He said to him, "If you do not let me weep now, I shall retreat to a place in which you have no right to enter, and there I shall weep." Said the Holy One, blessed be He, to the ministering angels, "Let's go and see what the enemies have done to my house." Forthwith the Holy One, blessed be He, and the ministering angels went forth, with Jeremiah before them. When the Holy One, blessed be He, saw the house of the sanctuary, he said, "This is certainly my house, and this is my resting place, and the enemies have come and done whatever they pleased with it!" At that moment the Holy One, blessed be He, wept, saying "Woe is me for my house! O children of mine—where are you? O priests of mine—where are you? O you who love me—where are you? What shall I do for you? I warned you, but you did not repent." Said the Holy One, blessed be He, to Jeremiah, "Today I am like a man who had an only son, who made a marriage canopy for him, and the son died under his marriage canopy. Should you not feel pain for me and for my son? "Go and call Abraham, Isaac, Jacob, and Moses from their graves, for they know how to weep." He said to them, "I don't know." Moses left him and went to the ministering angels, for he had known them from the time of the giving of the Torah. He said to them, "You who serve on high! Do you know on what account I am summoned before the Holy One, blessed be He? They said to him, "Son of Amram! Don't you know that the house of the sanctuary has been destroyed, and the Israelites taken away into exile?" So he cried and wept until he came to the fathers of the world. They too forthwith tore their garments and put their hands on their heads, crying and weeping, up to the gates of the house of the sanctuary. When the Holy One, blessed be He, saw them, forthwith: "My Lord God of Hosts summoned on that day to weeping and lamenting, to tonsuring and girding with sackcloth."

TOPIC AND PROPOSITION: The destruction of the Temple was mourned by God in heaven, who found himself engaged in debate by Jeremiah, Abraham, Isaac, Jacob, and Moses.

NARRATIVE CHARACTER: Attitudes and emotions figure, actions register, not only dialogue, and the players are treated as individuals, not merely as stick-figures. The narrative is autonomous of Scripture and its exegesis, and its principal point is that God wept at the destruction.

3. XXIV:ii.3. Said R. Samuel bar Nahman, "When the Temple was destroyed, Abraham came before the Holy One, blessed be He, weeping, pulling at his beard and tearing his hair, striking his face, tearing his clothes, with ashes on his head, walking about the temple, weeping and crying, saying before the Holy One, blessed be He, How come I am treated differently from every other nation and language, that I should be brought to such humiliation and shame!' When the ministering angels saw him, they too composed lamentations, arranging themselves in rows, saying, 'the highways lie waste, the wayfaring man ceases' (Isa. 33:8)." [The rest as given above.]

> TOPIC AND PROPOSITION: Continuous with the foregoing, this enormous narrative takes up the topic of God and the destruction, and repeats the proposition that God mourned, along with all of his hosts, on that occasion.
>
> NARRATIVE CHARACTER: The dialogue serves as the medium of the story: God and the angels, God and Abraham, Abraham and the letters of the alphabet, Isaac, Jacob, Moses, Jeremiah; there is ample described action; only when Rachel intervenes does God promise to restore Israel to the Land.

4. XXXV:v.2. Said R. Eleazar, "There was a case involving a caravan in which there was a merchant who was leading three hundred camels bearing pepper. He came by Tyre and found a certain tailor, sitting at the gate. He said to him, 'What are you selling?' He said to him, 'Pepper.' He said to him, 'Sell me a little.' He said to him, 'No, for all of it is for one [purchaser].' He said to him, 'You are going to sell it only to the Jewish town.' He came to the Jewish town and found another tailor sitting at the gate. He said to him, 'What are your camels carrying?' He said to him, 'Pepper.' He took him to a house, and showed him a pile of coins, saying to them, 'Look at this money. Does it circulate in your land?' [The other was satisfied and made the sale,] and he took his leave and went off in peace. After he had left, he went out to walk in the market place. He met one of his friends, who said to him, 'What are you bringing here?' He said to him, 'Pepper.' He said to him, 'If you have a little, sell it to me for a hundred denars, for I have a party to give.' He said to him, 'I have already sold it to a certain tailor, but I'll tell him to give you a little of it.' He went and found the house full of buyers, so that those who were in the first room secured an ounce each, and those in the second room half an ounce each, while those in the third received no attention at all."

Without the marker, *Ma'aseh*, translated, "case," we should have an authentic narrative, reaching its climax at the end-point, at which the point of the whole registers.

TOPIC AND PROPOSITION: The story deals with the prosperity and populous character of the Jewish towns of the Land of Israel, and its proposition is that there were many people (Lam. 1:1), who lived well.

NARRATIVE CHARACTER: He did this, he said that, with such-and-such a result—that simple pattern prevails.

5.   XXV:vii.3 There is the following case [*Ma'aseh*]. There was a Jerusalemite who went to a town, where he was received by a friend. He spent some time there. The time came for him [to die], and he entrusted his property into the hands of his friend by whom he had been received. He said to him, "If my son comes to you and wants this property, if he does not carry out three acts of wisdom, do not give him this property. The people had agreed that none of them would show the house of his father's friend to a stranger [who might ask for it]. The son heard and went to that place, and he knew the name of the man. He came and sat at the gate of the town. He saw someone carrying a load of twigs. He said to him, "Will you sell those twigs?"

TOPIC AND PROPOSITION: The wisdom of the Jerusalemite secures for the son the inheritance that the father has provided for him.

NARRATIVE CHARACTER: Dialogue carries the story, with the clever son of the Jerusalemite systematically overcoming the obstacles by solving the riddles his father left for him. The parts cohere as they unfold, the repeated pattern imposing cogency on the parts.

6.   XXXV:vii.4 Four Jerusalemites went to Athens and were received by someone there. In the evening he made a meal for them. After they had eaten and drunk, he set four beds for them, one of them damaged [and supported by the next]. After they had eaten and drunk, he said, "I'm going to listen, for the Jerusalemites are very smart. I'll go and lie down near them to know what they are saying." One of them woke up, the one sleeping in the damaged bed, and said, "Do you think that I am sleeping on a bed? I am sleeping only on the ground." The second woke up and said, "Are you surprised at that? The meat that we were eating tasted of dog." The third woke up and said, "Are you surprised at that? The wine that we drank tasted like the grave." The fourth awoke and said, "Are you surprised at that? The householder here is not the father of his son." At that moment the man said, "One of them spoke the truth, and three told lies."

7.   XXXV:vii.5. A Jerusalemite came to Athens, but no one wanted to extend him hospitality, so he went to a stall. After they had eaten and drink, he wanted to sleep there. The owner of the stall said to him, "We have made an agreement among us that no one from Jerusalem will sleep among us until he has jumped three jumps." He said to him, "I don't know how you people jump. You jump first, and I'll follow you." He took one jump, then another, and a third, and ended up outside the stall. The Jerusalemite went and locked the door after him. He said to him, "What's this?" He said to him, "What you wanted to do to me, I have done to you."

8.   XXXV:vii.6 An Athenian came to Jerusalem and went to the school house and found youngsters there, but their master was not present. They said to him, "Let us make a deal that whoever is asked a question and cannot answer it will lose a piece of clothing." They said to him, "Explain the following: Nine go out but eight come in, two pour out but one drinks, and twenty-four serve." He could not explain these things to them. They took away his clothes. He went to R. Yohanan, saying to him, "Is this how you act in your place? They strip guests naked." He said to him, "Go and tell them: [Cohen, p. 78:] the nine which go in are the nine months of gestation, and the eight that come out are the eight days of circumcision,

9.   XXXV:vii.7. An Athenian came to Jerusalem and came upon a child and gave him some money, saying to him, "Go, buy me cheese and eggs. When he came back, he said to him, "Tell me, as to these eggs, whence do they come, from a white chicken or a black one?"

10.   XXXV:vii.8. An Athenian came to Jerusalem and came upon a child and gave him some money, saying to him, "Go, buy me figs." There was an inferior portion, which the boy set before himself, and a better portion, before the visitor. He said to him, "Many thanks, well do people say that the Jerusalemites are very clever. Since the child knew that the money was mine, he chose the better portion and set it before me."

11.   XXXV:vii.9. An Athenian came to Jerusalem and came upon a child and gave him some money, saying to him, "Take this money and bring me something to eat now, with something left over for the way." He went and brought him salt.

12.   XXXV:vii.10. An Athenian came to Jerusalem and came upon a broken mortar. He took it and went to a tailor, saying to him, "Sew this broken mortar for me." He took out a handful of sand, saying to him, "Twist this into thread for me, and I'll sew the mortar."

13.   XXXV:vii.11. An Athenian came to Jerusalem and came upon a priest, saying to him, "How much of that load of wood will turn into smoke?" He said to him, "When it is damp, all of it, when it is dry, a third is smoke, a third ash, and a third fire."

14.   XXXV:vii.12. An Athenian came to Jerusalem and wanted to learn wisdom. When he came to leave, he bought a slave, blind in one eye. The one who had sold the slave said to him, "By your life, he

is very clever and can see at a distance." When they had come out of the gate, the slave said to him, "Make haste, so we may overtake the caravan. He said to him, "Is there a caravan before us?" He said to him, "Yes, and there is a she-camel in front of us, blind in one eye; it has twins in its womb; it is carrying two skin bottles, one with wine, the other, vinegar; it is four miles away, and the camel driver is a gentile."

15. XXXV:vii.13. Someone from Athens was making fun of the locals of Jerusalem. They said, "Who will go and bring him to us?" One of them said, "I'll bring him to you, with his head shaved." He went to Athens and stayed with him. He was walking in the market place, and one of his sandals broke. He gave it to a workman, saying, "Take this *tremis* [a sizable sum of money] and fix this sandal." He said to him, "Are sandals so costly where you live?" He said to him, "When they are expensive, they cost ten *denars,* and when cheap, eight."

> Topic and proposition: The composite of ten patterned narratives goes over the topic of the competition of Jerusalem and Athens for wisdom in solving riddles. The proposition is that the Israelites best the Athenians at wisdom.
> Narrative character: The narratives fully articulate the wisdom through action that is explained, expressed in exchanges of dialogue as well. Some are brief exchanges, others elaborate, but all adhere to the simple pattern: challenge, response, deed, dialogue, throughout.

16. XXXV:vii.14. A Samaritan set himself up as a dream-interpreter, ridiculing people. Said R. Ishmael b. R. Yosé, "I shall go and see how this Samaritan is ridiculing people." Someone came to him and said, "I saw in my dream an olive tree feeding oil." said to him, "The olive means light and oil means light; you will see a lot of light." R. Ishmael b. R. Yosé, "May your spirit explode! That man has known [has committed incest with] his mother."

17. XXXV:vii.15. A Samaritan said, "I want to go to see a certain sage of the Jews who makes fun of everybody. He said to him, "I saw in my dream four cedars, four sycamores, a hide stuffed with straw, and an ox riding on them."

18. XXXV:vii.16. Another came and said to him, "In planting season I dreamed of an olive tree." He said to him, "You will see a lot of light."

19. XXXV:vii.17. There was the case of a disciple who was in session before R. Yohanan, who explained matters to no avail. He said to him, "What's wrong that you don't understand?" He said to him, "I saw in my dream three bad things, and I don't know what they mean."

20. XXXV:vii.18.Another one said to him, "I dreamed that I did not have pants on." He said to him, "That is not a bad sign but a good

one. When the Festival [of Tabernacles] comes, you will have nothing."

21. XXXV:vii.19. Someone came to R. Yosé b. Halafta and said, "I was shown in my dream, 'Go to Cappadocia and find your father's property.'

22. XXXV:vii.20. There was the case of a woman who came to R. Eleazar and said, "I saw in my dream that the beam of the house was split."

23. XXXV:vii.21. Another time she came and did not find him there, but did find his disciples. She said to them, "Where is your master?" She said to them, "I saw in my dream that the beam of the house was split."

> TOPIC AND PROPOSITION: The topic of the eight anecdotes is dream-interpretation, and the proposition is that sages have the power to interpret dreams.
>
> NARRATIVE CHARACTER: The encounter between the dreamers and the interpreters is realized in exchanges of dialogue; these scarcely qualify as authentic narratives at all.

24. XXXV:vii. 22. There is the case of R. Joshua, who was walking on the way, and someone walking on the way saw him. He said to him, "What are you doing?" He said to him, "I am walking on the way." He said to him, "Well said, for robbers like you have trodden it [stealing private property and making it public property through usufruct]." He was walking along and found a child at a crossroad. He said to him, "What is the nearest way to town?" He said to him, "This way is near and far, and that is far and near."

25. XXXV.vii.23. It has been taught on Tannaite authority: They leave over peah of a dish prepared in a boiling pot and it goes without saying, of one prepared in a tightly covered stew pot. There is the following precedent: R. Joshua b. Hananiah lodged with a widow, and she brought him a dish on the first day, and he ate it and did not leave peah; the second day and he did not leave peah; and as to the third day, what did she do? She oversalted a dish of pounded grain, and when he tasted it, he did not touch it. She said to him, "Why did you leave aside the dish of pounded grain? He said to her, "I had already eaten during the day." She said to him, "If you had already eaten during the day, why didn't you decline the bread in the way in which you declined the grain? Maybe you left it over as peah? And why did you not leave peah from the two dishes you ate as you left it from this pounded grain?" Said R. Joshua, "No one ever got the better of me in an argument than those children and this widow and the little girl "so exemplifying the verse, 'she that was great among the nations.'"

> TOPIC AND PROPOSITION: The wisdom of the Israelite child

even exceeds the cleverness of the sage, who acknowledges
that fact.

NARRATIVE CHARACTER: Action and comment, action and
comment, set forth the riddle and then convey the resolution thereof.

26.   XXXIX:ii.2. In Jerusalem were three rich men, any one of whom
had the resources to feed the city for five years: Ben Sisit, Ben Kalba-
Shabua, and Naqdimon Ben Gurion. And there also was Ben
Battiah, son of Rabban Yohanan b. Zakkai's daughter, who was in
charge of the stores. He went and burned all the stores. Rabban
Yohanan ben Zakkai heard and cried, "Woe!" He sent and summoned him, saying to him, "Why did you cry, 'woe'?" He said to
him, "I did not say 'woe' but 'wow.'" Through the difference between "woe" and "wow," Rabban Yohanan ben Zakkai was saved.

27.   XXXIX:ii.3 Three days later Rabban Yohanan ben Zakkai went
out to stroll in the market, and he saw people boiling straw and
drinking the water. He said, "Can people who boil straw and drink
the water stand before the armies of Vespasian? The simple fact is
that I have to get myself out of here." Rabban Yohanan sent to Ben
Battiah, "Get me out of here." He said to him, "We have agreed
that no one is going to get out except for a corpse. He said to him,
"Get me out as a corpse." R. Eliezer carried him at the head, R.
Joshua at the feet, and Ben Battiah walked in front. When they got
to the gates, the guards wanted to stab the corpse. Ben Battiah said
to them, "Do you want people to say that when our teacher died,
they stabbed his body?" They let them pass.

28.   XXXIX:ii.4. Rabban Yohanan b. Zakkai emerged and went among
Vespasian's troops, saying to them, "Where is the king?" They went
and told Vespasian, "A Jew wants you." He said to them, "Bring
him along." When he came in, he said, *Vive domine Imperator!*"
Vespasian said to him, "You greet me as a king but I am not, and
if the king hears, he will assassinate me." He said to him, "If you
are not a king, you will be, because the temple will be destroyed
only by the power of a king: 'And Lebanon shall fall by a mighty
one' (Isa. 10:34)."

29.   XXXIX:ii.5. They took [Rabban Yohanan ben Zakkai] and put him
inside the innermost of seven rooms and asked him what time of
night it was. He told them. From his study [he kept repeating traditions, and these told him the passage of time].

30.   XXXIX:ii.6. They took [Rabban Yohanan ben Zakkai] and put him
inside the innermost of seven rooms and asked him what time of
night it was. He told them. From his study [he kept repeating traditions, and these told him the passage of time].

31.   XXXIX:ii.7. Three days later Vespasian went to wash at Gophna.
After he had bathed, he came out and put on his shoes. But when
he had put on one of his shoes, they brought him a writing from

Rome that the king had died and the citizens of Rome had crowned him king. He wanted to put on the other shoe and he could not put it on his foot. He sent for Rabban Yohanan ben Zakkai and asked, "Can you tell me why all these years I have been able to put on these shoes, but when I put on one of them and wanted to put on the other, it would not go on my foot?" He said to him, "You have heard good news: 'A good report makes the bones fat' (Prov. 15:30)."

32. XXXIX:ii.8. The generals began to speak in parables before him: "As to a cask in which a snake has nested, what is to be done with it?" He said to him, "Bring a charmer and charm the snake." Said Amgar [Cohen: Pangar], "Kill the snake and break the cask." If a snake nested in a tower, what is to be done with it?" Bring a charmer and charm the snake, and leave the tower be." Said Amgar, "Kill the snake and burn the tower."

33. XXXIX:ii.9. Vespasian said to Rabban Yohanan ben Zakkai, "Ask for something, and I shall give it to you." He said to him, "I ask you to leave the city and go away." He said to him, "The citizens of Rome did not make me king except to carry out public policy, and you tell me to leave the city and go away?! Ask something else, and I will do it." He said to him, "I ask you to leave the western gate, which leads to Lydda, and spare everyone who leaves up to the fourth hour."

34. XXXIX:ii.10. After he had come and conquered the city, he said to him, "If you have a relative there, send and bring him out." He sent R. Eliezer and R. Joshua to bring out R. Saddoq, whom they found at the city gate. When he came, Rabban Yohanan stood up before him. Vespasian asked, "Are you honoring this emaciated old man? He said to him, "By your life, if in Jerusalem there had been one more like him, even though your army were twice as big, you would not have been able to take the city."

35. XXXIX:ii.11. When they had conquered the city, he divided the destruction of the four ramparts to the four generals, with the western one to Pangar. Heaven had decreed that the western wall should never be destroyed. The three other generals destroyed their parts, but he did not destroy his. He said to him, "If I had destroyed my part as the others destroyed theirs, the kingdoms that will arise after you would never know about the great glory of what you have destroyed. But when people look [at the western wall], they will say, 'See the power of Vespasian from what he destroyed!'"

> TOPIC AND PROPOSITION: The topic is the destruction of the Temple, and the proposition is that the sage had the wisdom to survive and secure the survival of the Torah.
>
> NARRATIVE CHARACTER: A series of ten connected anecdotes are strong together, all of them fairly brief and self-contained, and the connections between one and the next

are formal, not substantive. The paramount medium is dialogue; there are very few sequences of described action.

36.   L.i.1. "For these things I weep; my eyes flow with tears; for a comforter is far from me, one to revive my courage; my children are desolate, for the enemy has prevailed" (Lamentations 1:16): Vespasian—may his bones be pulverized!—filled three ships with men and women of the nobility of Jerusalem, planning to place them in the brothels of Rome. When they had embarked on the sea, they said, "Is it not enough for us that we have angered our God in his holy house? Shall we now outrage him overseas as well?" They said, "Now if these, who are built for sexual relations, do not want it, as to us, how much the more so!" They said to them, "Do you think that if we throw ourselves into the sea, we shall have a portion in the world to come?" The Holy One, blessed be He, enlightened them with this verse: "The Lord said, I will bring them back from Bashan, I will bring them back from the depths of the sea" (Ps. 68:23). "I will bring them back from the depths of the sea:" this is meant literally.

TOPIC AND PROPOSITION: The topic is the aftermath of the destruction, the disposition of the captives, and the proposition is that the Israelites preferred death to profaning God's name, and they further attributed their fate to sin against God.

NARRATIVE CHARACTER: Dialogue serves as the medium for the narrative.

37.   L.i.2. "For these things I weep:" Hadrian—may his bones be pulverized—set up three guards, one in Emmaus, one in Kefar Leqatia, and the third in Bethel in Judah. He sent forth a proclamation, saying, "Wherever a Jew is located, let him come out, because the king wants to assure him." The heralds made this announcement and caught Jews, in line with this verse: "And Ephraim is become like a silly dove, without understanding" (Hos. 7:11). [The Jews who were caught were taunted:] "Instead of asking that the dead be resurrected, pray that those alive will not be caught." Those who understood did not come out of hiding, but those who did not gathered in the valley of Bet Rimmon. Hadrian] said to his general, "Before I am done eating this piece of cake and chicken leg, I want to be able to look for a single one of these yet alive and not find him." He surrounded them with the legions and slaughtered them, so the blood streams as far as Cyprus.

TOPIC AND PROPOSITION: The topic is the aftermath of the defeat by Hadrian, and the proposition is that it was cruel and bloody.

NARRATIVE CHARACTER: A combination of described action and dialogue sustains the narrative.

38. L.i.3. There was the case of one band that was hidden in a cave. They said to one of them, "Go out and bring us one of those who were killed," which they ate One day they said, "Let one of us go and if he finds something, let him bring it, and we shall have something to eat." He went out and found his father killed, and he buried him and marked the spot. He came back and said, "I found nothing." Another one of them went out, in the direction of that deceased and found the body and brought it back to them and they ate it. Afterward they said to him, "Where did you find this corpse? He said to them, "In such and such a place. "And what was the mark?" He told them. The other said, "Woe is me, I have eaten the flesh of my father."

> TOPIC AND PROPOSITION: The aftermath of the defeat by Hadrian produces a horror, and the proposition is that the prophecies of Scripture were realized in those days.
> NARRATIVE CHARACTER: They main action is carried by dialogue.

39. L.i.4 = CXIX.i.2 The wife of Trajan—may his bones be pulverized—gave birth to a child on the ninth of Ab, while the Jews were observing rites of mourning, and the child died on Hanukkah. They said to one another, "What shall we do? Shall we kindle the Hanukkah lights or not?" They said, "Let us light them, and what will be will be." They went and slandered the Jews to him, saying to his wife, "When your son was born, these Jews went into mourning, and when he died, they lit their lamps." She sent and said to her husband, "Instead of conquering the barbarians, come and conquer these Jews, who have rebelled against you. He had made a calculation that the trip would take ten days but the winds carried him and brought him in five days. He came into the synagogue and found the Jews occupied with this verse of Scripture: "The Lord will bring a nation against you from afar, from the end of the earth, as the vulture swoops down" (Dt. 28:49). He said to them, "I am he. I thought that I would come to you in ten days, but I came in five." He surrounded them with his legions and killed them.

> TOPIC AND PROPOSITION: The defeat by Trajan is followed by blood suppression and martyrdom. The proposition is, Scripture has foretold these things.
> NARRATIVE CHARACTER: The dialogue is augmented by described action, and the whole is guided by Scripture, which reveals to Trajan what he is to do.

40. L.i.5. There was the case of the two children of R. Saddoq, high priest, who were taken captive, one a boy, the other a girl, each

falling to a different officer. This one went to a whore and handed
over the boy as her fee [for sex]. That one went to a storekeeper
and handed over the girl as his fee for wine. This exemplifies the
verse of Scripture, "And they have given a boy for a harlot and sold
a girl for wine" (Joel 4:3). After some days the whore went to the
storekeeper and said to him, "I have a Jewish boy and he is ready
for that girl you have. Let's match them up with one another, and
whatever they produce as a child we can divide among us. They
did so. They closed them up in a room, and the girl started crying.
The boy asked her, "Why are you crying?" She said to him, "Woe
for this daughter of the high priest who has gone and wed a slave."
He said to her, "Who is your father?" She said to him, "I am the
daughter of Saddoq, the high priest." He said to her, "Did you have
a brother or sister?" She said to him, "I had a brother, with a mole
on his shoulder. When he would come home from school, I would
uncover it and kiss it." He said to her, "If you were to see it, would
you recognize it? She said to him, "Yes." He bared his shoulder,
and they recognized one another, embraced, and kissed, until their
souls expired.

> TOPIC AND PROPOSITION: The topic is the fate of the cap-
> tives, and the proposition is that virtue of the Israelite
> captives persists even in captivity.

> NARRATIVE CHARACTER: Dialogue bears the narrative
> burden.

41.   L.i.9 There was the case of Miriam, daughter of Tanhum, who was
taken captive with her seven sons with her. The ruler took and im-
prisoned them within seven rooms. Then he went and brought the
eldest and said to him, "Bow down before the idol. He said to him,
"God forbid! I will not bow down before the idol." "Why not?"
"Because it is written in the Torah, 'I am the Lord your God' (Ex.
20:2)." He forthwith had him taken off and killed....Then he went
and brought the youngest and said to him, "My child, bow down
before the idol." He said to him, "God forbid! I will not bow down
before the idol. "Why not?" "Because it is written in the Torah,
'Know this day and lay it to your heart that the Lord, he is God in
heaven above and on earth beneath, there is none else' (Dt. 4:39).
"Furthermore, we have taken an oath to our God that we will not
exchange him for any other: 'You have sworn the Lord this day to
be your God' (Dt. 26:17). And as we swore to him, so he swore to
us not to exchange us for another people: 'And the Lord has sworn
you this day to be his own treasure' (Dt. 26:18)."

> TOPIC AND PROPOSITION: "The ruler" unnamed martyrs
> the Israelites for declining to bow down to idols, engag-
> ing in a detailed disputation on matters of theological truth
> in the process. The proposition is, the pagan ruler is cruel

and the Israelite sons and their mother valiant.

NARRATIVE CHARACTER: The mixture of dialogue and action is made up mostly of dialogue, which bears the main burden of the tale: the refutation of the views of paganism.

42.   L.i.14. The following case sustains the position of R. Yudan in the name of R. Aibu: There was a man who was ploughing, and one of his oxen lowed An Arab came by and said to him, "What are you?" He said to him, "I am a Jew." He said to him, "Untie your ox and your plough because the house of the sanctuary of the Jews has been destroyed." He said to him, "How do you know?" He said to him, "I know from the lowing of your ox." While he was engaged with him, the ox lowed again. He said to him, "Harness your ox and tie on your plough, for the redeemer of the Jews has been born." He said to him, "What is his name?" He said to him, "His name is Menahem [Redeemer]." "And as to his father, what is his name?" He said to him, "Hezekiah." He said to him, "And where do they live? He said to him, "In Birat Arba in Bethlehem in Judah." That man went and sold his oxen and sold his plough and bought felt clothing for children. He went into one city and left another, went into one country and left another, until he got there. All the villagers came to buy from him. But the woman who was the mother of that infant did not buy from him. He said to her, "Why didn't you buy children's felt clothing from me?" She said to him, "Because a hard fate is in store for my child, because at his coming the house of the sanctuary was destroyed."

TOPIC AND PROPOSITION: The topic is the destruction and restoration of the Temple, and the proposition is, just as at the Messiah's coming, the Temple was destroyed, so at his coming it will be rebuilt.

NARRATIVE CHARACTER: While dialogue predominates, there are important actions in the exposition, involving the sale of the ox and purchase of clothing as a way of finding the Messiah-child.

43.   LVIII:ii.10. For three and a half years Hadrian besieged Betar. R. Eleazar the Modiite was sitting in sack cloth and ashes, praying, and saying, "Lord of all the ages, do not sit in judgment today, do not sit in judgment today." Since [Hadrian] could not conquer the place, he considered going home. There was with him a Samaritan, who said to him, "My lord, as long as that old cock wallows in ashes, you will not conquer the city. But be patient, and I shall do something so you can conquer it today." He went into the gate of the city and found R. Eleazar standing in prayer. He pretended to whisper something into his ear, but the other paid no attention to him. People went and told Bar Koziba, "Your friend wants to be-

tray the city." He sent and summoned the Samaritan and said to
him, "What did you say to him?" He said to him, "If I say, Caesar
will kill me, and if not, you will kill me. Best that I kill myself and
not betray state secrets." Nonetheless, Bar Koziba reached the conclusion that he wanted to betray the city. When R. Eleazar had
finished his prayer, he sent and summoned him, saying to him,
"What did this one say to you?" He said to him, "I never saw that
man." He kicked him and killed him.

> TOPIC AND PROPOSITION: The arrogance of Bar Kokhba is
> the topic, and the proposition is that the humility of the
> sage could have saved Betar, but the arrogance of Bar
> Kokhba is the cause of its fall.

> NARRATIVE CHARACTER: Dialogue supplemented by de-
> scribed action as required carries the narrative.

44.   LVIII:ii. 19. There were two brothers in Kefar Haruba, and no
Roman could pass by there, for they killed him. They decided, "The
whole point of the thing is that we must take the crown and put it
on our head and make ourselves kings. They heard that the Ro-
mans were coming to fight them. They went out to do battle, and
an old man met them and said, "May the Creator be your help
against them." They said, "Let him not help us nor hinder us!"
Because of their sins, they went forth and were killed. They went,
carrying his head to Hadrian. He said, "Who killed this one?" They
said, "One of the Goths killed him," but he did not believe them.
He said to them, "Go and bring me his body." They went to bring
his body and found a snake around the neck. He said, "If the God
of this one had not killed him, who could have vanquished him?"

> TOPIC AND PROPOSITION: The arrogance of the Israelite war-
> riors is the topic, and the proposition is the same as the
> foregoing.

> NARRATIVE CHARACTER: As above, action supplements the
> dialogue that conveys the narrative.

45.   LXXXIV.i.5. R. Judah b. Betera came to Nisibis on the eve of the
great fast [the Day of Atonement]. He ate and finished [eating prior
to the fast]. The head of the community came to him to invite him.
He said to him, "I have already eaten and completed eating [prior
to the fast]." He said to him, "Pay attention to me so that people
should not say that the master paid no attention to me." Since he
insisted, the other went with him. The head of the community there-
upon instructed his young servant, saying, "Any course which you
serve us once must not be repeated." They brought before them
eighty courses, and he took a small taste of each, and drink a cup
of each jar of wine.

> TOPIC AND PROPOSITION: The topic is hospitality, and the

proposition is, the aggressive host is boastful.

NARRATIVE CHARACTER: The narrative is carried out through the deeds of the host and his staff and the comments and dialogue thereon.

46. XCVIII.i.1 Hadrian—may his bones rot!—proclaimed, "Whoever does not greet the king will be put to death. "A Jew passed by and greeted him. He said, "Who are you?" He said to him, "A Jew." He said to him, "You, a Jew, pass the king and greet him! Take him out and kill him." Then another one passed by and did not greet him. The king asked, "Who are you?" "A Jew." He said to him, "You, a Jew, pass the king and do not greet him! Take him out and kill him." The senators said to him, "We don't really know what your policy is. This one who did not greet you, you kill, and that one who greeted you, you kill." He said to them, "Let me be! I know precisely how I am going to kill my enemies."

TOPIC AND PROPOSITION: The harsh repression of Hadrian is the topic, and the proposition is, God knows what is being done to Israel and will avenge their blood.

NARRATIVE CHARACTER: The narrative depends entirely on dialogue for exposition.

47. CII:ii.1. There was the case of a man who was in Jerusalem and made a banquet. He said to his messenger, "Go and bring my friend, Qamsa." He went and brought to him his enemy, Bar Qamsa. He said to him, "How is it that you are my enemy and you sit in my house? Get out of here." He said to him, "Since I have come, don't humiliate me. I'll pay you back for the cost of whatever I eat." He said to him, "You are not to recline at this banquet. Bar Qamsa then left. He said to himself, "Since these are feasting in luxury, I am going to go and inform against them at court." What did he do? He went to the ruler and said to him, "These sacrifices that you contribute [to the temple] they eat, and they offer others in their place [which are inferior]."

TOPIC AND PROPOSITION: The theme is the cause of the destruction of Jerusalem, and the proposition is that enmity within Israel and cruelty of one Israelite to another led to acts of sedition that culminated in the destruction of the Temple.

NARRATIVE CHARACTER: Dialogue is the principal vehicle for telling the story.

48. CII:i.2.Another matter concerning "The precious sons of Zion, [worth their weight in fine gold, how they are reckoned as earthen pots, the work of a potter's hands!]:" 3. There was the case of Joshua b. Hananiah, who went to Rome. He was told that there was a boy in prison, kept there for pederasty. He went and saw there a young-

ster of beautiful eyes, a lovely face, curly locks, who was used for
pederasty. He stood by the door to find out his character, reciting
to him this verse, "Who gave Jacob for a spoil, and Israel to the
robbers" (Isa. 42:24). The boy responded, "Did not the Lord? He
against whom we have sinned, and in whose ways they would not
walk, neither did they obey his Torah" (Isa. 42:24). When he heard
this, he wept and recited the verse, "The precious sons of Zion,
[worth their weight in fine gold, how they are reckoned as earthen
pots, the work of a potter's hands!]"

> Topic and proposition: The fate of the captives is the
> theme, and the proposition is, the knowledge of Torah is
> what saved the captives from their fate.

> Narrative character: The exchanges of dialogue, in-
> cluding verses of Scripture, form the means for telling the
> story.

49.   CXL:i.1 = Sifré Deuteronomy XLIII:iii.7-8 "for Mount Zion which
       lies desolate; jackals prowl over it" (Lamentations 5:18): Rabban
       Gamaliel, R. Joshua, R. Eleazar b. Azariah, and R. Aqiba went to
       Rome. They heard the din of the city of Rome from a distance of
       a hundred and twenty miles. They all begin to cry, but R. Aqiba
       began to laugh. They said to him, "Should we not cry, that idola-
       tors and those who sacrifice to idols and bow down to images live
       securely and prosperously, while the footstool of our God has been
       burned down by fire and become a dwelling place for the beasts of
       the field? So shouldn't we cry?" He said to them, "That is precisely
       the reason that I was laughing. For if those who outrage him he
       treats in such a way, those who do his will all the more so!" (2). There
       was the further case of when they were going up to Jerusalem. When
       they came to the Mount of Olives they tore their clothing. When
       they came to the Temple mount and a fox came out of the house
       of the Holy of Holies, they began to cry. But R. Aqiba began to
       laugh.

> Topic and proposition: The topic is the destruction of
> the Temple, and the proposition is, just as prophecy of
> destruction is realized, so prophecy of restoration is sure
> to come true.

> Narrative character: Dialogue the whole way.

Now to revert to the purpose of this survey: do we find a correlation between the theological message of the document and the narrative medium? In other words, have the compilers responded to a
documentary program in the selection of narration for a particular
message? To answer that question, let us review the rather unre-
fined results in hand. What we see is that the themes of the Midrash-

compilation and of the biblical book to which it attends have defined the paramount themes of the narratives collected therein.

1. TORAH-STORY
No. 1 (anecdote)
2. PROSPERITY OF ISRAEL PRIOR TO THE DESTRUCTION
No. 4 (several sequences of action, realized in dialogue)
3. DESTRUCTION OF THE TEMPLE; ISRAEL'S SUFFERING AND MARTYRDOM IN CONSEQUENCE; THE MESSIAH & RESTORATION
No. 2 (protracted narrative); No. 3 (protracted narrative); Nos. 26-35 (sequence of connected anecdotes [chapters], action and dialogue combined; No. 36 (dialogue, interspersed with verses of Scripture); No. 37 (described action and dialogue); No. 38 (described action and dialogue); No. 39 (described action and dialogue); No. 40 (anecdote realized through described action and dialogue); No. 41 (protracted sequence of connected, patterned exchanges between principals); No. 42 (action and dialogue); No. 43 (action and dialogue); No. 44 (action and dialogue, anecdote); No. 44 (as before); No. 46 (anecdote, as before); No. 47 (protracted account, with motivation and characterization, to account for the war against Jerusalem); No. 48 (Torah-knowledge saves Israelites in captivity; anecdote); No. 49 (protracted, balanced accounts, realized in dialogue deriving from verses of Scripture)
4. THE WIT OF JERUSALEMITES OR ISRAELITE CHILDREN/THE OBTUSE-NESS OF ATHENIANS
No. 5-15, 24-25 (several sequences of action, realized in dialogue);
5. DREAM INTERPRETATION
Nos. 16-23 (brief, anecdotal, effected entirely in *he said to him...he said to him...*)
6. HOSPITALITY
No. 45 (anecdote: action and dialogue)

The two large blocks of narrative materials, Nos. 3 and 4, attend to the capacious, encompassing theme, Israel among the nations. They moreover directly respond to the theological issues of the book of Lamentations. No. 2 explicitly joins in that discussion, and No. 5 is tacked on for reasons that are clear in context. So a rule of composition governing Lamentations Rabbah is, narrative materials will focus on the condition of Israel among the nations in general, and the specific historical events that make Israel's condition among the nations an acute crisis and frame the theological challenges implicit therein.

The criterion—thematic congruence—on its own presents no surprise: what else should we expect except that a document's compilers will choose what pertains to the document? Why find astonishing that the compilers of exegesis of a document will on the whole limit themselves to topically pertinent items? The answer to both questions is, because other documents' compilers accomplish their goals through other kinds of writing than through authentic narratives, which elsewhere are few, hardly important in proportion to the whole of the other documents, e.g., Song of Songs Rabbah or the Mishnah or Sifra. Not only so, but the Fathers According to Rabbi Nathan Text A, for its part chooses stories of a quite different character—specific, fixed chapters in lives of important sages, their origins, Torah-study, death-scenes for example—to accomplish its goals. In other words, on its own, the program of Lamentations Rabbah cannot be understood as consequential, its choices as to modes of narrative writing significant. But when compared and contrasted with other canonical compilations, the document at hand is seen to effect choices and respond to a documentary assignment.

That raises the question: why this, not that? Why the enormous corpus of authentic narratives in a document, the companions of which contain, proportionately, only modest proportions of authentic narratives, or none at all? In other words, why has the authorship of Lamentations Rabbah chosen a medium for accomplishing its goals that other documents ignore or treat as only marginally useful? In the present context, the question may be framed simply: why does Song of Songs Rabbah (which we met in chapter three) opt for exegetical parables, while Lamentations Rabbah prefers protracted, complex, authentic narratives, many of them enormous and beautifully articulated? Asked in this way, the question answers itself. Song of Songs Rabbah comments on a parabolic text and chooses the pseudo-narrative medium of exegetical parables to respond thereto. So it reads the Song of Songs the way the Song of Songs reads Israel's relationship to God: as a simile, as a parable. Lamentations Rabbah addresses the large theological questions raised in the book of Lamentations. That dirge in the manner of biblical prophecy from Joshua through Kings uses historical narrative to frame a theology of history. So it reads the book of Lamentations the way Lamentations reads Israel's history: as the tragic outcome of Israel's own conduct, *but also as a tragedy in the biography of God: God wept.*

How else say so, then by telling the story? And what effect is achieved, if the story is not told? To be told, "God wept," effects no empathetic relationship. To be shown in the context of a dual narrative—Scripture's and the Rabbinic sages'—how God wept— that is another matter altogether!

So in formulating protracted, enormous, continuous stories, one after another, the framers of Lamentations Rabbah have matched the book on which they comment with the kind of writing—sustained, narrative history—that dominates in the passages of Scripture subject to amplification. Just as these represent theology in the medium of historical narrative, so authentic, historical narrative serves as the chosen medium for theology of history in Lamentations Rabbah. Scripture with its focus upon the theological meaning of concrete, specific historical events, forms the model. In both cases, the Midrash-compilers, those of Song of Songs Rabbah and of Lamentations Rabbah respond in their choices of narrative writing to the book of Scripture assigned to them by carrying forward the very modes of thought and expression of that book, selecting, respectively, the one, the exegetical parable, the other, the (historical) narrative.

D. The Mashal/Parable

What we shall now find is that the framers of Lamentations Rabbah gave preference to the authentic narrative over other available media of conveying their theological structure. They did not find the parable-form equivalently promising; compilers of other documents of theology and Aggadah did. Specifically, after reviewing forty-nine authentic narratives of various kinds, some of them remarkable for their articulation, we find that the corpus of exegetical parables is paltry. In Lamentations Rabbah the parable proves a subordinated medium of exegesis and exposition, eighteen entries in all against forty-nine authentic stories, many of them enormous. We find fourteen exegetical parables, a pair in the Halakhic realm occurs, and an—in this context—unfamiliar utilization of the parable makes its appearance as well.

When we recall that Song of Songs Rabbah required no fewer than fifty-six exegetical parables, but yielded only seven authentic narratives, none of them comparable to the massive constructions we have just examined, the picture is clear. The compilers of each document knew precisely what types of narratives they required, and they accordingly subordinated the narrative to documentary purposes. The distinctive messages of the theological structure set forth in Lamentations Rabbah are matched by the emphatic preference for authentic (teleological) narrative.

1. *The Halakhic Mashal*

These are the only items that carry forward the now-ancient resort
to parables to clarify, by concretizing, the transactions implicit in
Halakhic rulings.

1.   LXXXI.i.3 R. Aha and Rabbis. R. Aha said, "Whoever says his prayers
      with the congregation finds that his prayer is heard. To what may
      the matter be compared? To the case of <u>ten men who made a
      crown for the king, and a poor man came along and helped out.
      What did the king say? 'Shall I not put on this crown [merely] on
      account of that poor man?' The king forthwith accepts the crown
      and puts it on his head</u>. So if there are ten righteous persons standing
      in the synagogue and saying their prayers, and a wicked man is
      standing with them, what does the Holy One, blessed be He, say?
      On account of that wicked man shall I not accept the prayer? I
      shall accept it as is.'"

> How the Halakhic parable illustrates the primacy of
> praying in a quorum of ten is not fully clear. The point
> is ten righteous persons' prayers are not rejected be-
> cause of the presence of one wicked person. The com-
> parison is then drawn to the case of the ten men who
> made the crown and a poor man who helped out—
> not a close parallel to the case that is rendered. That
> the king does not reject the crown of the ten who made
> the crown because of the participation of the poor man
> who helped out hardly corresponds to the matter of the
> wicked eleventh man.

2.   LXXXI.i.3 And rabbis say, "Whoever says his prayers after the con-
      gregation says theirs finds that his actions are spelled out [and scru-
      tinized in detail]. To what may the matter be compared? To the
      case of <u>a king, whose sharecroppers and staff came before his pres-
      ence to honor him. One person came late. Said the king, 'Let the
      wine bottle be stopped up for him.' What made this [insult] come
      about? That the man came late.</u> So too, whoever says his prayers
      after the congregation says theirs finds that his actions are spelled
      out [and scrutinized in detail]."

> Here is a much more exact parallel. Now the Halakhic
> parable has someone who comes late and who is pun-
> ished on that account, having called attention to him-
> self by his lateness. The application is then precise.

These two items deal with the Halakhic preference for prayer in a
quorum over prayer individually recited. They do not deal with

detail, only with the general principle, and one of them does not exactly match the transaction it is meant to realize. They represent a considerably less successful utilization of the parable for Halakhic discourse than the counterparts in the Halakhic Midrash-compilations, such as Sifré to Numbers. That is hardly surprising in the present context.

2. *The Exegetical Mashal*

At issue once more is whether the exegetical parable matches its setting and responds to its assignment or is free-standing and adapted for its present purpose. The criterion, as before, is whether the details track the exegetical task or correspond to them only approximately. We shall see that most, though not all, of the exegetical parables originate in the particular task at hand and concretize, in generic figures, the transaction portrayed by the verse subject to amplification. The recurrence of the king/God, the queen or the prince/Israel once more marks the parable as a convention of constructing similes, some static, some dynamic, rather than as a genre of narrative writing (if the distinction makes a difference).

3. II.ii.2. ["Alas! Lonely sits the city once great with people!" (Lamentations 1:1):] "Thus says the Lord of hosts: 'Summon the dirge-singers, let them come; send for the skilled women, let them come.' [Let them quickly start a wailing for us, that our eyes may run with tears, our pupils flow with water. For the sound of wailing is heard from Zion, How are we despoiled! How greatly are we shamed!]" (Jer. 9:16-18). R. Yohanan said, "The matter [of the exile of Israel, then Judah] may be compared to the case of <u>a king who had two sons. He lost his temper with the first, took a stick and beat him and threw him out of the house. He said, 'Woe for this one! From what luxury he has been thrown out!' He lost his temper with the second, took a stick and beat him and threw him out of the house. He said, 'I am the one [who is at fault], for my way of bringing them up is no good.'</u> So when the Ten Tribes went into exile, the Holy One, blessed be He, began to recite for them the following verse: 'Woe is they, for they have strayed from me' (Hos. 7:13). But when Judah and Benjamin went into exile, it is as though the Holy One, blessed be He, said, 'Woe is me for my hurt' (Jer. 10:19)."

4. II.ii.3. R. Simeon b. Laqish said, "The matter may be compared to the case of <u>a king who had two sons. He lost his temper with the first, took a stick and beat him and the son writhed and perished. He then lamented for him. He lost his temper with the second,</u>

took a stick and beat him and the son writhed and perished. He
said, 'Now I don't have the strength to lament for them, but summon the dirge-singers, let them come; send for the skilled women,
let them come.' So when the Ten Tribes went into exile, the Holy
One, blessed be He, began to lament for them: 'Hear you this
word that I take up in lamentation over you, O house of Israel'
(Amos 5:1). But when Judah and Benjamin went into exile, it is as
though the Holy One, blessed be He, said, 'now I do not have the
strength to lament for them, but "Summon the dirge-singers, let
them come; send for the skilled women, let them come." Let them
quickly start a wailing for us, [that our eyes may run with tears,
our pupils flow with water].'

5.   II.ii.4. Rabbis say, "The matter may be compared to the case of a
king who had twelve sons, and two of them died. He began to
take comfort in the ten. Then another two died, and he began to
take comfort from the eight. Then when all of them had died, he
began to mourn for them [all]: 'Alas! Lonely sits the city once great
with people!'"

> The exegetical parables, particular to the case, take up
> the amplification of Jer. 9:6-18. The key language is
> "how greatly we are shamed," and the point is, with
> the first exile, God blamed the Israelites, but with the
> second, he blamed himself. The second parable picks
> up on "send for the skilled women...," and the third
> moves us back to our base-verse. This is a rather com-
> plex composite, dealing with a single theme in response
> to two clauses of one verse and another verse altogether
> as well. But there can be no doubt that the parables
> respond to the challenge of exegesis.

6.   XXXV:v.3. ["How lonely sits] the city that was full of people:"] If
you wish to know how many multitudes there were in Jerusalem,
you can ascertain it from the priests. R. Joshua of Sikhnin in the
name of R. Levi said, "To what may the matter be compared?
To a large heap that stood in the marketplace, and no one could
estimate its volume. There was a smart man there, who said to
them, 'If you want to come to an estimate of its volume, you may
come to an estimate based on the amount of priestly ration that
is separated from it.' So if you want to estimate the population of
the Israelites you make an estimate based on the priesthood.

> The point of the parable is explicitly stated and links
> the parable to its exegetical setting. There can be no
> doubt as to what provoked the composition of the
> parable.

7.   L.ii.2. Said R. Abba b. Kahana in the name of R. Levi, "It is written, 'And God said, 'Let the waters under the heavens be gathered together into one place' (Gen. 1:9). The Holy One, blessed be He, said, 'Let the waters gather themselves to me for the purpose that I will achieve through them.' Said R. Haggai in the name of R. Isaac, "The matter may be compared to the case of <u>a king who built a palace and gave residences in it to people who lacked the power of speech. They would get up in the morning and greet the king by making appropriate gestures with their fingers and with flag-signals. The king thought to himself, 'Now if these, who lack the power of speech, get up in the morning and greet me by means of gestures, using their fingers and flag-signals, if they had full powers of speech, how much the more so!' So the king gave residences in the palace to people possessed of full powers of speech. They got up and took possession of the palace [and seized it]. They said, 'This palace no longer belongs to the king. The palace now belongs to us!' Said the king, 'Let the palace revert to its original condition.'</u> So too, from the very beginning of the creation of the world, praise for the Holy One, blessed be He, went upward only from water. That is in line with the verse of Scripture which states, 'From the roar of many waters' (Ps. 93:4). And what praise did they proclaim? 'The Lord on high is mighty' (Ps. 93:4). Said the Holy One, blessed be He, 'Now if these [waters], which have neither mouth nor power of speech, so praise me, when mortals are created, how much the more so!' The generation of Enosh went and rebelled against him, the generation of the flood went and rebelled against him, the generation of the dispersion went and rebelled against him. The Holy One, blessed be He, said, 'Let these be taken away and let those [that were here before, that is, the primeval waters] come back.' That is in line with the following verse of Scripture: 'And the rain was upon the earth forty days and forty nights' (Gen. 7:12)."

> Here is a more conventional exegetical parable, but a story is told through verses of Scripture, "So too...when mortals are created. how much the more so... Enosh... dispersion...flood..., then the flood..." In that context, the parable replicates the story, in abstract terms. Now we do not have specific figures, e.g., the generation of Enosh, but a comparable transaction. But the parable can lay claim to an autonomous standing and is not wholly dependent, detail by detail, on the exegetical setting.

8.   L.ii.3. But it is only the Holy One, blessed be He, who said it, for he never sleeps: "Behold, he who keeps Israel neither slumbers nor

sleeps" (Ps. 121:4). R. Judah b. R. Simon said, "The matter may
be compared to <u>a shepherd who had only a staff and basket. He
went and gathered a flock for himself. On one occasion wolves
came and tore the flock to pieces. He said, 'I shall go back to my
staff and basket.'</u> So the shepherd is the Holy One, blessed be He.
The sheep are Israel: 'And you are my sheep, the sheep of my
pasture' (Ezek. 34:31. Wolves came and tore the flock into pieces'
refers to the enemies who entered the temple. At that moment,
the Holy One, blessed be He, said, 'Oh that my head were waters, and my eyes a fountain of tears that I may weep day and
night for the slain of the daughter of my people' (Jer. 8:23)."

> The shepherd weeps for the loss of all his possessions
> but the staff and basket, just as God, having lost Israel
> to the wolves, weeps for the loss of whatever he had.
> It is hard to see the parable as exegetical, since the key
> action, "wolves came..." is left without a verse to am-
> plify or clarify. And "At that moment..." is left hang-
> ing, since it is not part of the parable. Something is awry
> in this exposition of the verses and the parable of the
> bereft shepherd.

9.   LV.i.2. "Hear how I groan; there is none to comfort me. All my en-
       emies have heard of my trouble; they are glad that you have done
       it. Bring the day you have announced and let them be as I am"
       (Lamentations 1:21): "they are glad that you have done it:" This
       may be compared to the case <u>of a noble lady to whom the king
       said, "Do not lend anything to your neighbors. Do not borrow
       from them anything either." One time the king lost his temper
       with her and drove her out of the palace. She made the rounds
       of all her neighbors but they would not accept her. She went back
       to the palace. Said the king to her, "You have nerve to come back!"
       She said to him, "You are the one who did it. For you said, 'Do
       not lend anything to your neighbors. Do not borrow from them
       anything either.' Had I been lending to them or borrowing from
       them, and something of mine was in their domain or theirs in mine,
       wouldn't they have received me?"</u> So too when the Temple was
       destroyed, [the nations of the world sent word everywhere to which
       the Israelites fled and shut them out, so they appealed to God,]
       said Holy One, blessed be He, to Israel, "You have nerve to come
       back to me!" They said to him, "Lord of the world, did you not
       write in your Torah, 'Neither shall you make marriage with them,
       your daughter you shall not give to his son, nor his daughter shall
       you take for your son' (Dt. 7:3). If we had intermarried with them,
       would they not have accepted us? you have done it."

>   The exegetical parable explains why "there is none to

comfort me...they are glad you have done it..." Why Israel can blame God for her isolation is clear: by keeping his will, Israel isolated herself from the nations and when God turned against her, there was no where to turn. The parable tracks the exegesis; we should be hard put to understand the outcome were we to tell the parabolic story without the concrete application.

10.   LVII:iii.2. ["How the Lord in his anger has set the daughter of Zion under a cloud! He has cast down from heaven to earth the splendor of Israel; he has not remembered his footstool in the day of his anger" (Lamentations 2:1): "He has cast down from heaven to earth the splendor of Israel:" R. Huna bar Aha in the name of R. Hanina b. R. Abbahu: "The matter may be compared to the case of <u>a king who had a son. The son cried, so he put him on his knees. He cried some more, so he held him in his arms. He cried some more, so he put him up on his shoulders. The boy dirtied the father, so he threw him to the ground, and he was not thrown down in the way that he was lifted up. The lifting up was step by step, but the throwing down was in a single angry gesture.</u> So it is said, 'And I, I taught Ephraim to walk, taking them by their arms' (Hos. 11:3). Then: 'I will make Ephraim ride, Judah shall plow, Jacob shall break his clods' (Hos. 10:11). And finally: 'He has cast down from heaven to earth the splendor of Israel.'"

> The relationship of God to Israel, conveyed in Lam. 2:1, is translated into the exegetical parable, sustained by further verses of Scripture. Here the verses mark the stages in the king's relationship to the child.

11.   LVII:iii.3=LXIII.i.1. Another comment on the verse, "He has cast down from heaven to earth the splendor of Israel:" R. Joshua b. R. Nahman said, "The matter may be compared to the case <u>of townsfolk who made a crown for the king. They angered him, but he took it, and they angered him again, but he took it. Finally]</u> he said, '<u>Are the town-folk not irritating me only because of the crown that is set on my head? Here, take it, it's thrown in your face!</u>' So said the Holy One, blessed be He, 'Isn't it the fact that the Israelites are angering me only because of the icon of Jacob that is engraved on my throne? Here, take it, it's thrown in your face!'

> The exegetical parable takes up another component of the base-verse, "the splendor of Israel." Why the parable should yield Jacob as the crown/splendor of Israel is not clear; that is a given.

12.   LXXIX:ii.1. "I am the man [who has seen affliction under the rod of

his wrath; he has driven and brought me into darkness without any light; surely against me he turns his hand again and again the whole day long]" (Lamentations 3:1-3):" The matter may be compared to the case of <u>a noble lady, against whom the king grew angry. He drove her out of the palace. What did she do? She went and pressed her face against the pillar. The king passed by and saw her and said to her, 'You have gall [to cling to the palace after you were driven out]! She said to him, 'My lord, king, this is proper for me, this is good for me, this is right for me, for no other woman took you but for me.' The king said to her, 'No, but I am the one who rejected all other women on account of you.' She said to him, 'No, but they are the ones who did not accept you.'</u> So the Holy One, blessed be He, said to the community of Israel, 'You have gall. The community of Israel replied, 'Lord of the world, this is proper for me, this is good for me, this is right for me, for no other nation accepted the Torah except for us.' He said to her, 'No, but I am the one who rejected all other nations on account of you.' She said to him, 'How come you went with your Torah around to all the other nations for them to reject it?'

> At issue in the exegetical parable is God's insistence that he chose Israel, and Israel's insistence that the nations rejected God and that Israel was the only nation that accepted the Torah. Then the parable tracks the exegetical problem very closely, and captures Israel's merit in continuing to remain loyal to God even after the expulsion.

13. LXXXV.i.2. "My soul continually thinks of it and is bowed down within me" (Lamentations 3:19): Hiyya taught, "The matter may be compared to the case of <u>a king who went to battle and took his sons with him. One time they angered him, and he took an oath not to take them along again. Then he remembered them and wept, saying, 'Would that my sons were with me, even though they anger me!'</u> The king is the Holy One, blessed be He, and the sons are Israel. When the Israelites went forth to battle, the Holy One, blessed be He, would go with them. But when they angered him, he did not accompany them. When Israel was no longer in the land, he said, 'Would that Israel were with me, even though they anger me.'

> Here is an exegetical parable that precisely matches the case it is meant to realize, with an explicit statement to that effect ("the king is...the sons are...").

14. LXXXV.i.4. "But this I call to mind and therefore I have hope" (Lamentations 3:21): R. Abba bar Kahana said in the name of R. Yohanan, "The matter may be compared to the case of <u>a king</u>

who took a wife and wrote out for her a document specifying a very large marriage-settlement: 'So many state-apartments I am making ready for you, so many purple garments I am giving you.' Then he left her for many years and went overseas, and her neighbors aggravated her, saying, 'The king has abandoned you, has gone overseas and will never return.' She wept and sighed, but she would go into her room and open and read her marriage-settlement. When she saw in the document, 'So many state-apartments I am making ready for you, so many purple garments I am giving you,' she took comfort. After days and years had gone by, the king came home. He said to her, 'My daughter, I am surprised that you were able to wait for me all these years.' She said to him, 'My lord, king, were it not for the marriage-settlement that you wrote out for me, with its generous settlement, my neighbors would have misled me.' So the nations of the world aggravate Israel, saying to them, 'Your God does not want you any more, he has hidden his face from you, he has removed his Presence from your midst and will return to you no more. Come to us and we shall appoint you dukes, lords, and generals. And when the Israelites go into their synagogues and study houses and recite in the Torah: 'And I shall have respect for you and make you fruitful and multiply you...and I will set my tabernacle among you...and I will walk among you' (Lev. 26:9-11), they take comfort. Tomorrow, when the redemption comes, the Holy One, blessed be He, will say to the Israelites, 'My children, I am surprised that you were able to wait for me all these years.' And they will reply to him, 'Lord of all the ages, were it not for your Torah, which you have given to us, the nations of the world would long ago have led us astray from you.'

> The nations correspond to the neighbors, God to the king, Israel to the queen, and the transaction—Israel's hope despite it all—is exactly captured in this nearly perfect match. The one detail not followed in the parable is the "Come to us and we shall appoint you...." In that important detail, the parable adds up to less than the case it is supposed to replicate, and it is an important difference.

15. LXXXVI.i.5. "'The Lord is my portion,' says my soul, 'therefore I will hope in him'" (Lamentations 3:24): R. Abbahu in the name of R. Yohanan said, "The matter may be compared to the case of a king who came into a town, and with him were his dukes, lords, and generals. The chief citizens of the town were sitting in the midst. This one said, 'I will take a duke to my house,' and another, 'I will take a lord to my house,' and a third, 'I will take a general to my house.' Now there was one astute fellow there, who said, 'I shall take only the king alone, for all of the others

pass on, but he never passes on.' So of the nations of the world, these serve the sun, those the moon, others wood, others stone. But the Israelites serve only the Holy One, blessed be He: 'The Lord is my portion,' says my soul, 'therefore I will hope in him,'"

> The exegetical parable captures Israel's insistence on God as her portion, while the nations accept lesser beings, because God is eternal.

16. CXI.i.2 "and he kindled a fire in Zion, which consumed its foundations" (Lamentations 4:11): It is written, "A Psalm of Asaph. O God, the gentiles have come into your inheritance" (Ps. 79:1). What is required is not "psalm" but "a weeping of Asaph" or "a lament of Asaph" or "a dirge of Asaph." So why say, "A psalm of Asaph"? The matter may be compared to the case of <u>a king who prepared a bridal canopy for his son. He fixed it up, plastered it, cemented and decorated it. But the son angered the father, so he tore it down. He went into the room, tore the curtains, broke the rods. The son's pedagogue began to sit and play [using a piece of rod as a flute]. They said to him, "The king has destroyed this chamber, and you are sitting and playing a song?" He said to him, "I am playing a song because the king has poured out his anger on his son's bridal chamber, but not on his son."</u> So people said to Asaph, "The Holy One, blessed be He, has destroyed his sanctuary, and you are sitting and singing a psalm?" He said to them, "That is precisely why I am singing a song, for the Holy One, blessed be He, has poured out his anger on wood and stones, but not on Israel." That is in line with this verse: "and he kindled a fire in Zion, which consumed its foundations."

> There is no understanding the transaction of the parable without knowledge of the problem taken up by the exegete, Ps. 79:1's reference to a Psalm in response to the nations' having come into God's inheritance. Then the parable solves that problem, leaving no space between the problem and the solution, an exact transaction.

The distinction between the exegetical parable that responds to the problem defined by the verses and the sage's reading of them, and the exegetical parable that stands autonomous of its particular setting, registers with a minimum of subjective judgment.

3. *The Mashal Recapitulating a Narrative, Neither Halakhic Nor Exegetical*

A type of parable that is found in the present document and not seen in the Mishnah, Tosefta, Sifra, the two Sifrés, or Song of Songs Rabbah—is what I call "recapitulative," in that it goes back over the elements of an established narrative. That is, in a simile of a dynamic character, this type recapitulates a free-standing narrative, hence, it is classed as the narrative-recapitulative parable. It invokes no base-verse and does not realize the articulated result of the interpretation of Scripture at all. There are two blatant instances in which neither a Halakhic nor an exegetical task frames the assignment assumed by a parable. Rather, the narrative-recapitulative parable is comprised by a story responsive to a story, thus: the parable that renders abstract and general the principal parts of a concrete, specific narrative.

17.   XLIII.i.5. There was a priest who went to someone who had many children and said to him, "Such and such a statue has told me to come to you, for I have heard that you have many children, so you should offer up one of them." He said to him, "They are not subject to my domination. One works in gold, one in silver, one with sheep, one with herds. I have one young son, who is in the house of his master. Wait until he comes from the house of his master, and I shall give him to you, and you may go and offer him up." Said to him the Holy One, blessed be He, "Of all the sons that you had, you could offer to an idol only this one, who is consecrated to Heaven!" R. Judah b. R. Simon in the name of R. Levi b. Parta: "The matter may be compared to the case of a noble woman to whom her lover said, 'Warm some food up for me.' She took the portrait of the king and burned it up to heat the food. Said the king to her, 'Of all the things you had in the palace, you could heat up food for your lover only with my portrait!' So said the Holy One, blessed be He, to that wicked man, 'Of all the sons that you had, you could offer to an idol only this one, who is consecrated to my name!'

It is difficult to imagine a more exact replication of the case than in the narrative-recapitulative parable, but it is not exegetical in a narrow sense, not being tied up to a particular verse of Scripture. Rather, we have a story that is perfectly clear in its own terms, followed by a metaphor built on the model of the transactions of the story—an odd construction indeed. Clearly, the

study of the classification of parables here finds a classification distinct from the Halakhic and the exegetical types.

18.   XLIV.i.1. You find that when the gentiles entered the sanctuary, with
them came the Ammonites and Moabites. Everyone was running
to plunder the silver and gold, but the Ammonites and Moabites
went running to plunder the scroll of the Torah, as to remove from
there the statement, "An Ammonite and a Moabite shall not enter
the assembly of the Lord" (Dt. 23:4). R. Judah b. R. Simon in the
name of R. Levi bar Parta: "To what may they be compared?_a
fire that happened in the palace of the king, and everybody ran
to plunder the silver and gold, but the slave ran to plunder his
title deed. So when the gentiles entered the sanctuary, with them
came the Ammonites and Moabites. Everyone was running to
plunder the silver and gold, but the Ammonites and Moabites went
running to plunder the scroll of the Torah, so as to remove from
there the statement, 'An Ammonite and a Moabite shall not enter the assembly of the Lord' (Dt. 23:4)."

The parable once more matches a narrative, "So when
the gentiles...," with the transaction of the narrative
repeated in the parable.

I do not know what to make of this imaginative extension of the
possibilities of the parable beyond its Halakhic and exegetical frameworks.

4. *The Parabolic Components of Lamentations Rabbah*

Let me summarize the classification of the parables that I have set
forth:

EXEGETICAL PARABLES: 3, 4, 5, 6, 7, 8, 9, 10, 11, 12, 13, 14, 15, 16
HALAKHIC PARABLES: 1, 2
NARRATIVE-RECAPITULATIVE PARABLES: 17, 18

Of the eighteen parables that I have identified, fourteen are particular to the exegetical setting. Those that on the surface can serve
for some purpose other than the specific one at hand involve a more
elaborate transaction than those particular to the terms of the verse
that is amplified or the Halakhic ruling that is clarified.

HALAKHIC PARABLES OF LAMENTATIONS RABBAH
Parable particular to its Halakhic setting: 2
Parable not particular to its Halakhic setting: —
EXEGETICAL PARABLES LAMENTATIONS RABBAH

Parable particular to its exegetical setting: 14
Parable not particular to its exegetical setting: — [possibly 2, Nos. 8 and 14]
>   NARRATIVE-RECAPITULATIVE PARABLES OF LAMENTATIONS
RABBAH
Exegetical setting does not pertain: 17, 18

Our sample is limited and sustains no global generalization. Not only so, but the proportion of the document as a whole that we have reviewed in this rubric is negligible. We do not deal with a principal part of the document. But it is equally clear that Lamentation Rabbah's framers have found uses for the *Mashal*, both Halakhic and exegetical, and now narrative-recapitulative, that escaped the attention of the compilers of the Mishnah and the Tosefta. Though the number of entries is modest, it is also well-delineated and each of the types bears uniform traits.

E. The Ma'aseh

Lamentations Rabbah contains a negligible number of *Ma'asim*, which ordinarily, though not always, serve as precedents attached to laws. It is not a preferred narrative form. And most of the instances we do have serve a single documentary purpose. In this compilation of exegeses of a particular book of Scripture, the *Ma'aseh* signals a case that illustrates or realizes the point of a particular verse of Lamentations. The marker, *Ma'aseh*, signals a case, not a fully realized, authentic narrative, that is adapted to the documentary program. That is what we see in most of the following entries.

Here, then, the *Ma'aseh* forms the counterpart to the exegetical parable. But the entries here exhibit this fixed difference: the parable introduces a nameless, generic stick-figure, while the *Ma'aseh* cites a particular person; both are exemplary. So both in the exegetical parable and in the exegetical *Ma'aseh* the documentary vocation governs.

[1.   XXXV:v.2. is marked as a *Ma'aseh*, but I have classified it as an authentic story.]
[2.   XXXV:vii.3 is marked as a *Ma'aseh*, but I have classified it as an authentic story.]
3.   XXXVIII.i.1. "The roads to Zion mourn, for none come to the appointed feasts (Lamentations 1:4):" Said R. Huna, "Everyone seeks its proper mate. There was a case in which a wild bitch who climbed up a rock to mate with a male."

Here *Ma'aseh* signals not a Halakhic precedent or an
example but a datum drawn from nature, illustrating
the proposition of Huna.

4.   L.i. 6. There was the case of Miriam, daughter of Boethus, that she
was betrothed to Joshua b. Gamla, and the king appointed him high
priest. One time she said, "I shall go and see how he reads in the
Torah on the Day of Atonement." What did they do for her? They
brought out carpets from the door of her house to the door of the
house of the sanctuary, so that her feet should not be exposed.
Nonetheless, her feet were exposed. When her husband died, sages
decreed for her [a settlement of her marriage contract involving]
two *seahs* of wine a day. Said R. Eleazar bar Saddoq, "May I not
see consolation, if I did not see that the troops tied her hair on the
tails of horses and made her run from Jerusalem to Lud. "In her
regard I cited this verse: 'The tender and delicate woman among
you, who would not set the sole of her foot on the ground because
of delicateness and tenderness' (Dt. 28:56)."

The *Ma'aseh* here realizes or embodies the cited verse
of Deuteronomy, thus serves as the equivalent to a
parable.

5.   L.i.7. There was the case of Miriam, daughter of Naqdimon, for
whom sages allotted the sum of five hundred gold *denars* for the
purchase of perfumes daily. Said R. Eleazar b. R. Saddoq, "May I
not see consolation, if I did not see her gathering barley from beneath the hooves of the horses in Akko. "In her regard I cited this
verse: 'If you do not know, O you fairest among women, go forth
by the footsteps of the flock and feed your kids' (Song 1:8).

Here again, the requirements of the exegesis are met
by an example, not a generic embodiment such as a
parable provides. But the cited verse has dictated the
striking detail of the *Ma'aseh* .

6.   L.i.8. There is the case of Miriam, daughter of Tanhum, who was
taken captive and ransomed in Akko. They brought her a shift, and
she went down to immerse in the sea, and the waves came and swept
it off, so she got another and went down to immerse in the sea, and
the waves came and swept it off. When she saw this, she said, "Let
the Collector [God] collect the debt. [The waves exact punishment
for my sins.]" Since she had accepted the divine decree upon herself, the Holy One, blessed be He, gestured to the sea and it returned her garments.

The point of the *Ma'aseh* is articulated, "Since she had
accepted...." Here we have a specific incident that
embodies the stated principle. Here what is realized is

not the exegesis of a verse of Scripture but the theological outcome of the same matter.

7.   LXVII.i.1. "My eyes are spent with weeping" (Lam. 2:11): But the
tears caused by the death of an adult child are worst of all." There
was the case of a woman whose adult son died. She wept over him
nightly, until her eyelashes fell out. She went to a physician, who
said to her, "Paint your eyes with this eye-paint that I give you, and
you will recover."

> The *Ma'aseh* illustrates the mourning for the death of
> an adult child by invoking a specific case, the whole
> serving an exegetical purpose, in connection with Lam.
> 2:11: why the tears caused by the death of an adult
> child are worst of all.

8.   LXVII.i.2. "my soul is in tumult, my heart is poured out in grief
because of the destruction of the daughter of my people" (Lam. 2:11):
There was the case of a man whose adult son died, and he wept
over him nightly, until his liver dropped. He said, "My liver has
dropped from weeping over him, but it has made no difference."

> As above.

9.   LXVIII.i.2. [They cry to their mothers, "Where is bread and wine?"
as they faint like wounded men in the streets of the city, as their
life is poured out on their mothers' bosom (Lamentations 2:12):"
"as they faint like wounded men in the streets of the city, as their
life is poured out on their mothers' bosom:" There is the case of a
woman who said to her husband, "Take a bracelet or earring, go
to the market, and buy something so we shall eat and not die." He
did so, but found nothing to buy, writhed, and died. She said to
her son, "Go, see what your father is doing." He went to the market and found him dead in the market place, began weeping for him,
writhed and died by his side.

> As above, an explicit exegesis through an exemplary
> case.

10.   LXXXIV.i.1. "He has made my teeth grind on gravel and made
me cower in ashes" (Lamentations 3:16): There is the case of the
son of R. Hanina b. Teradion, who joined up with guerillas. He
snitched on them, and they killed him. His father went and found
him in the wilderness, with his mouth full of dirt and gravel. A few
days later they put him in a coffin and out of respect for his father,
they wanted to have a eulogy said for him. The father would not
permit it. He said to them, "Let me speak concerning my son." He
commenced by citing this verse: "Neither have I hearkened to the
voice of my teachers, nor inclined my ear to those who taught me.
I was well nigh in all evil in the midst of the congregation and as-

sembly" (Prov. 5:13-14). His mother commenced by citing this verse over him: "A foolish son is a vexation to his father, and bitterness to her that bore him" (Prov. 17:25) His sister cited this verse: "Bread of falsehood is sweet to a man, but afterwards his mouth will be filled with gravel" (Prov. 20:17).

The case illustrates the verse of Scripture, with special reference to Lam. 3:16/Prov. 20:17.

11. LXXXIV.i.4. [He has made my teeth grind on gravel and made me cower in ashes; my soul is bereft of peace, I have forgotten what happiness is; so I say, "Gone is my glory, and my expectation from the Lord" (Lamentations 3:16-18)] [A further illustration of the verse, "my soul is bereft of peace, I have forgotten what happiness is:" Said R. Eleazar b. R. Yosé, "There was the case of a woman who brought her son to a cook and said to him, 'Teach my son the trade. He said to her, 'Leave him with me for five years, and I shall teach him how to make five hundred kinds of omelets.'" Rabbi [Judah the Patriarch] heard and said, "That kind of luxury we have never seen" [after the destruction of the Temple, thus "my soul is bereft of peace, I have forgotten what happiness is"].

What is illustrated is how the luxurious life prior to the war gave way to extreme want.

12. CVIII.i.3. Said R. Eliezer b. R. Sadoq, "There is the case of a poor man who came and stood at the door of father's house. Father said to me, 'My son, go and see whether or not he is a Jerusalemite.' I went and found a woman, whose hair had fallen out, so that you could not tell whether it was a man or a woman. She asked only for a preserved fig. That illustrates the verse: 'their skin has shriveled upon their bones, it has become as dry as wood.'"

Once more, the *Ma'aseh* serves an exegetical purpose.

The purpose of the *Ma'aseh* in Lamentations Rabbah is primarily exegetical. The pseudo-narrative is asked to tell an illustrative story that closely responds to the attitude or doctrine of the cited verse of Scripture, or that tells a story showing its realization. The document decides what it wants out of a given narrative form, and since this is an exegetical document, the *Ma'aseh* serves to bear the burden of illustrating the meaning of a verse. That's what it does, and it is pretty much all that it does. The upshot is, the prior conventions associated with the marker, *Ma'aseh*, have completely vanished; there is no instance in Lamentations Rabbah in which the marker signals a case or a precedent of a Halakhic character.

F. Not Classified

1. L.i.10 = LXXVI:i.1 They said concerning Doeg, son of Joseph, that he died and left a young son to his mother, who would measure him by handbreadths and give his weight in gold to Heaven year by year. When the earthworks besieged Jerusalem, she slaughtered him by her own hand and ate him.

    > What is awry is the marker, "they said concerning...." With the substitution of *Ma'aseh*, we should have the sort of exemplary case of an exegetical character that the compilers of Lamentations Rabbah prefer and occasionally introduce.

iii. *Lamentation Rabbah's Narratives in Canonical Context*

These results yield an economical response to the questions that precipitate this study: does narrative writing bear a particular proposition, carry out a distinctive task in Lamentations Rabbah? I have already signaled my judgment and the foundations for it: the authentic narratives signal their claim to a position integral to, characteristic of, the document at hand. What is the theological statement possible only through authentic narratives and not possible through other types of story (parable, *Ma'aseh*), let alone through the medium of Halakhic discourse at all?

The authentic narratives of the destruction and its aftermath, on earth and in heaven, find story-telling the sole appropriate medium for their message. How else to portray God as mourning for the destruction, how else to engage the patriarchs, Moses, Jeremiah, and Rachel, in the confrontation with God on what God has brought about, I cannot begin to imagine. But the argument for divine pathos is not negative only. The substance of the message addresses things that have happened—God did these things or permitted them to happen, but deeply mourned the outcome nonetheless—and the medium fo÷rm a perfect match. And it is a medium accessible only with the whole of the written part of the Torah in hand, Abraham alongside Jeremiah, Rachel at the apex.

So the principal component of non-documentary writing in the form of authentic narrative presents itself as unique to the document, because it and it alone can say what the compilers wish to say in response to Lamentations and the events it portrays. Here through authentic narrative we see the sustaining outline of a theological structure. It is the Rabbinization of the destruction and its lessons for restoration, part of a cogent theology embodied also in the Rabbinization of Qohelet, a structure at the foundations of the Aggadah throughout.

The theological structure sets forth monotheism in mythic medium as I said at the outset. The monotheist doctrine responds within the very covenantal relationship of God and Israel to narratives of the calamities brought about by that one and only God that makes himself known in the Torah. It is only through the authentic narratives of the destruction and its aftermath that the particular issues of the events at hand can be sorted out. God did it, but God shared with Israel in the anguish of what he did, however justly, in response to Israel's sins. Along with Abraham, Isaac, Jacob, Moses, and Jeremiah, and Rachel, and all by himself also, God wept. That is the unique message of this document. Only through narrative can the Torah make that statement: in any other medium, as mere proposition for example, it defies all imagining.

iv.   *The Perfection of the Torah through the Match of the Medium and Message in the Aggadah and the Halakhah*

The message of monotheism was one and the same throughout: the God proclaimed by Israel is the one, the only, the unique God of all the world. But the Torah in its perfect form, Written and Oral reconstituted into a single statement, expressed monotheism in two different media. The philosophical formulation took abstract form, and the mythic, concrete. The one realized in systematic norms of behavior the structure and order of the Israelite social order integrated with the order of the world of nature. The other announced in episodic narratives chapters of the monotheism embodied in moments in Israelite history and eternity. So each medium was particularly suited to the data as well as the message. Philosophical monotheism addressed the timeless world of regularity and order. Mythic monotheism took up the time-bound events of disruption and disorder. Working together, the two media for the monotheism message constructed a seamless universe, created and ruled by the one eternal God made known in the Torah.

We began with the simple premise on how the Oral Torah relates to the Written Torah: *the Rabbinic sages' setting forth of the Oral*

Torah is the outcome of their possessing whole and complete the written part of the Torah. Without the Written Torah, the Oral Torah lacks context and coherence. The Rabbinic sages read Scripture forward from Creation to their own day. Their presentation of the Oral Torah came forth as the outcome of that coherent reading.

In chapter one we considered one fundamental result of such a continuous reading: the construction of a complete, cogent legal (Halakhic) system of the social order. Working back from the details to the whole, we could recover the main lines of that system.

In chapter two we identified that comprehensive message that the medium of the Halakhah sets forth: the philosophical monotheism, embodied in patterns of action. These patterns revealed the oneness of being: the possibility of finding the one in the many, and the many in the one. Given the capacity of the Halakhah to repeat a simple message in many, complex forms, we found reason to affirm the Halakhah as a remarkable medium for the chosen message of monotheism: God at the apex, all things emanating from the Creator, all things flowing back to the Creator.

Now, how do we know that a counterpart systematic reading yielded structure that was realized in the Aggadic narrative and that we can identify in its main lines?

In chapter three we saw how the Rabbinic sages perfected the Torah in its Aggadic aspect. This they did by showing that in detail important scriptural books that seem anomalous in fact conform to the cogent system that animates the whole of the Torah, written and oral. What signals the presence of a governing theological structure? In our encounter with Qohelet and Song of Songs as recapitulated by documents of the Oral Torah, we noted the implicit markers of a theological structure. That structure imparted coherence to the messages that the Torah conveyed in its diverse narrative, prophecy, and exhortation. It is the theological structure to which the Midrash-compilations, Leviticus Rabbah and Song of Songs Rabbah, transitively accommodated the anomalous Scriptural books, Qohelet and Song of Songs, respectively.[6] Both cases attested to a theological structure, one of cogent convictions, that envelops the nar-

---

[6] Other books of Scripture that required transitive accommodation include Job and Proverbs and, for its diversity of viewpoint, Psalms. What they all have in common is failure to invoke resurrection, judgment, and eternal life, which the Rabbinic sages identified as critical to the Torah and showed through exegesis is fully exposed by the written Torah, including the prophets.

rative, exhortation, and prophecy of Scripture within encompassing patterns. These patterns convey theological doctrine, attitude and belief. Now, it is clear, that cogent structure comes to expression in the Aggadic portions of the Oral Torah.

The medium identified in chapter four, the authentic narrative, perfectly matches the message of the theological structure of the Aggadah by reason of its governing logic of coherent, that of teleology, as well as its theological task. That was to address the meaning of events, to cope with the disruption of the particular event, to naturalize into the Torah those data that most disturb Israel's wholeness, its peace. Only through the medium of narrative could the message of God's unity, his responsibility for all that happens and the perfect justice of his actions, register. In the encounter with catastrophe, philosophical theology falls silent, its message of God's intentionality and justice being too much to bear. Mythic theology finds its voice for its message: the story of how, along with Israel, God suffered, wept, but determined on redemption in response to repentance, atonement, regeneration.

So our work is done. Through affirmative and explicit cases of the medium of theology, I have identified the distinctive merit of narrative in delivering the theological message of monotheism, as I succeeded in showing how the medium of law bears a unique task for conveying the philosophical message of monotheism. The Torah attains perfection when it is whole and complete, specifically, when the media and the messages match. For the matter of the two modalities of monotheism, I have shown that they do.

To summarize what I think I have made manifest: the Halakhah served as the perfect medium for the message of *philosophical* monotheism, and the Aggadah with special reference to narrative formed the perfect medium for the message of *mythic* monotheism. The one ordered social norms, enduring rules of governance, the other regularized historical exceptions, noteworthy events, singular moments that disrupted the social norms. The media of Halakhah, hierarchized classifications of law, and of Aggadah, authentic narratives of exceptions, exhibiting a teleological character, match each the requirements of its respective message.

To state what I have not yet resolved: in the preface I introduced the considerations of context and circumstance. By context I referred to the political setting in which the Oral Torah was given written form by the Rabbinic sages who received the tradition from Sinai.

Circumstance pertained to the disarray of ancient patterns of culture. But I have not doubled back to ask about how philosophical and mythic monotheism in the formulation of the Rabbinic sages addresses the context and circumstance of this defeated people.

Why the insistence upon imputing to the one, all powerful God the traits of justice and mercy, as the Rabbinic sages do in so many words in document after document? That vanquished people, like many other losers through history but with a success enjoyed by only a few of the losers, undertook the task of cultural reconstruction in accord with an established model—and succeeded. They lost for an interval, but, time has shown, they won a position of permanence in the history of humanity, and, they would claim, a critical position at that. Enduring Israel, the people of the Torah (within the mythic language of the Rabbinic sages) clearly hope to recapitulate the redemptive component of the pattern of exile and return that animates and imparts structure and system to Scripture's narratives, laws, and exhortations. How philosophical and mythic monotheism figured in the realization of that aspiration remains to be investigated in requisite detail, but in proper proportion. That I have not done.

The relationship between ideas and the social circumstance of those who hold those ideas has long interested the study of the interplay of religion and the order of society and culture. In these pages we have considered details—important details to be sure. But that main problem—the power of monotheism (in theory at least) to impart structure and system to the Israelite social order, coherence and cogency to its animating intellect, awaits study.

INDEX OF SUBJECTS

INDEX OF ANCIENT SOURCES

THE BRILL REFERENCE LIBRARY

OF

JUDAISM

The Brill Reference Library of Ancient Judaism *presents research on fundamental problems in the study of the authoritative texts, beliefs and practices, events and ideas, of the Judaic religious world from the sixth century B.C.E. to the sixth century C.E. Systematic accounts of principal phenomena, characteristics of Judaic life, works of a theoretical character, accounts of movements and trends, diverse expressions of the faith, new translations and commentaries of classical texts – all will find a place in the* Library.

1. Neusner, Jacob, *The Halakhah. An Encyclopaedia of the Law of Judaism.*
   5 Vols. 2000. ISBN 90 04 11617 6 (*set*)
   Vol. I. Between Israel and God. Part A. ISBN 90 04 11611 7
   Vol. II. Between Israel and God. Part B. Transcendent Transactions: Where Heaven and Earth Intersect. ISBN 90 04 11612 5
   Vol. III. Within Israel's Social Order. ISBN 90 04 11613 3
   Vol. IV. Inside the Walls of the Israelite Household. Part A. At the Meeting of Time and Space. ISBN 90 04 11614 1
   Vol. V. Inside the Walls of the Israelite Household. Part B. The Desacralization of the Household. ISBN 90 04 11616 8
2. Basser, Herbert W., *Studies in Exegesis.* Christian Critiques of Jewish Law and Rabbinic Responses 70-300 C.E. 2000. ISBN 90 04 11848 9
3. Neusner, Jacob, *Judaism's Story of Creation.* Scripture, Halakhah, Aggadah. 2000. ISBN 90 04 11899 3
4. Aaron, David H., *Biblical Ambiguities.* Metaphor, Semantics and Divine Imagery. 2001. ISBN 90 04 12032 7
5. Neusner, Jacob, *The Reader's Guide to the Talmud.* 2001.
   ISBN 90 04 1287 0.
6. Neusner, Jacob, *The Theology of the Halakhah.* 2001. ISBN 90 04 12291 5.
7. Schwartz, Dov, *Faith at the Crossroads.* A Theological Profile of Religious Zionism. Translated by Batya Stein. 2002. ISBN 90 04 12461 6
8. Neusner, Jacob, *The Halakhah: Historical and Religious Perspectives.* 2002.
   ISBN 90 04 12219 2
9. Neusner, Jacob, *How the Talmud Works.* 2002. ISBN 90 04 12796 8
10. Gruenwald, Ithamar, *Rituals and Ritual Theory in Ancient Israel.* 2003.
    ISBN 90 04 12627 9
11. Boyarin, Daniel, *Cultural Rabbinic Essays.* 2003. ISBN 90 04 12628 7
12. Strange, James F., (*in preparation for 2003*). ISBN 90 04 12626 0
13. Neusner, Jacob, *The Perfect Torah.* 2003. ISBN 90 04 13033 0
14. Neusner, Jacob, *Rabbinic Narrative. A Documentary Perspective.* Volume One: Forms, Types and Distribution of Narratives in the Mishnah, Tractate Abot and the Tosefta. 2003. ISBN 90 04 13023 3

15. Neusner, Jacob, *Rabbinic Narrative. A Documentary Perspective.* Volume Two: Forms, Types and Distribution of Narratives in Sifra, Sifré to Numbers, and Sifré to Deuteronomy. 2003. ISBN 90 04 13034 9

16. Neusner, Jacob, *Rabbinic Narrative. A Documentary Perspective.* Volume Three: Forms, Types and Distribution of Narratives in Song of Songs Rabbah and Lamentations Rabbah and a Reprise of Fathers According to Rabbi Nathan Text A. 2003. ISBN 90 04 13035 7

17. Neusner, Jacob, *Rabbinic Narrative. A Documentary Perspective.* Volume Four, The Precedent and the Parable in Diachronic View. 2003. ISBN 90 04 13036 5

ISSN 1566-1237